DANIEL
In God I Trust

A COMMENTARY BY
PRACTICAL CHRISTIANITY FOUNDATION
L. L. SPEER, FOUNDER

GREEN KEY BOOKS

HOLIDAY, FLORIDA

DANIEL: IN GOD I TRUST

©2004 by the Practical Christianity Foundation. All Rights Reserved.

International Standard Book Number: 1932587446

Cover Art: The Resource Agency, Franklin, Tennessee
Production and prepress: JJ Graphics/Impact Productions

Printed in the United States of America

For information:
Green Key Books
2514 Aloha Place
Holiday, Florida 34691
www.greenkeybooks.com

Library of Congress Cataloging-in-Publication Data available on request.

CONTENTS

PREFACE

From the conception of the Practical Christianity Foundation, it has been the goal of the organization to convey the truth in Scripture through verse-by-verse devotional studies such as this one. As part of that goal, we agree in an attempt neither to prove nor disprove any traditional or alternative interpretations, beliefs, or doctrines, but rather to allow the Holy Spirit to reveal the truth contained within the Scriptures. Any interpretations relating to ambiguous passages that are not directly and specifically verifiable by other scriptural references are simply presented in what we believe to be the most likely intention of the message based upon those things that we are specifically told. In those instances, our conclusions are noted as interpretive, and such analyses should not be understood as doctrinal positions that we are attempting to champion.

This study is divided into sections, usually between six and eight verses, and each section concludes with a "Notes/Applications" passage, which draws practical insight from the related verses that can be applied to contemporary Christian living. The intent is that the reader will complete one section per day, will gain a greater understanding of the verses within that passage, and will daily be challenged toward a deeper commitment to our Lord and Savior Jesus Christ. Also included at certain points within the text are "Dig Deeper" boxes, which are intended to assist readers who desire to invest additional time to study topics that relate to the section in which these boxes appear. Our prayer is that this study will impact the lives of all believers, regardless of age, ethnicity, or education.

Each of PCF's original projects is a collaborative effort of many writers, content editors, grammatical editors, transcribers, researchers, readers, and other contributors, and as such, we present them only as products of the Practical Christianity Foundation as a whole. These works are not for the recognition or acclamation of any particular individual but are written simply as a means to uphold and fulfill the greater purpose of our Mission Statement, which is "to exalt the Holy Name of God Almighty by declaring the redemptive message of His Son, the Lord Jesus Christ, to the lost global community and equipping the greater Christian community through the communication of the Holy Word of God in its entirety through every appropriate means available."

Practical Christianity Foundation
Value Statements

1. We value the Holy Name of God and will strive to exalt Him through godly living, committed service, and effective communication. *"As long as you live, you, your children, and your grandchildren must fear the Lord your God. All of you must obey all his laws and commands that I'm giving you, and you will live a long time"* (Deuteronomy 6:2).

2. We value the redemptive work of the Lord Jesus Christ for a lost world and will strive to communicate His redemptive message to the global community. *"Then Jesus said to them, 'So wherever you go in the world, tell everyone the Good News'"* (Mark 16:15).

3. We value the Holy Word of God and will strive to communicate it in its entirety. *"¹⁶Every Scripture passage is inspired by God. All of them are useful for teaching, pointing out errors, correcting people, and training them for a life that has God's approval. ¹⁷They equip God's servants so that they are completely prepared to do good things"* (2 Timothy 3:16–17).

4. We value spiritual growth in God's people and will strive to enhance that process through the effective communication of God's Holy Word, encouraging them to be lovers of the truth. *"But grow in the good will and knowledge of our Lord and Savior Jesus Christ. Glory belongs to him now and for that eternal day! Amen"* (2 Peter 3:18).

5. We value the equipping ministry of the church of the Lord Jesus Christ and will strive to provide resources for that ministry by the communication of God's Holy Word through every appropriate means available. *"¹¹He also gave apostles, prophets, missionaries, as well as pastors and teachers as gifts to his church. ¹²Their purpose is to prepare God's people to serve and to build up the body of Christ"* (Ephesians 4:11–12).

INTRODUCTION

The book of Daniel focuses upon many of God's past and future judgments upon His people, the Israelites. The prophet Daniel lived during the same time period as Ezekiel, Ezra, and Jeremiah, and a study of these books reveals several coinciding accounts and prophecies. However, the book of Daniel is also a discourse on world history from the Babylonian Empire to the second coming of the Lord Jesus Christ and the beginning of His eternal reign as King of kings.

During its time, Babylon was the greatest city in the world. Ancient historians have calculated that the city's wall was sixty miles in circumference, fifteen miles on each side, three hundred feet high, and eighty feet thick. It also extended thirty-five feet below the ground to prevent enemies from tunneling underground. The massive wall featured over two hundred towers and one hundred brass gates. In addition, the waters of the Euphrates River flowed through the city and provided water for the city's moat. This large moat ran along the city wall and somewhat protected Babylon from invasion.[1]

Nabopolassar, king of Babylon, led a revolt against the Assyrians and established the Babylonian Empire in 625 B.C. In 609 B.C.,

Necho II, the pharaoh of Egypt, invaded Palestine to protect his political interests there. Necho then fought King Josiah of Israel at Megiddo in 608 B.C. As a result, Josiah was killed, and Necho II returned victoriously to Egypt with a large army and extended his territory to the Euphrates River:

> ²⁹*In Josiah's days Pharaoh Necoh (the king of Egypt) came to help the king of Assyria at the Euphrates River. King Josiah went to attack Necoh. When Pharaoh saw him at Megiddo, Pharaoh killed him.* ³⁰*His officers put his dead body in a chariot and brought it from Megiddo to Jerusalem. They buried Josiah in his tomb. (2 Kings 23:29–30)*

In 605 B.C., Nabopolassar sent his son Nebuchadnezzar to fight Necho's Egyptian army. This bloody battle at Carchemish drove the Egyptians back to their own land and subjugated Judah to Babylon. During this time, Nebuchadnezzar received news that his father had died; therefore, Nebuchadnezzar returned to ascend Babylon's throne. After its subjection, Judah rendered tribute to Nebuchadnezzar for three years and then revolted:

> ¹*During Jehoiakim's reign King Nebuchadnezzar of Babylon attacked [Judah], and Jehoiakim became subject to him for three years. Then Jehoiakim turned against him and rebelled.* ²*The* LORD *sent raiding parties of Babylonians, Arameans, Moabites, and Ammonites against Jehoiakim to destroy Judah as the* LORD *had predicted through his servants the prophets. (2 Kings 24:1–2)*

In response, Nebuchadnezzar went to Palestine to suppress this revolt and then returned to Babylon after defeating Jehoiakim, king of Judah and son of Josiah. Nebuchadnezzar dispersed the Jewish captives to different parts of the Babylonian Empire and thereby obtained the slave labor needed to construct his numerous projects, including the Great Wall of Babylon, several majestic temples, and a magnificent palace. In addition, he commissioned the construction of the Hanging Gardens of Babylon, one of the seven wonders of the ancient world, for his wife. He also built a great reservoir for irrigation that records indicate measured 140 miles in circumference and 180 feet deep.[2]

This brings us to the time when Daniel, as a teenager, was transported with the other captive Jews to Babylon. The name *Daniel* means "my judge is God," and at this time, God's judgment did fall upon Israel.[3] Daniel was a man both tested and exalted. However, regardless of external circumstances, his commitment to the Lord God Almighty never fluctuated. He relied upon God for both life-saving miracles and the smallest of provisions. As we begin to study this intriguing book, we will see this one man's unwavering faith in his God, beginning from the time that he arrived in Babylon as a young Jew and continuing throughout his years of service under the authority of several kings and kingdoms. There is perhaps no better example of godly faith, dependency, trust, and worship than in the character of the prophet Daniel.

DANIEL 1

Daniel 1:1–7

1:1 *In the third year of the reign of King Jehoiakim of Judah, King Nebuchadnezzar of Babylon came to Jerusalem and attacked it.*

Jehoiakim began his rule of Judah in 609 B.C. This verse dates itself as 606 B.C., the third year of his reign. The Hebrew name *Jehoiakim* means, "Jehovah will set up."[1] We know from other Scriptures that Jehoiakim became king when he was twenty-five years of age, and that he collected heavy taxes for the pharaoh of Egypt (*2 Kings 23:35–36*). Jeremiah, a prophet of God who lived during Daniel's time, warned Jehoiakim of divine judgment unless retribution was made. God gave this king three years to repent, but Jehoiakim treated the matter with contempt (*Jeremiah 36:1–3*). Therefore, in the third year of Jehoiakim's reign, God judged Jehoiakim by allowing Nebuchadnezzar to besiege Jerusalem.

Sometimes, we associate the word *besiege* with a swift, violent overthrow. In this situation, though, Nebuchadnezzar came to Jerusalem to conquer the city and to make its inhabitants loyal to

him. Up to this point, the confrontation had been relatively nonvio-
lent, though later there would be much bloodshed.

1:2 *The Lord handed King Jehoiakim of Judah and some utensils from God's temple over to Nebuchadnezzar. Nebuchadnezzar
took the utensils to the temple of his god in Babylonia and put
them in the temple treasury.*

Solomon's temple, which Nebuchadnezzar looted, was magnificent, as were all of its furnishings. Riches like these had
not been seen since Solomon's actual reign. The sto-
len vessels were ornaments that the king had made specifically for the temple, so they were all exceptionally beautiful
(*2 Kings 24:13; 2 Kings 25:15*). Nebuchadnezzar carried these goods
into the land of Shinar in which the city of Babylon was located.
"*Nebuchadnezzar also brought some of the utensils of the Lord's temple to
Babylon. He put them in his palace in Babylon*" (*2 Chronicles 36:7*).

1:3 *The king told Ashpenaz, the chief-of-staff, to bring some of
the Israelites, the royal family, and the nobility.*

Ashpenaz was the master of the eunuchs, loyal servants of the king.
As a requirement, eunuchs were castrated so that they would not
desire women, least of all the king's wives and his daughters.[2]
    The fact that Ashpenaz was asked to bring royal Israelites meant
that they were descendants of King David, the second king of Israel
who received God's promise that his family would always rule. David
was from the tribe of Judah, so also was Daniel and his friends.

1:4 *They were to be young men who were healthy, good-
looking, knowledgeable in all subjects, well-informed, intelligent,
and able to serve in the king's palace. They were to be taught the
language and literature of the Babylonians.*

The king further directed Ashpenaz to choose young men who were
without physical blemish. They were to be physically attractive and

"knowledgeable in all subjects," which indicated that they were to display discernment and sensibility in words and in actions.

In addition, they were to possess the intellectual aptitude to learn the Chaldean language, customs, and culture. In the Babylonian Empire, the Chaldeans were the dominant race and were considered extremely intelligent. These captives, with their ability to learn and to understand the Chaldean language and culture, ranked among the elite of the Jewish captives. They were to be young people competent to stand in the king's court as physically, morally, and mentally exceptional individuals, those of whom the king could be proud.

These men were chosen because they possessed these qualities as judged by their fellow man, yet they were given these characteristics by Almighty God. They were God's chosen people, singled out and set apart by Him. Because of their Jewish heritage and their special relationship with Jehovah, they could trust His leading in every aspect of their lives, even as they experienced the cruel circumstances of captivity.

1:5 *The king arranged for them to get a daily allowance of the king's rich food and wine. They were to be trained for three years. After that, they were to serve the king.*

Once these young people were chosen, they were brought into the king's palace in Babylon and served the choicest meats and the finest wines. Their meals were selected by and suitable for the king himself. By worldly standards, this was the best food and drink available since they were the same provisions consumed by the king.

This was not just a special favor that happened every so often. It was a daily regimen. For three years the captives were to partake of this food. At the end of that time, they were to stand before King Nebuchadnezzar as beautiful, seemingly perfect human beings.

1:6 *Among these young men were some Judeans: Daniel, Hananiah, Mishael, and Azariah.*

Among the young men who were taken captive, four were sin-
gled out: Daniel, whose Hebrew name means "my judge is God";
Hananiah, whose Hebrew name means "the grace of Jehovah";
Mishael, whose Hebrew name means "who is what God is?"; and
Azariah, whose Hebrew name means "helped of Jehovah." These
Hebrew children were from the tribe of Judah. Judah means "He
shall be praised," and these four men certainly would praise God
throughout their lifetimes in Babylon.[3]

1:7 *The chief-of-staff gave them Babylonian names: To Daniel
he gave the name Belteshazzar. To Hananiah he gave the name
Shadrach. To Mishael he gave the name Meshach. And to Azariah
he gave the name Abednego.*

These four—and presumably all of the captives—received new
Babylonian names. This was probably an attempt to dissociate the
captives from their Jewish culture and identity. Daniel's new name,
Belteshazzar, means "lord of the straitened's treasure." Hananiah's
name, *Shadrach,* means "the breast was tender." Mishael's new
name, *Meshach,* means "waters of quiet." Azariah's name, *Abednego,*
means "servant of brightness."[4] The king delegated the mundane
task of renaming the Jewish captives to the head eunuch.

Notes/Applications
King Nebuchadnezzar seized the Israelites and carried them back
to his kingdom in Babylon. As a result, the Israelite captives found
themselves in a foreign land and strange culture. Not only were they
forced to leave their homeland, but they were also expected to deny
their native religion and to embrace the Babylonian pagan gods.
*"'I will punish them for these things,' declares the Lord. 'I will punish this
nation'"* (*Jeremiah 5:9*). Among these captives were Daniel, Hananiah,
Mishael, and Azariah. It seems quite likely that these four and the
other Israelites became homesick for Judah, their homeland.

When we ask Jesus Christ to forgive our sins and to be the Lord and Savior of our lives, we identify ourselves with Him. Being His children puts us at conflict with the world, its people, and its values. *"18If the world hates you, realize that it hated me before it hated you. 19If you had anything in common with the world, the world would love you as one of its own. But you don't have anything in common with the world. I chose you from the world, and that's why the world hates you"* (John 15:18–19). However, as children of God, we need to remember that we, like the captive Israelites in Babylon, are not at home in this world. God has something much better in store for us. *"Instead, these men were longing for a better country—a heavenly country. That is why God is not ashamed to be called their God. He has prepared a city for them"* (Hebrews 11:16). Our eternal home is with God in heaven as "fellow citizens" with our Christian friends and loved ones. *"That is why you are no longer foreigners and outsiders but citizens together with God's people and members of God's family"* (Ephesians 2:19).

Are we homesick today for our promised home in heaven? We should be. This life is not the end but the beginning of our journey. We are just passing through this world on our way to a glorious eternity!

Daniel 1:8–14

1:8 *Daniel made up his mind not to harm himself by eating the king's rich food and drinking the king's wine. So he asked the chief-of-staff for permission not to harm himself in this way.*

Daniel's decision surely seemed reckless because it was culturally inexcusable to disobey the king's orders. However, Daniel did not want to defile ("harm") his body with substances that God specified in the Law of Moses not to eat. The Hebrew word translated as *harm* means "to pollute; to stain" and carries with it a spiritual emphasis more than a physical one.[5] Although the request that Daniel made of the eunuch was in direct opposition to what the king had ordered the eunuch to do, Daniel stood firm in his convictions.

1:9 *God made the chief-of-staff kind and compassionate toward Daniel.*

Because of God's work in his heart, the chief-of-staff granted Daniel special privilege. He did this even though Daniel was a captive stranger that the chief had only known for a short time. In this way, God used Daniel and his friends to influence the Babylonian authorities. God is all-powerful and can use anyone, even someone without faith, to accomplish His will. Any benevolence granted to Daniel by the chief was, as this verse confirms, a direct result of God's intervention.

1:10 *The chief-of-staff told Daniel, "I'm afraid of my master, the king. The king determined what you should eat and drink. If he sees that you look worse than the other young men your age, he would have my head cut off."*

The chief of the eunuchs feared disobeying the king's command and the consequences that could result. One of the consequences that the chief dreaded most, as indicated by his response, was execution by beheading. Ashpenaz feared that the king might be able to look upon the faces of Daniel and his friends and see that they had been disobedient. He was afraid that their faces would look whiter, more drawn, or in some other way less healthy than the other young men.

1:11–12 *11The chief-of-staff put a supervisor in charge of Daniel, Hananiah, Mishael, and Azariah. Daniel said to the supervisor, 12"Please test us for ten days. Give us only vegetables to eat and water to drink.*

Daniel appealed to the proper authorities through the proper channels. He was not able to convince Ashpenaz, the chief of the eunuchs, but he did not lose heart. Instead, Daniel petitioned the steward who was placed directly in charge of his group.

Daniel pleaded with the steward to consider his petition, at least for a reasonable trial period. Willing to put his conviction to the test if the steward would permit this ten-day trial, Daniel's regimen? Vegetables and water.

1:13 *Then compare us to the young men who are eating the king's rich food. Decide how to treat us on the basis of how we look."*

Daniel invited the steward to compare his and his friends' appearances with those that had eaten the king's food after ten days. He did not suggest that their faces would appear healthier than those who had eaten the king's provisions; he merely encouraged the steward to see for himself. At that time then, the steward could determine what the king's men would serve the Israelites from then on.

Daniel's trust in God's faithfulness was so steadfast that he agreed with whatever action the steward deemed appropriate at the end of the ten-day trial, whether that meant submissive compliance with the king's diet or even punishment for their conduct. This is the first of many examples in which Daniel boldly placed his life in God's hands, regardless of the outcome, with uncompromising obedience.

1:14 *The supervisor listened to them about this matter and tested them for ten days.*

The steward eventually permitted the request. Daniel, Hananiah, Mishael, and Azariah ate only vegetables and water for ten days in an effort to be true to their faith convictions even in a foreign world.

Notes/Applications

In this passage, Daniel "made up his mind" not to eat the food of the king's table. Other versions (such as the King James Version) say that Daniel decided "in his heart" not to eat the king's food. The heart is often considered the very core of a person, and in this verse, the description *in his heart* refers to Daniel's total commitment to God's Law rather than to an emotional decision that he made based upon his own preferences. Like Daniel, our decisions must be made in the heart if we are to remain committed to those decisions. *"I wholeheartedly searched for you. Do not let me wander away from your commandments"* (Psalm 119:10). *"God does not see as humans see. Humans look at outward appearances, but the Lord looks into the heart"* (1 Samuel 16:7b). If we rely upon our human emotions or intellect, we will find ourselves aligned with the world's practices and against God's precepts.

Although Daniel knew that God would not want him to eat the king's food, he did not act defiantly against the king's orders. Instead, Daniel asked for permission to refrain from eating the food, provided a reasonable alternative, and left room for input from those in authority. Christians are not to rebel against the orders of those placed in authority over us. *"⁵Slaves, obey your earthly masters with proper respect. Be as sincere as you are when you obey Christ. ⁶Don't obey them only while you're being watched, as if you merely wanted to please people. But obey like slaves who belong to Christ, who have a deep desire to do what God wants them to do"* (Ephesians 6:5–6). If these orders contradict God's Word, we should try to change policies and procedures but do so with a godly attitude and spirit.

Daniel meekly stood upon his convictions. Likewise, we need to decide in our hearts to live according to God's instructions in His Holy Word. In what areas of our lives do we need to abandon our own desires and fully, with our whole heart, mind, and soul, commit to applying God's principles to our lives?

Daniel 1:15–21

1:15 *After ten days they looked healthier and stronger than the young men who had been eating the king's rich food.*

At the end of the ten-day trial period, Daniel, Hananiah, Mishael, and Azariah actually appeared healthier and "healthier and stronger" than any of the Jewish young people who ate the king's diet. This was because the four friends obeyed the guidelines the Lord had given regarding eating proper foods. It's important to remember that these young men chose this particular diet out of obedience to God rather than according to their own personal tastes.

> *[1]When you sit down to eat with a ruler, pay close attention to what is in front of you, [2]and put a knife to your throat if you have a big appetite. [3]Do not crave his delicacies, because this is food that deceives you. (Proverbs 23:1–3)*
> *Do not let me be persuaded to do anything evil or to become involved with wickedness, with people who are troublemakers. Do not let me taste their delicacies. (Psalm 141:4)*

1:16 *So the supervisor took away the king's rich food and wine and gave them vegetables.*

Because the results at the end of the ten days so favored Daniel and his three friends, the steward allowed them to continue with their special diet instead of the king's provisions. Although according to verse eleven, it is a possibility that Daniel still might not have secured Ashpenaz's approval, he did have the consent of the one who had been placed directly over this particular group of Jewish captives. In addition, Daniel did not fear the possible consequences of his actions because he knew that he was doing the right thing according to God's standards. Similarly, the steward was not afraid to continue providing their simple diet because he had seen the positive results, so the steward's life would not be threatened. He trusted that both Ashpenaz and Nebuchadnezzar would be pleased.

1:17 *God gave these four men knowledge, wisdom, and the ability to understand all kinds of literature. Daniel could also understand all kinds of visions and dreams.*

Daniel, Hananiah, Mishael, and Azariah possessed knowledge and intelligence in liberal portion. Ashpenaz had gone into Israel looking for such qualities in those who were chosen to serve his king. Daniel also possessed that something extra—the gift of understanding in all visions and dreams. As we will see throughout this book, Daniel sought God for proper interpretation of visions and dreams. It was not something he was able to do on his own; it was a gift from God to be used for God's glory.

1:18 *At the end of the three-year training period, the chief-of-staff brought all the young men to Nebuchadnezzar.*

We know from verse five that these Israelites had lived in captivity for three years when their period of grooming and training ended. During this period, they had received the finest food, exercise, and training in all matters of education and culture. They had been given the best preparation the ancient world could offer. At the end of the three years, Ashpenaz brought them before Nebuchadnezzar so that the king could select the finest among them for his court.

1:19 *The king talked to them and found no one like Daniel, Hananiah, Mishael, and Azariah among all of them. So these four men served the king.*

Essentially, the king interviewed the captives. He likely asked them particular questions to evaluate each candidate's worthiness. Given that it took three years to groom and educate these men, we can presume that these questions were difficult. The experience may have been almost like an oral exam.

Out of all of the young captives, none compared to Daniel, Hananiah, Mishael, and Azariah. They excelled above all the other participants. The goal explained in verse five—the training of all the

Jewish captives in order to find the most commendable individuals worthy to serve before the king—had been fulfilled in these four Israelites.

1:20 *Whenever the king asked them about things that required wisdom and insight, he found that they knew ten times more than all the magicians and psychics in his whole kingdom.*

The Lord continued to bless the obedience of his four servants. The king apparently tested their wisdom and knowledge in many different aspects, and in all matters, these four (whose wisdom and intelligence were from God) were found to be far superior to any of the king's magicians and astrologers (whose intelligence was of the world). Therefore, Daniel and his friends were, even by the king's worldly standards, the most intelligent men in the Babylonian Empire. The king was certainly thrilled to have these four great men in his court, and many times, as we will see throughout the study of Daniel, Nebuchadnezzar praised God for them.

1:21 *Daniel served the royal palace until the first year of King Cyrus of Persia.*

Though we are not sure about Hananiah, Mishael, and Azariah, we know Daniel remained in the king's court. This does not mean that

Daniel's presence ended at the first year of the new king, for we know from other Scriptures that he continued on into Darius' reign:

> ¹*Darius decided it would be good to appoint 120 satraps to rule throughout the kingdom. ²Over these satraps were three officials. Daniel was one of these officials. The satraps were to report to these three officials so that the king wouldn't be cheated. ³This man, Daniel, distinguished himself among the other officials and satraps because there was an extraordinary spirit in him. The king thought about putting him in charge of the whole kingdom. (Daniel 6:1–3)*

We can also conclude from other biblical records that Daniel's position was not always as prominent nor his reputation as well known as when he served under Nebuchadnezzar *(Daniel 5:10–16)*.

King Cyrus came to power at the end of the seventy years of the Jewish exile *(Jeremiah 25:11–12; 29:10; Ezra 1:1–3)*. Daniel, therefore, had remained in the court for at least those seventy years. At that point he would have been around eighty-six years old. In all those years, the cunning, ungodly forces that tried to abolish his godly example within the king's court many times threatened Daniel's life.

Notes/Applications

Does God really care how we spend our money? Do the foods we eat really matter to God? Does God really care which person we marry? Does He care how we earn a living? We may think that God does not care about these personal areas of our lives. However, not only does God care, He calls us to be obedient to Him by applying the principles in His Word to every area of our lives—the little things and the big things. *"Everything you say or do should be done in the name of the Lord Jesus, giving thanks to God the Father through him" (Colossians 3:17)*. Obedience to God means that, out of our love for Him, we follow Him in all that we say and do.

In this chapter, four of the Jewish captives did not partake of the king's foods because they knew that this was in conflict with the guidelines God had previously given them. To us, eating the king's meats might seem trivial. What harm would have been done if Daniel and his friends had eaten the king's delicacies? Would they have been struck by lightning? Probably not, since there are no indications that such consequences ever befell the other Israelite children. However, in the Hebrew law, God specifically instructed His children not to eat from the king's table because these meats were considered unclean. Because of Daniel and his friends' obedience in this seemingly simple matter, God made them physically healthier than the other captive children and ten times wiser than the king's magicians and astrologers. Therefore, if they had disobeyed God, these four may have robbed themselves of God's blessings.

We are saved by God's grace. Certainly, the Christian walk is not a formula. Doing x and y may not always yield result z. However, God's Word outlines several basic principles that we should follow in order to live obedient, godly lives. Our works do not save us, but they do reveal for Whom we are working.

> *15Then what is the implication? Should we sin because we are not controlled by laws but by God's favor? That's unthinkable! 16Don't you know that if you offer to be someone's slave, you must obey that master? Either your master is sin, or your master is obedience. Letting sin be your master leads to death. Letting obedience be your master leads to God's approval (Romans 6:15–16).*

Are there any areas of our lives that we have held back from God? Have we mistakenly believed that He does not care about trivial things? Have we thought we could handle those situations on our own? Do we obey God out of our love and devotion to Him or out of a sense of duty?

> *18Dear children, we must show love through actions that are sincere, not through empty words. 19This is how we will know that we belong to the truth and how we will be reassured in his presence. 20Whenever our conscience condemns us, we will be*

reassured that God is greater than our conscience and knows everything. ²¹Dear friends, if our conscience doesn't condemn us, we can boldly look to God ²²and receive from him anything we ask. We receive it because we obey his commandments and do what pleases him. (1 John 3:18–22)

According to these verses, what spiritual blessings does God bestow upon those who obey Him?

DANIEL 2

Daniel 2:1–7

2:1 *During the second year of Nebuchadnezzar's reign, he had some dreams. He was troubled, but he stayed asleep.*

This chapter reveals the first recorded dream of King Nebuchadnezzar. God gave Nebuchadnezzar's visions, but the king didn't recognize their source. The fact that the first vision occurred during the second year of the king's reign in Babylon is telling. It rewinds the clock a few years from where the first chapter of Daniel concluded. Putting the whole time line together, we know that Daniel and his friends had not yet completed their three years of training when Nebuchadnezzar's vision came.

From the phrasing of this verse, we can infer that Nebuchadnezzar dreamed several intense dreams that disturbed his spirit. Whenever he laid his head down at night to sleep, Nebuchadnezzar's rest was interrupted by these terrible dreams, and as a result, his whole being was troubled.

2:2 *The king sent for the magicians, psychics, sorcerers, and astrologers so that they could tell him what he had dreamed. So they came to the king.*

Nebuchadnezzar summoned the service of the psychics, core magicians, astrologers, and sorcerers to interpret the meaning of his dreams. These men were viewed as the intellectual elite of their culture, but they sought their wisdom from ungodly sources.

> **DIG DEEPER:** *All The King's Men*
> The term *magician* comes from the Hebrew word *hartumim*, which means "drawers of magical lines and circles," such as those who drew diagrams to explain something divine. Astrologers—from the Hebrew word *ashshaph*, which means, "a conjurer"—were priests who received their enlightenment by reading the stars.[1] The sorcerers cast spells, practiced occult magic, and performed visual "miracles." Throughout biblical history, "wise men" of this sort, who obtained their power from ungodly sources, have never been able to match the true power of Almighty God. *(Genesis 41; Exodus 8; Daniel 4)*

2:3 *The king said to them, "I had a dream, and I'm troubled by it. I want to know what the dream was."*

The king admitted that he recently had a dream, and although he could not remember it, the dream troubled him deeply. When the king said, "I want to know what the dream was," he confirmed that his agitation drove his compelling desire to know its meaning. Surely, his summoning of these wise men for such a seemingly trivial matter revealed the king's desperation. Therefore, he demanded that the wisest men in his kingdom tell him what his dream concerned.

2:4 *The astrologers spoke to the king in Aramaic, "Your Majesty, may you live forever! Tell us the dream, and we'll interpret it for you."*

The astrologers spoke to the king first. Speaking to him in the Syrian language, they said, "Your Majesty, may you live forever," which was, as evidenced throughout this book, a traditional greeting of a servant toward a reigning potentate. They then urged the king to tell them his dream so that they could interpret it for him. Appeasing the king would have been simple under these circumstances since each astrologer could have offered his own interpretation of the dream with no regard for accuracy. The problem, however, persisted because the astrologers did not know what the king had dreamed and, therefore, could not even suggest an interpretation for him.

2:5 *The king answered the astrologers, "I meant what I said! If you don't tell me the dream and its meaning, you will be torn limb from limb, and your houses will be turned into piles of rubble.*

It seems that the astrologers' responses spurred Nebuchadnezzar's aggravation because these were, supposedly, the wisest men in his kingdom. Nebuchadnezzar impatiently reiterated his need for someone to recount the dream's details. The king then threatened the astrologers by saying that he would kill them by cutting them into pieces and that he would also destroy their homes if they could not tell him his dream. Apparently, he fully intended to carry out his threats.

2:6 *But if you tell me the dream and its meaning, I will give you gifts, awards, and high honors. Now tell me the dream and its meaning."*

The king enticed the mystics with promises of gifts, money, and public praise as a reward for revealing the events of his dream and its interpretation. The wise men were surely tempted by these promises of wealth and stature, which certainly captivated them with visions of the public honor that might be bestowed upon them. If possible, they likely would have fabricated a reply, whether true or not.

However, even with serious threats upon their lives, they refrained from lying to the king, for if they were found to be deceitful, they would have undoubtedly lost their lives. Though Nebuchadnezzar waved great temptations as well as threats, these men were unable to do what only God could do.

2:7 *Once more they said, "Your Majesty, tell us the dream, and we'll tell you its meaning."*

Probably by this point, the material rewards offered by the king seemed inconsequential to the men, who now only sought to escape from the predicament with their lives. Because of their inability to answer the king accurately, they stalled for more time. They again begged the king to tell them his dream, so they could interpret it for him. Still, Nebuchadnezzar simply could not remember the dream, and his wise men's response only further irritated him.

Notes/Applications
According to these verses, Nebuchadnezzar sought the advice of his wise men, while the wise men sought the king's praise. Even today, people barter away their souls for the approval of others.

The need for acceptance is deeply rooted within the heart of every person. We all want to be recognized as someone of significance. Our deepest needs for acceptance, however, can only be met by the heavenly Father. He alone fully understands us. He alone is equipped to meet our need for approval because He alone has the capability to love unconditionally.

Individual performance does not determine a person's importance. A Christian's identity and sense of worth lies not in even his most holy works. As believers, our worth is reflected in the price that God paid when He bought our redemption through the sacrifice of His Son, the Lord Jesus Christ. *"You were bought for a price. So bring glory to God in the way you use your body"* (1 Corinthians 6:20).

Have we grown tired of performing for the approval of others? Our search for significance ends when we remember that being "precious in His sight" renders us forever priceless to the one who really matters.

Daniel 2:8–15

2:8 *The king replied, "I'm sure you're trying to buy some time because you know that I meant what I said.*

Nebuchadnezzar sensed the struggle of the men before him. The king reiterated that the remembrance of the dream escaped him, and although the mystics believed the king, they desperately delayed the process to prolong their lives. Neither Nebuchadnezzar nor the wise men realized it, but God eliminated Nebuchadnezzar's remembrance of the dream to give Daniel the opportunity to glorify his God—the one true God.

2:9 *If you don't tell me the dream, you'll all receive the same punishment. You have agreed among yourselves to make up a phony explanation to give me, hoping that things will change. So tell me the dream. Then I'll know that you can explain its meaning to me."*

Nebuchadnezzar rightly accused the men of scrambling for more time. Therefore, he no longer trusted anything they said. The king was quickly losing his patience (though he seemed low on patience from the beginning). Nevertheless, patience or not, he granted the astrologers and wise men one last opportunity and commanded them to tell him his dream immediately.

2:10 *The astrologers answered the king, "No one on earth can tell the king what he asks. No other king, no matter how great and powerful, has ever asked such a thing of any magician, psychic, or astrologer.*

The astrologers finally confessed their inability to the king. They daringly suggested that Nebuchadnezzar's requirements were unrealistic, something that no man on earth could do. They argued that regardless of the authority given to a particular person—whether king, lord, or other ruler—he should know better than to ask for the impossible, even from the wisest men in the world.

2:11 *What you ask is difficult, Your Majesty. No one can tell what you dreamed except the gods, and they don't live with humans."*

The astrologers continued to reason with Nebuchadnezzar in spite of his irrational expectations. The wise men admitted that only the gods could solve this mystery. In admitting that none of the resources at their disposal were able to help them answer the king's request, they were also inadvertently admitting that they had no access to such a true god, if indeed they even believed one existed. Unwittingly, Nebuchadnezzar and the astrologers set the stage for Daniel to honor the only true God when they acknowledged that this revelation could not be accomplished by a mere person.

2:12 *This made the king so angry and furious that he gave an order to destroy all the wise advisers in Babylon.*

At this point, Nebuchadnezzar lost control of his emotions. In his rage, he set forth a command to kill all of Babylon's wise men because they could not do what he asked. The king decided to destroy them all without any regard for the unreasonableness of his request.

2:13 *So a decree was issued that the wise advisers were to be killed, and some men were sent to find Daniel and his friends and kill them.*

At the king's word, the decree that ordered the deaths of every wise man throughout Babylon was enacted. The consequences of this order also fell upon Daniel, his three friends, and the other young Jewish men who belonged to the king's court, even though the king had apparently never consulted them regarding the dream. This was more than just a ploy to coerce these wise men; the killing had already begun. Therefore, Daniel and his three friends were in imminent danger.

2:14–15 *¹⁴While Arioch, the captain of the royal guard, was leaving to kill the wise advisers in Babylon, Daniel spoke to him using shrewd judgment. ¹⁵He asked Arioch, the royal official, "Why is the king's decree so harsh?" So Arioch explained everything to Daniel.*

Alarmed by the decree, Daniel addressed Arioch, the captain of the king's guard. Arioch, whose name means "lion-like," was in charge of executing the wise men throughout the Babylonian Empire.[2] Daniel, who spoke with godly wisdom and discernment, inquired about the hastiness of the decree and the deliberate speed with which it was being carried out. It was then that Arioch revealed that no one had successfully described the dream itself, much less any interpretation attached to it.

Notes/Applications
In these passages, Nebuchadnezzar became so furious with the wise men's inability to tell him his dream that he sentenced them to death. Obviously, by allowing his temper to cloud his rationale, the king acted hastily.

People often hastily said or done something in anger that we later regretted? Are the consequences to losing our tempers usually worth the emotional relief that we feel by venting those feelings? Decisions that we make while we are angry are generally hasty ones. After our anger subsides, we may change our mind about a situation, but we can never change the ramifications of what we said or did in the midst of the tantrum. *"A hothead stirs up a fight, but one who holds his temper calms disputes"* (Proverbs 15:18).

People often use the excuse of "righteous anger" to justify their incensed emotions, but God is very clear about His aversion to anger. *"Also get rid of your anger, hot tempers, hatred, cursing, obscene language, and all similar sins"* (Colossians 3:8). We need to maintain control of our emotions and always strive to exemplify the meek—strength under control—and loving Spirit of Christ within us. *"Better to get angry slowly than to be a hero. Better to be even-tempered than to capture a city"* *(Proverbs 16:32).*

Daniel 2:16–21

2:16 *Daniel went and asked the king to give him some time so that he could explain the dream's meaning.*

When Daniel approached the king, he assured Nebuchadnezzar that, if given time, he would interpret the king's dream. According to following verses, the king granted Daniel's request for additional time and also temporarily lifted his decree against Babylon's wise men until Daniel was either found to be helpful in the matter or found to be another fraud. As a result of this exchange between Daniel and Nebuchadnezzar, Daniel delayed the deaths of the remaining wise men of Babylon.

2:17–18 *¹⁷Then Daniel went home and told his friends Hananiah, Mishael, and Azariah about this matter. ¹⁸He told them to ask the God of heaven to be merciful and to explain this secret to them so that they would not be destroyed with the rest of the wise advisers in Babylon.*

To interpret the dream, Daniel first needed to know the dream. That information could only come from God. Daniel did not know when God would help him, but he knew that in God's time he would receive divine guidance. Therefore, as soon as the king granted Daniel the time, Daniel went back to his house and confided in his brothers of faith—Hananiah, Mishael, and Azariah—seeking their prayer support. Together, they prayed for God to reveal the king's dream.

The four young men asked God for mercy, although they knew they did not deserve it. Nevertheless, they sought the answer to this secret in order to be delivered from the decree with the rest of the Babylonian wise men. Daniel made no public display of his prayers to God. He simply returned to his house and gathered his three friends, whereupon they collectively, fervently prayed, believing God for the answer that would come.

2:19 *The secret was revealed to Daniel in a vision during the night. So Daniel praised the God of heaven.*

In a vision that night, while Daniel's mind was free from the cares and concerns of the day, God gave Daniel the message of Nebuchadnezzar's dream. This is the first recorded use of Daniel's God-given gift of understanding visions and dreams. *"God gave these four men knowledge, wisdom, and the ability to understand all kinds of literature. Daniel could also understand all kinds of visions and dreams"* *(Daniel 1:17).* He knew the source of the vision, so he could take no credit for the dream. Daniel simply rendered himself as God's instrument, and he blessed the Lord God of heaven before he shared the secret with the king.

2:20 *He said, "Praise God's name from everlasting to everlasting because he is wise and powerful.*

Daniel's first reaction to God's revelation of the king's dream was to thank the Lord, the faithful God who answered their prayers, granted them mercy, and spared their lives. Daniel exclaimed, "Praise God's name," thereby exalting God's holy name; he declared that God's name should be revered "from everlasting to everlasting," thereby acknowledging God's infinitude and eternality. Daniel also attributed all wisdom and strength to God alone.

2:21 *He changes times and periods of history. He removes kings and establishes them. He gives wisdom to those who are wise and knowledge to those who have insight.*

Daniel praised God for His power as the one in control of time and seasons. *"Jesus told them, 'You don't need to know about times or periods that the Father has determined by his own authority'"* *(Acts 1:7).* He declared that God sovereignly determines all earthly authorities, even the wicked leaders of the world. Again, Daniel acknowledged that God alone bestows discernment and insight upon those who are perceived as wise and knowledgeable. *"The Lord gives wisdom. From his mouth come knowledge and understanding"* (Proverbs 2:6). *"He disciplines nations. Do you think he can't punish? He teaches people. Do you think he doesn't know anything?"* (Psalm 94:10).

Notes/Applications

Daniel appealed for time to find the answers that the king so desperately sought. The king granted Daniel's request, so Daniel returned home and listened for God's voice. In the stillness of the night, God answered Daniel's prayer.

We, too, must learn to stop, look, and listen for God's guidance. *"Let go of your concerns! Then you will know that I am God"* (Psalm 46:10a). In his insightful book, *Victorious Christian Living,* Allen Redpath challenges the believer to "dare to stand still" until he knows the direction that God would have him to go:

> Never, never, never trust your own judgment in anything. When common sense says that a course is right, lift your heart to God, for the path of faith and the path of blessing may be in a direction completely opposite to that which you call common sense. When voices tell you that action is urgent that something must be done, immediately refer everything to the tribunal of Heaven. Then, if you are still in doubt, dare to stand still. If you are called on to act, and you do not have time to pray, don't act. If you are called on to move in a certain direction and cannot wait until you have peace with God about it, don't move. Be strong enough and brave enough to dare to stand and wait on God, for none of them that wait on God shall ever be ashamed. That is the only way to outmatch the devil.[3]

No one who waits upon God ever regrets doing so. He will not miss the boat, train, bus, or any opportunity, but he may very well bypass the heartache and confusion that accompany hasty actions. Recognizing that God is faithful and trustworthy to answer each of our prayers according to His perfect will and in His perfect timing, do we dare to stand still until we know His will?

Daniel 2:22–28

2:22 *He reveals deeply hidden things. He knows what is in the dark, and light lives with him.*

Daniel continued praising the Lord for answering their prayers and for sparing their lives. God is light, and He knows what is "in the dark," those things unknown to any other. Daniel knew that God held in the palm of His hand the answers to each of life's questions, but he also knew that God would disclose only the things that He wished to reveal. What a blessing that God had chosen to divulge such secrets to him!

2:23 *God of my ancestors, I thank and praise you. You gave me wisdom and power. You told me the answer to our question. You told us what the king wants to know."*

In a nation of many false gods, Daniel audaciously served the only true God, the God of his fathers, Who had been faithful to His people from generation to generation. He magnified God as the one Who had given him the wisdom and strength to appear boldly before Nebuchadnezzar. The plural pronoun "us" used in this verse describes how Daniel thanked God for unveiling "the answer to our question." Daniel recognized that it was an answer to several prayers and not just his own.

2:24 *Then Daniel went to Arioch, whom the king had appointed to destroy Babylon's wise advisers. Daniel told him, "Don't destroy Babylon's wise advisers. Take me to the king, and I'll explain the dream's meaning to him."*

After Daniel offered praise and thanksgiving to the Lord, he went directly to Arioch, the man who was given the assignment of executing the death decree. He asked Arioch to take him before the king so that he could recite the interpretation of the dream. Arioch certainly must have thought Daniel was insane because he, too, knew what the king had requested and that an interpretation could not be accomplished unless the dream was known. He, like the others in the king's court, realized no human could accomplish this miracle.

2:25 *Arioch immediately took Daniel to the king. He told the king, "I've found one of the captives from Judah who can explain the dream's meaning to you, Your Majesty."*

There are several possible reasons that Arioch promptly took Daniel to see the king. Arioch would have been in a position to understand just how desperately Nebuchadnezzar wanted to learn his dream. Arioch certainly could have responded for the sake of the king's peace of mind. Nevertheless, having the possible solution to the king's problem put Arioch in a position of power. He told the king that he, himself, had found the solution when in fact Daniel had volunteered his services. Arioch, with visions of possible rewards showered upon him, probably hoped to appease the king. Another reason that Arioch rushed Daniel before the king could be that he, like the others, knew the resulting death sentence of the king's unreasonable request. Perhaps even this chief executioner, aware of his role in the executions, was anxious to spare lives that he would be required to take. Whatever the reason, Arioch quickly took Daniel before the king.

2:26 *The king asked Daniel (who had been renamed Belteshazzar), "Can you tell me the dream I had and its meaning?"*

Nebuchadnezzar, seemingly unable to believe such good news, asked Daniel if he was truly able to reveal the dream and explain its interpretation. The king, now a skeptic, had likely given up on knowing his dream and its interpretation, for he had ordered the deaths of every wise man in Babylon for the failures of a few.

2:27 *Daniel answered the king, "No wise adviser, psychic, magician, or fortuneteller can tell the king this secret.*

Daniel first stated what Nebuchadnezzar already knew. For example, the king was unable to find an answer from the psychics, astrologers, magicians, and fortunetellers. None of these men could recount the forgotten dream or reveal its interpretation. Daniel again referred to the dream as a "secret" to emphasize that its truth existed beyond the realm of human knowledge.

2:28 *But there is a God in heaven who reveals secrets. He will tell King Nebuchadnezzar what is going to happen in the days to come. This is your dream, the vision you had while you were asleep:*

Daniel, however, also assured the king that the God of the Israelites, the only true God, held the key to such secrets and had unveiled this mystery to Daniel. Before Daniel explained the dream, he left a small clue—the dream was about the days to come. It seems apparent by the interpretation of the vision given later in this book that this description refers to the end of the world, but that can't be clearly identified from Daniel's words at this point.

Notes/Applications

Daniel proclaimed God as the source of knowledge and wisdom. The *American Heritage Dictionary* defines *knowledge* as "the state or fact of knowing; understanding gained through experience or study; learning." It defines *wisdom* as "understanding what is true, right, or lasting; common sense; good judgment; scholarly learning."[4]

How can a person know and consistently practice true, right, and lasting discernment outside of the absolute authority of an eternal and unchanging God? Many people can retain the knowledge of facts, but only those who intently seek to apply biblical principles can attain true wisdom. True wisdom comes from God alone and cannot be manifested in an individual unless he rids himself of all humanistic predispositions and becomes fully dependent upon the Lord. *"²⁰Where is the wise person? Where is the scholar? Where is the persuasive speaker of our time? Hasn't God turned the wisdom of the world into nonsense? ²¹The world with its wisdom was unable to recognize God in terms of his own wisdom. So God decided to use the nonsense of the Good News we speak to save those who believe"* (1 Corinthians 1:20–21).

God promises that He will generously give us discernment in our daily situations if we humble ourselves and seek His ways. *"If any of you needs wisdom to know what you should do, you should ask God, and he will give it to you. God is generous to everyone and doesn't find fault with them"* (James 1:5). Still, so many times we postpone or even avoid asking God for understanding. We look instead to the society around us and think that social reform, money, relationships, or something else can provide us with a plan or a purpose for our existence, but these are temporary, earthly imitations of the genuine spiritual truth.

Which of these adequately satisfies thirst: a glass of pure water or a glass of sour vinegar? The answer is obvious. Likewise, our souls thirst for what only God can supply. Therefore, we must not settle for the world's "misunderstanding" but seek God's answers with our whole heart, mind, body, and soul. *"Take my discipline, not silver, and my knowledge rather than fine gold"* (Proverbs 8:10).

Daniel 2:29–35

2:29 *Your Majesty, while you were lying in bed, thoughts about what would happen in the future came to you. The one who reveals secrets told you what is going to happen.*

Daniel knew the circumstances. He confirmed that the dream occurred while Nebuchadnezzar was in his bed, presumably while he was asleep, and that it concerned future events. He then clarified that God Himself imparted this dream to Nebuchadnezzar as a warning of certain future events.

2:30 *This secret wasn't revealed to me because I'm wiser than anyone else. It was revealed so that you could be told the meaning and so that you would know your innermost thoughts.*

Daniel immediately admitted that this dream had not been revealed to him based upon any superior intelligence that he possessed. He was not speaking because he on his own had authority greater than the other wise men. Rather, he emphasized the dream had been *given* to him so that the king would finally understand the things that greatly troubled him and, in turn, would show mercy to Daniel and to his companions.

2:31 *"Your Majesty, you had a vision. You saw a large statue. This statue was very bright. It stood in front of you, and it looked terrifying.*

Daniel began to tell the dream to Nebuchadnezzar, explaining in great detail what the king had seen in his dream. Nebuchadnezzar had seen an awesome image, magnificent, beautiful, and enormous in measure.

2:32–33 *³²The head of this statue was made of fine gold. Its chest and arms were made of silver. Its stomach and hips were made of bronze. ³³Its legs were made of iron. Its feet were made partly of iron and partly of clay.*

Next, Daniel described the image to the king. The head was molded of refined gold, its upper torso and arms of silver, its lower torso and upper legs of brass, its lower legs of iron, and its feet partly of iron and partly of clay. The completed description of this image revealed a composite of materials whose value and strength progressively diminished from head to toe.

2:34 *While you were watching, a stone was cut out, but not by humans. It struck the statue's iron-and-clay feet and smashed them.*

A stone not made with human hands pummeled the image by crushing its feet into countless fragments.

Remember that the image consisted of gold, silver, brass, iron, and clay. What would happen if an enormous structure were actually made of these materials and constructed in this order? The specific gravity of any given material is determined by a ratio of that material's mass compared to the mass of an equal volume of water.[5] More specifically, gold's specific gravity is 19:32 (or is 19:32 times heavier than the same volume of water), silver is 10:47, brass is 8:92, iron is 7:92, and clay is 1:93.[6] Gold, therefore, is about 10 times heavier than clay. Consequently, this image was extremely top-heavy with a poor foundation. If one actually attempted to build such an object in the physical world, it could not stand.

2:35 *Then all at once, the iron, clay, bronze, silver, and gold were smashed. They became like husks on a threshing floor in summer. The wind carried them away, and not a trace of them could be found. But the stone that struck the statue became a large mountain which filled the whole world.*

The whole image collapsed into dust, beginning with the iron and clay feet and ending with the head of gold. What was once an imposing image was quickly reduced to husks on a threshing floor. When wheat is threshed, the naked husk of the wheat, because of its virtual weightlessness, is blown away by the wind. When this occurred in the dream, the wind scattered the remaining dust to places where it would never be found. The stone that destroyed the image became a mountain that filled the whole earth.

> **DIG DEEPER:** *The Stone*
>
> Throughout the Scriptures, the Lord Jesus Christ is referred to as the "Cornerstone" spoken of in Psalm 118:22 (*Matthew 21:42–44; 1 Peter 2:7–8*). Christ, the perfect embodiment of the Law, has never filled the whole earth, but He will one day when He returns (*Revelation 2:27–29*).

Notes/Applications

God revealed the dream to Daniel but not according to Nebuchadnezzar's or even to Daniel's timeline. It is obvious that God's plan for revealing the dream and its interpretation served a far greater purpose than appeasing Nebuchadnezzar's restlessness. According to verses twenty-nine and thirty, why did God reveal this information to Daniel?

We are not much different than Nebuchadnezzar. We, too, grow impatient. Still, our Lord reminds us to grow anxious for nothing. *"Never worry about anything. But in every situation let God know what you need in prayers and requests while giving thanks"* (*Philippians 4:6*). When we long to see a purpose for life's predicaments and when it seems that we have waited and waited for our prayers to be answered, we must trust that Father God knows our needs better than we do. He will provide for our needs better than we can ever provide for ourselves. *"Wait with hope for the Lord. Be strong, and let your heart be courageous. Yes, wait with hope for the Lord"* (*Psalm 27:14*).

What burdens weigh heavily on our hearts today? May we commit each of those needs to Him in prayer. Let's thank Him for the assurance that in His timing He will take care of us.

Daniel 2:36–42

2:36 *This is the dream. Now we'll tell you its meaning.*

Daniel completed his account of Nebuchadnezzar's dream by telling the king that "we" would explain the interpretation. In using this phrasing, Daniel alluded to his three companions, whose prayers had also been answered by the revelation of the king's dream and its interpretation.

2:37 *"Your Majesty, you are the greatest king. The God of heaven has given you a kingdom. He has given you power, strength, and honor.*

Daniel directly addressed Nebuchadnezzar, describing him as a king among kings. *"This is what the Almighty Lord says: 'From the north I'm going to bring King Nebuchadnezzar of Babylon against you, Tyre. He is the greatest king. He will bring horses, chariots, war horses, many people, and many troops'"* (Ezekiel 26:7). At this point in history, Nebuchadnezzar had only recently begun his reign as Babylon's king. By the end of his reign, however, he had made the Babylonian Empire the most powerful kingdom in the world, with its dominion stretching over other powerful nations such as Egypt, Arabia, and Syria. Everyone and everything in the region submitted to the authority of Nebuchadnezzar.[7] Nevertheless, Daniel strongly reminded the king that the God of heaven had given the king this empire and all the benefits that came with it.

2:38 *He has given you control over people, wild animals, and birds, wherever they live. He has made you ruler of them all. You are the head of gold.*

While emphasizing Nebuchadnezzar's God-ordained power, Daniel told the king that he was not only ruler of all people but that he also had dominion over the animals of the earth and the birds of the air. God divinely appointed Nebuchadnezzar as commander and controller over all of creation. Daniel then explained that the golden head of the image in the dream represented Nebuchadnezzar and his empire.

2:39 *Another kingdom, inferior to yours, will rise to power after you. Then there will be a third kingdom, a kingdom of bronze, that will rule the whole world.*

The duration of Nebuchadnezzar's reign would be limited. Nebuchadnezzar was not told *how* another kingdom would succeed his own. He was only told that one would, and that it would have an inferior governmental structure, as indicated by the silver chest and arms in the king's vision. History has since proven this empire to be the kingdoms of the Medes and the Persians. The Medo-Persian Empire was a limited monarchy, meaning that the king of this empire would not have full control to do as he pleased but was accountable to other leaders.

Nebuchadnezzar was then told that a third empire, represented in the image by the brass belly and thighs, would follow the second one. This kingdom, we now know, was the Greco-Macedonian Empire. The government of Alexander the Great, the epitome of the Greco-Macedonian Empire at its height of power, was a limited monarchy ruled by military aristocracy. As brass is weaker than silver, the type of leadership of this third kingdom would prove to be inferior to that of the kingdom before it.

2:40 *There will also be a fourth kingdom. It will be as strong as iron. (Iron smashes and shatters everything.) As iron crushes things, this fourth kingdom will smash and crush all the other kingdoms.*

The iron legs of the image represented the fourth kingdom, the Roman Empire. This seems to be the general governing style that prevailed; it is the model for many present-day forms of government that are autocratic democracies, wherein the people determine, by the election of their leaders, those who govern them. We are told in this verse that iron, as when fashioned into tools, can subdue all things. The implication here is that this fourth and final kingdom will end the dominion of the kingdoms that preceded it. Furthermore, though seemingly strong and powerful, we will see in the verses that follow that this fourth kingdom's strength was compromised by the inherent weaknesses that accompany this style of government.

2:41 *You also saw the feet and toes. They were partly potters' clay and partly iron. This means that there will be a divided kingdom which has some of the firmness of iron. As you saw, iron was mixed with clay.*

It is important to remember the prophetic nature of Nebuchadnezzar's dream. In fact, the fulfillment of the dream's prophecy has not yet occurred. The iron and clay mixture represents the ultimate deterioration and loss of strength of the fourth empire. As long as there is at least some iron in the mixture, some strength remains. As illustrated by this particular description of the feet of Nebuchadnezzar's image, the weaker the foundation of a structure, the weaker the integrity of the structure as a whole will also be. This symbolizes the Roman style of government with its divided authority, whereby the strength of its authority is undermined.

2:42 *The toes were partly iron and partly clay. Part of the kingdom will be strong, and part will be brittle.*

The Roman Empire fell, but its form of government remains strong around the world. However, what is often perceived as the strength of this type of government—the power of the general public in its influence over its leaders—will ultimately lead to its demise because man will always make selfish decisions on his own behalf rather than for the benefit of the people. Man, who from birth is at contention with God, will rule himself contrary to God's ways. This image, therefore, illustrates the decline in mankind's regard for God and an increased disobedience to His laws and His will.

Notes/Applications

In order for an orchestra to play harmoniously, every musician must follow the same leader—the conductor. If even one musician plays his own music in his own timing, the result sounds like chaotic jumble rather than a harmonious blending. The last type of government depicted in the image is a system of shared authority, represented by the weakest element in the image's construction because, as with an orchestra that is out of sync, this system of rule produces confusion.

As Christians, we must submit to God's supremacy by recognizing that He has ordained every detail of our lives, including the earthly rulers who administer over us. *"No government would exist if it hadn't been established by God. The governments which exist have been put in place by God"* (Romans 13:1b). The authority figures in our lives—church leaders, employers, spouses, teachers, and so forth—hold us accountable to the laws and standards of our society. Frankly, if we think that we please God yet constantly rebel against the boundaries that He has ordained, we deceive ourselves. Being submissive, however, is not synonymous with being weak. Quite the contrary is true. By respecting the authority figures in our lives, we ultimately honor God, our highest authority.

> *¹³Place yourselves under the authority of human governments to please the Lord. Obey the emperor. He holds the highest position of authority. ¹⁴Also obey governors. They are people the emperor has sent to punish those who do wrong and to praise those who do right. ¹⁵God wants you to silence the ignorance of foolish people by doing what is right. ¹⁶Live as free people, but don't hide behind your freedom when you do evil. Instead, use your freedom to serve God.* (1 Peter 2:13–16)

Daniel 2:43–49

2:43 *As you saw, iron was mixed with clay. So the two parts of the kingdom will mix by intermarrying, but they will not hold together any more than iron can mix with clay.*

These individual kingdoms will be weakened when they "mix" with their respective societies. In this context, *mixed* means "blended" as to form a new compound.[8] Therefore, these ten kingdoms represented by the ten toes of the image will dilute their own power by the interaction with and influence from the people over whom they are supposed to govern.[9] It seems apparent that the inevitable result of governmental democracies is the watering down of the governing authorities by the surging influence of the common people.

2:44 *"At the time of those kings, the God of heaven will establish a kingdom that will never be destroyed. No other people will be permitted to rule it. It will smash all the other kingdoms and put an end to them. But it will be established forever.*

Almighty God will usher in His indestructible kingdom after all the other kingdoms have been destroyed. Rulership of God's kingdom will not be left to any man, and this kingdom, a holy monarchy whose King is Jesus Christ, will endure forever.

2:45 *This is the stone that you saw cut out from a mountain, but not by humans. It smashed the iron, bronze, clay, silver, and gold. The great God has told you what will happen in the future, Your Majesty. The dream is true, and you can trust that this is its meaning."*

The ten kingdoms, represented by ten toes, will be ten earthly kingdoms, world powers that will be completely demolished with one great blow by the Stone. Apparent by what the Stone accomplishes and by its description of not having been formed by human hands, the great stone that crushes this image symbolizes Jesus Christ, the

Son of God.[10] Therefore, Jesus Christ will subdue all the earth and will be in complete, perfect control.

> [42]*Jesus asked them, "Have you never read in the Scriptures: 'The stone that the builders rejected has become the cornerstone. The Lord is responsible for this, and it is amazing for us to see'?* [43]*That is why I can guarantee that the kingdom of God will be taken away from you and given to a people who will produce what God wants.* [44]*Anyone who falls on this stone will be broken. If the stone falls on anyone, it will crush that person." (Matthew 21:42–44)*

Daniel concluded the interpretation of the dream by telling the king, "The great God has told you what would happen in the future." Daniel assured Nebuchadnezzar of the validity of the dream and its interpretation.

2:46 *King Nebuchadnezzar immediately bowed down on the ground in front of Daniel. He ordered that gifts and offerings be given to Daniel.*

The king fell on his face as though worshipping Daniel, which was certainly an uncharacteristic way for a "king of kings," as Nebuchadnezzar had been titled, to behave toward a common man. Evidently, Nebuchadnezzar believed all that Daniel had told him. Surely, the king was so relieved to understand this dream that had deeply burdened him that he expressed his gratitude to Daniel by lavishly rewarding him with abundant luxuries.

2:47 *The king said to Daniel, "Your God is truly the greatest of gods, the Lord over kings. He can reveal secrets because you were able to reveal this secret."*

Despite the rewards that Nebuchadnezzar bestowed upon Daniel, the king acknowledged that Daniel himself did not deserve the credit. Nebuchadnezzar recognized the source of the revelation, Daniel's God, Who had proven Himself to be the true God of gods.

> **DIG DEEPER:** *God of gods*
>
> Nebuchadnezzar saw how God worked in Daniel's life, and it pro-
> voked him to call Daniel's God "the God of gods" (*Deuteronomy*
> *10:17*). Imagine the impact that we Christians could have on the
> world if we allowed God to boldly demonstrate His power through us
> the way that Daniel did! (*Matthew 5:16; Colossians 4:5–6*)

2:48 *Then the king promoted Daniel and gave him many won-*
derful gifts. Nebuchadnezzar made Daniel governor of the whole
province of Babylon and head of all Babylon's wise advisers.

The king offered Daniel many "wonderful gifts," which included a
prestigious position as ruler over the province of Babylon, second
only to Nebuchadnezzar and over all of the wise men. This extremely
distinguished position would have honored any man, let alone a captive Jew.

Daniel was able to rule with wisdom because he daily relied upon
God, and despite his vast material possessions, Daniel never denied
his dependence upon the Lord.

2:49 *With the king's permission, Daniel appointed Shadrach,*
Meshach, and Abednego to govern the province of Babylon. But
Daniel stayed at the king's court.

Daniel did not forget his three friends—Shadrach, Meshach, and
Abednego—who had prayed with him for God to reveal the dream
and to spare lives through His mercy. They had certainly endured
many hard times together. Therefore, Daniel appealed to Nebuchadnezzar that they, too, be rewarded, so the king obliged and also
recompensed them for their faithfulness by appointing them as ministers over the affairs of Babylon. Nebuchadnezzar ruled autocrati-
cally (with absolute power), yet he yielded much of this power to
Daniel, the first in command under him.

Notes/Applications

Daniel did not allow the king's rewards to obstruct his relationship with God because he knew that all of his possessions were imparted to him by God's mercy. Many people who have great riches think that they do not need God. However, material wealth is only temporary and, except for God's grace, can vanish instantly. Money cannot buy health, happiness, peace, or most importantly, an entrance into heaven.

What would others say is the most important thing to us? What would others say motivates us to do the things that we do? Is it so that we can impact more people for the Lord or so that we can have more? Success is not a matter of how much time, talent or money we possess because none of these goods determines our usefulness to God. God created each of us for a special purpose: to have fellowship with Him, and a relationship with Him. When we seek intimacy with Him more than any other earthly commodity, we purchase a genuine treasure that appreciates in value throughout eternity.

> [17]*You say, "I'm rich. I'm wealthy. I don't need anything." Yet, you do not realize that you are miserable, pitiful, poor, blind, and naked.* [18]*I advise you: Buy gold purified in fire from me so that you may be rich. Buy white clothes from me. Wear them so that you may keep your shameful, naked body from showing. Buy ointment to put on your eyes so that you may see.* [19]*I correct and discipline everyone I love. Take this seriously, and change the way you think and act.* [20]*Look, I'm standing at the door and knocking. If anyone listens to my voice and opens the door, I'll come in and we'll eat together.* (Revelation 3:17–20)

DANIEL

Daniel 3:1-7

3:1 *King Nebuchadnezzar made a gold statue 90 feet high and 9 feet wide. He set it up in a recessed area in the wall in the province of Babylon.*

At some point during his reign, Nebuchadnezzar built this golden image. Though the years of the king's reign are not cited, it can be inferred that this occurred after Daniel and his three friends had been appointed to their positions of leadership *(chapter two)*. The king set up this idol so those who came to worship it would see it from a great distance. Some expositors have speculated that Nebuchadnezzar had this image erected in response to Daniel's interpretation of the vision recorded in chapter two. They have concluded that the king constructed this image entirely of gold to portray his empire as a permanent kingdom rather than a temporary one.[1]

This image measured approximately ninety feet tall and nine feet wide, using calculations of one cubit equaling about eighteen inches. The measurement ratio given in this verse suggests that the statue was unusually slim in proportion to its height, which leads some scholars to believe that the measurement of the image's elevation possibly included the dimensions of a pedestal upon which the symmetrical idol stood.[2] In addition, the statue was probably not made of solid gold because an image of such proportions, even if creating and pouring such a mold were feasible, would have been virtually immovable due to its excessive weight.[3] Rather, it is more likely that the image was plated with gold as was the custom for such massive structures *(1 Chronicles 29:4; Isaiah 40:19)*. It must have certainly been an impressive image, although larger statues of ancient times, such as the Colossus at Rhodes, did exist.[4]

3:2 *King Nebuchadnezzar sent messengers to assemble the satraps, governors, mayors, military advisers, treasurers, judges, officers, and all the other provincial officials to dedicate the statue he had set up.*

The king summoned every person in the kingdom that served in an official capacity to attend the dedication of the image. *Satrap* is an archaic Persian word that refers to a provincial governor who ruled over a distinct region, either a small prominent city or a larger territorial district.[5] We can only speculate the precise responsibilities of each of these official positions, but we can be sure that this gathering was comprised of Babylon's elite.

3:3 *Then the satraps, governors, mayors, military advisers, treasurers, judges, officers, and all the other provincial officials assembled to dedicate the statue King Nebuchadnezzar had set up. They stood in front of the statue.*

This verse essentially repeats verse two except in the action of the sentence. In the previous verse these men were to be present together. In this verse, they were gathered before the enormous statue erected by King Nebuchadnezzar.

3:4-5 *⁴The herald called out loudly, "People of every province, nation, and language! ⁵When you hear the sound of rams' horns, flutes, lyres, harps, and three-stringed harps playing at the same time with all other kinds of instruments, bow down and worship the gold statue that King Nebuchadnezzar has set up.*

The herald's duty was to proclaim the king's decrees and to guarantee that the commands were heard and understood by the people. He might have repeated the message in several languages to ensure that every captive group in Babylon understood the command. It is just as likely, though, since these captives were trained to be among the elite of the kingdom, that the herald spoke in Chaldean.

Once Babylon's officials assembled for the dedication of the image, the herald announced the king's message. Only this multitude of gathered officials actually heard the decree, but the mandate extended to each and every inhabitant of Babylon, as evidenced in the address to "people of every province, nation, and language." Upon hearing the decree, these officials were to relay the message to their respective subordinates and would enforce the decree within their specific realm of authority.

These instruments are individually listed probably as a representative cross-section of the most common instruments of that time and culture, though modern versions of the horn, flute, and harp are popular instruments still today. The lyre and psaltery were similar harp-like stringed instruments.⁶ The herald then clearly explained the proclamation and its relevance to these instruments. Whenever the people of the Babylonian Empire heard any kind of music, they were to "bow down and worship the gold statue."

3:6 *Whoever doesn't bow down and worship will immediately be thrown into a blazing furnace."*

The consequence for disobeying the king's decree was severe. Anyone found refusing to fall down and worship the golden image was to be thrown immediately into a fiery furnace. This form of capital punishment was not uncommon in Babylon *(Jeremiah 29:22)*. These furnaces may have been the same large ovens used to bake bricks and melt gold. It is just as likely, though, based upon Nebuchadnezzar's evident proneness to extremes, that the king had built these furnaces solely for this purpose.[7] Whatever the origin, it seems that the furnaces were continually stoked to consume anyone that did not comply with the king's command.

3:7 *As soon as they heard the sound of rams' horns, flutes, lyres, harps, and three-stringed harps with all other kinds of instruments, all the people from every province, nation, and language bowed down and worshiped the gold statue King Nebuchadnezzar had set up.*

After the king's declaration, the playing of the music began, and as commanded, people of all nationalities and languages immediately fell down and worshipped the golden image. In light of what we have learned about the king's personality and by virtue of the severity of the punishment, we can presume that Nebuchadnezzar intended this to be as strict and uncompromising a decree as any he had ever given.

Notes/Applications

These passages serve as the first example of how Nebuchadnezzar had witnessed and testified to God's great power yet eventually returned to his own selfish, prideful ways. Nebuchadnezzar became so intoxicated with ego that it ultimately led to his ruin.

"Pride goes before the fall" has become a common cliché, but it's not just a warning. It is a biblical promise. *"Pride precedes a disaster, and an arrogant attitude precedes a fall"* *(Proverbs 16:18)*. Simply stated, pride is a condition where a person, consumed by his own desires, does not acknowledge God's supremacy or live in obedience to God's principles. Pride, like a parasite that eats away at its host, blinds us to God's abundant grace and more importantly to our need for His healing touch upon our sin-sickened lives. "*²¹Evil thoughts, sexual sins, stealing, murder, ²²adultery, greed, wickedness, cheating, shameless lust, envy, cursing, arrogance, and foolishness come from within a person. ²³All these evils come from within and make a person unclean*" (Mark 7:21–23). Essentially, pride, the root of other sinful desires, is a symptom that reveals our depravity and need for a complete heart transplant by the Master Physician, the Lord Jesus Christ.

Obviously, this absorption with self infects every one of us. None of us is immune from it. Therefore, our primary way to battle the spread of pride to every area of our life and to keep it from destroying us, as it did Nebuchadnezzar, is to give God total glory on a daily basis for Who He is and for what He has done. What are some aspects of God's character for which we can offer our praise? For what blessings can we offer God our thanksgiving today?

Daniel 3:8–15

3:8 *After that happened, some astrologers came forward and brought charges against the Jews.*

Apparently, some Chaldeans knew of the Jews' devotion to God and His laws because they seized this opportunity to find fault in the Israelites. Ironically, these Chaldeans would not have noticed certain Jews' refusal to bow if they had been worshipping the image as the king previously commanded. These Chaldeans evidently went to the king to incriminate the Jews, who are specifically identified in later verses as Shadrach, Meshach, and Abednego.

3:9 *They addressed King Nebuchadnezzar, "Your Majesty, may you live forever!*

The Chaldeans spoke with Nebuchadnezzar about the matter, though they knew the king favored these Jews because they were Daniel's friends. They began with the customary greeting. This statement by these Chaldeans may or may not have been sincere. The repetitiveness of this greeting throughout the book of Daniel suggests that such was simply "standard operating procedure" when a subject approached the king.

3:10 *Your Majesty, you gave an order that everyone who hears the sound of rams' horns, flutes, lyres, harps, and three-stringed harps playing at the same time with all other kinds of instruments should bow down and worship the gold statue.*

The Chaldeans repeated to the king his own decree as if to ensure its inevitable enforcement against those in defiance, regardless of status. They also gave Nebuchadnezzar total credit for creating the decree. He was the king and had final, complete authority.

3:11 *Your order said that whoever doesn't bow down and worship will be thrown into a blazing furnace.*

The Chaldeans also reiterated the king's predetermined penalty against those that violated the decree. Certainly, Nebuchadnezzar had not forgotten such specifics, considering the time and energy required in constructing the image. Rather, the Chaldeans seemed to provoke the king to wrath to ensure their desired results for Shadrach, Meshach, and Abednego.

3:12 *There are certain Jews whom you appointed to govern the province of Babylon: Shadrach, Meshach, and Abednego. These men didn't obey your order, Your Majesty. They don't honor your gods or worship the statue that you set up."*

The Chaldeans then pinpointed three Jews that the king had appointed to positions of authority over the province of Babylon and who now refused to obey this decree. They accused Shadrach, Meshach, and Abednego likely because they were despised as Jewish captives who had been promoted to high positions of authority.[8] Apparently, the Chaldeans reserved no gratitude toward these three men who had played an integral role in saving the lives of all the wise men of the kingdom *(chapter two)*.

Interestingly, this is one of only two chapters in the book of Daniel where Daniel's name is not mentioned. In the other chapter, chapter twelve, the text is obviously written by Daniel who was describing a future time period and, therefore, did not refer to himself. Did Daniel, God's instrument, worship this pagan idol? Surely not. Some commentators suggest that he may have been away from Babylon on the king's business during this time.[9] It seems more probable, though, that Daniel had been promoted to a position of authority above the Chaldeans and was, therefore, beyond their reproach and out of their immediate observation.[10]

Furthermore, this account specifically records the charges against Shadrach, Meshach, and Abednego but does not necessarily negate the possibility that few, several, or many other captive Jews also refused to bow to the image. It is not improbable that many Jews could have been found in defiance and even executed in the same fiery furnace for their convictions. However, the fact that these three served as members of the king's court makes this specific account so relevant.

3:13 *Then, in a fit of rage and anger, Nebuchadnezzar summoned Shadrach, Meshach, and Abednego. Immediately, they were brought to the king.*

The king became enraged with the things he heard. How could these same Israelites that he previously promoted from the disgrace of captivity to the prominence of authority dare to defy his decree? Nebuchadnezzar commanded the men of his court to bring Shadrach, Meshach, and Abednego before him so that he could personally question them.

3:14 *Nebuchadnezzar asked them, "Shadrach, Meshach, and Abednego, is it true that you don't honor my gods or worship the gold statue that I set up?*

Nebuchadnezzar bluntly asked Shadrach, Meshach, and Abednego if they had refused to serve his gods and worship the golden image. More importantly, however, he probably questioned the intention of their actions. He was very fond of these men because they were Daniel's friends, so perhaps at this point they could have simply denied the allegations, and the king might have spared them.

3:15 *When you hear the sound of the rams' horns, flutes, lyres, harps, and three-stringed harps playing at the same time with all other kinds of instruments, will you bow down and worship the gold statue I made? If you don't worship it, you will immediately be thrown into a blazing furnace. What god can save you from my power then?"*

The king offered them another chance before they responded to his first question. He prompted the three Jews toward the answer that he wanted to hear by repeating the punishment for those who refused to obey the decree. Surely, most men would have been frightened into begging the king's forgiveness with the assurance that it would never happen again. Not these men. Nebuchadnezzar assumed that not even their God could deliver them from his punishment when he said, "Who is the god who will deliver you from my hands?"

Notes/Applications

Though they did not realize it, Shadrach, Meshach, and Abednego were being watched by ungodly spies who wanted to slander them. Often this is the case with us as well. Many evil forces lie in wait hoping to find fault in Christians who claim to be "changed," and these observers exploit those situations for selfish gain.

If we live Christ-centered lives, it is probable that some will hate us because we live according to God's principles. In fact, it is more than probable. The Scriptures promise that this kind of persecution will certainly befall us. Therefore, we can count it joy to know that persecution for our faith can be an indicator that we are living Christ-centered lives.

> *18 [Jesus said], "If the world hates you, realize that it hated me before it hated you. 19If you had anything in common with the world, the world would love you as one of its own. But you don't have anything in common with the world. I chose you from the world, and that's why the world hates you" (John 15:18–19).*

> *Those who try to live a godly life because they believe in Christ Jesus will be persecuted (2 Timothy 3:12).*

Also, just as Nebuchadnezzar did with Shadrach, Meshach, and Abednego, the world may sometimes offer us an escape from peril by demanding that we conceal or even deny our faith, but we must not cower from proclaiming what we believe. Blending in with the world can be enough to keep others from seeing the Spirit that should be evident in our lives. *"Don't become like the people of this world. Instead, change the way you think. Then you will always be able to determine what God really wants—what is good, pleasing, and perfect" (Romans 12:2).* The world constantly observes us with its private, accusing eyes. However, regardless of whether or not we think we are under the skeptical, watchful eyes of others, we should always strive to be Christ-like in speech and in action in order to impact our world for Christ.

> [13]*You are salt for the earth. But if salt loses its taste, how will it be made salty again? It is no longer good for anything except to be thrown out and trampled on by people.* [14]*You are light for the world. A city cannot be hidden when it is located on a hill.* [15]*No one lights a lamp and puts it under a basket. Instead, everyone who lights a lamp puts it on a lamp stand. Then its light shines on everyone in the house.* [16]*In the same way let your light shine in front of people. Then they will see the good that you do and praise your Father in heaven.* (Matthew 5:13–16)

Daniel 3:16–22

3:16 *Shadrach, Meshach, and Abednego answered King Nebuchadnezzar, "We don't need to answer your last question.*

Shadrach, Meshach, and Abednego immediately and boldly answered the king. They must have known that their response would not please him; nevertheless, the three Jews asserted that they were not afraid to answer the king truthfully.

> **DIG DEEPER:** *Be Not Ashamed*
>
> As exemplified by the lives of Shadrach, Meshach, and Abednego, the Lord calls us to serve and obey Him with uncompromising boldness (Hebrews 13:6). Let us never be ashamed of the One Who has delivered our souls from a fiery fate (*Luke 9:23–26; Romans 1:16*)!

3:17 *If our God, whom we honor, can save us from a blazing furnace and from your power, he will, Your Majesty.*

The three Jews then explained why they were not afraid to answer truthfully. Again, they remained respectful in how they addressed the king, but they purposely declared that if God so chose He could save them from the furnace and from the hand of Nebuchadnezzar.

3:18 *But if he doesn't, you should know, Your Majesty, we'll never honor your gods or worship the gold statue that you set up."*

The faith and allegiance to God that these three possessed empowered them to proclaim that even if God did not deliver them from the furnace they still would not worship the king's gods or bow to his golden idol. Their emphasis in saying "but if he doesn't" demonstrated their unconditional faith in whatever God's will was for their lives. They did not disrespect their earthly king, but they would not disobey their heavenly King, no matter the consequences.

3:19 *Nebuchadnezzar was so filled with anger toward Shadrach, Meshach, and Abednego that his face turned red. He ordered that the furnace should be heated seven times hotter than normal.*

We may assume by his reaction that Nebuchadnezzar took the response of Shadrach, Meshach, and Abednego as a blow to his pride. They chose to be obedient to their God rather than to Nebuchadnezzar as their king. Ironically, the king had once bowed before these three who participated with Daniel in interpreting the king's former dream, but Nebuchadnezzar now punished Daniel's friends for worshipping the same God, the true God, who had answered their prayers by revealing the meaning of Nebuchadnezzar's vision.

Consequently, the king became so enraged with the three men that "his face turned red." Nebuchadnezzar's fury soared to the point that the punishment he had deemed suitable for those who disobeyed his decree no longer sufficed. As a result, he ordered his servants to heat the furnace seven times hotter than usual, although its normal temperature would have been hot enough to consume anything within it. This was done solely for the king's satisfaction in thinking that he could multiply the men's punishment.

3:20 *He told some soldiers from his army to tie up Shadrach, Meshach, and Abednego so that they could be thrown into the blazing furnace.*

Nebuchadnezzar instructed the mightiest men in his service to restrain Shadrach, Meshach, and Abednego, so they could not escape. They were bound, probably hand and foot, and then thrown into the fiery furnace.

What went through their minds as they were being bound and while they waited for the furnace to reach its increased temperatures? Might they have wondered how soon God would deliver them? With every passing moment that drew them closer to being thrown into the furnace, did they question whether God really intended to deliver them at all?

3:21 *Then the three men were thrown into the blazing furnace. They were wearing their clothes, hats, and other clothing.*

The three men's mobility and movement were restricted as they were tied up with their own clothing, which would have the same effect as being restrained in straight jackets. To be bound in this manner would also cause them to burn more quickly.

3:22 *The king's order was so urgent and the furnace was so extremely hot that the men who carried Shadrach, Meshach, and Abednego were killed by the flames from the fire.*

The heat from the furnace was so intense that the men who threw Shadrach, Meshach, and Abednego into the fire perished just by being so near to it. Certainly by that point, the fire should have also immediately consumed Shadrach, Meshach, and Abednego.

Ironically, by having the furnace heated seven times hotter than usual, the king inadvertently added to the glory that God would receive for delivering Shadrach, Meshach, and Abednego from such intense circumstances. There would be no doubt as to the validity of the miracle, and Nebuchadnezzar would never be able to discredit the marvel by saying that the furnace had not been made hot enough.

Notes/Applications
What a remarkable faith Shadrach, Meshach, and Abednego had! They knew their God, the God of their fathers, could save them from the furnace. However, God, in His sovereignty, allowed them to be sentenced to the fiery chambers. So what happened? Did God abandon them? Did they curse God as they approached the intense heat of the blazing furnace? It appears that their faith did not waiver even as they stood face-to-face with the fire.

The Bible defines faith as "the substance of things hoped for, the evidence of things not seen" *(Hebrews 11:1, NKJV)*. The issue here was not the amount of faith that Daniel's friends possessed but the object of their faith. Even when the object—Almighty God—could not be seen with the naked eye, they trusted that He would accomplish His plan for them through this ordeal. Ultimately, God did not save them from the furnace, but He certainly saved them within the furnace.

God delivered Shadrach, Meshach, and Abednego in a way unimaginable by human design but in a way that glorified Himself. God still wants to work this way in our lives today. Despite our pressing circumstances, God is accomplishing His dynamic plan and perfect will for our lives, and He will not leave us alone in the belly of the furnace. We can walk confidently into fiery trials because God Himself stands with us in the midst of the fire. *"A person's fear sets a trap for him, but one who trusts the Lord is safe" (Proverbs 29:25).* *"No one can please God without faith. Whoever goes to God must believe that God exists and that he rewards those who seek him" (Hebrews 11:6).*

What is the object of our faith? Is it powerful enough to save us in the midst of fiery trials and loving enough to stand with us in them?

Daniel 3:23-30

3:23 *So these three men—Shadrach, Meshach, and Abednego— fell into the blazing furnace. They were still tied up.*

As these three were thrown into the furnace's fierce heat, they were at the mercy of God. The fire not only had no effect upon their bodies, but it did not burn the clothing that chained them either! They fell down in the midst of the furnace, still bound but completely unscathed from the extreme heat of the roaring flames surrounding them.

3:24 *Then Nebuchadnezzar was startled. He sprang to his feet. He asked his advisers, "Didn't we throw three men into the fire?" "That's true, Your Majesty," they answered.*

Evidently, the king took a spectator's seat nearby because we are told that he quickly jumped to his feet while observing this spectacle. Many of his counselors and leaders accompanied him as we will read in verse twenty-seven. It seems as though the king intended to make sport of this horrible display.

Nebuchadnezzar obviously thought that his eyes deceived him because he asked those around him to confirm that they had thrown three men into the fires of the furnace. Those accompanying the king assured him that he was correct.

3:25 *The king replied, "But look, I see four men. They're untied, walking in the middle of the fire, and unharmed. The fourth one looks like a son of the gods."*

Nebuchadnezzar exclaimed that he saw four men loose and walking amidst the furnace and unaffected by the fire. The four in the furnace were not harmed in the least, but we also know that they were not in some type of protective bubble because these verses tell us that they walked around "in the middle of the fire."

How could all of this be, and who was this fourth person? Even Nebuchadnezzar, a prideful leader who served false gods, recognized the identity of this fourth person as the very Son of God, Whose presence redeemed the captives from the furnace's death grip. Such an appearance of the Lord in the Old Testament prior to His earthly birth in Bethlehem is called a "Christophany." Apparently, the Son of God had loosened the garments and ropes and enabled the captives to walk around freely within the furnace.

Regardless of the things Shadrach, Meshach, and Abednego might have been thinking prior to being thrown into the fire, what were they thinking at this moment? Surely, they praised the miraculous, awesome God that they served! He had proven Himself to be far more powerful than they could have ever imagined! The Lord could have caused the great flames to be extinguished, yet this miracle brought even more glory to Him.

3:26 *Then Nebuchadnezzar went to the door of the blazing furnace and said, "Shadrach, Meshach, and Abednego—servants of the Most High God—come out here." Shadrach, Meshach, and Abednego came out of the fire.*

Nebuchadnezzar approached the mouth of the furnace, still unable to believe what he saw, and called for the Jews to come out of the furnace. As he neared the entrance of the furnace, he called each of the three men individually by name and corporately as "servants of the Most High God." Because of the conviction and determination displayed by these three, God received the glory.

3:27 *The king's satraps, governors, mayors, and advisers gathered around the three men. They saw that the fire had not harmed their bodies. The hair on their heads wasn't singed, their clothes weren't burned, and they didn't smell of smoke.*

Many important leaders witnessed this incredible spectacle. The fire had not touched Shadrach, Meshach, or Abednego in the least.

Neither their skin nor clothes were burned. Not a hair on their heads was singed, and their clothes did not even smell of smoke! It was as if they were never even near the flames!

3:28 *Nebuchadnezzar said, "Praise the God of Shadrach, Meshach, and Abednego. He sent his angel and saved his servants, who trusted him. They disobeyed the king and risked their lives so that they would not have to honor or worship any god except their own God.*

After Nebuchadnezzar inspected the men, he blessed the God Who saved them. As previously stated, this absolute monarch could seemingly do anything in the world that he pleased. However, God will allow man, even an absolute earthly monarch, to go only as far as His sovereign will permits.

The king fully and accurately acknowledged the role of God's power in the entire situation. The God of Israel had not only spared the lives of these men, but more importantly, He delivered them because they demonstrated obedience to Him by not worshipping other gods.

3:29 *So I order that people from every province, nation, or language who say anything slanderous about the God of Shadrach, Meshach, and Abednego will be torn limb from limb. Their houses will be turned into piles of rubble. No other god can rescue like this."*

Nebuchadnezzar immediately made another decree, and in so doing, seemingly rescinded the earlier decree that required all people to worship his golden image. However, this was not a decree that required the worship of the God of Shadrach, Meshach, and Abednego, but simply a mandate that forbade anyone to speak against their God. Anyone found speaking against the God of the Israelites would be cut into pieces and would have his home utterly destroyed by fire.

As a witness to God's ultimate power over the elements of the earth and protective power over these faithful servants, Nebuchadnezzar experienced a slight adjustment in his thinking because he realized that no other god could have delivered these men like this all-powerful God.

3:30 *Then the king promoted Shadrach, Meshach, and Abednego to higher positions in the province of Babylon.*

Shadrach, Meshach, and Abednego already held high positions in the government, according to chapter two of the book of Daniel. In the Chaldean language of the original texts, the word for *promoted* as used here is *tselach*, which means "to advance," indicating that they prospered while serving in Nebuchadnezzar's court.[11]

Notes/Applications

This passage is another example of Nebuchadnezzar's fluctuating "spirituality." At the end of chapter two the king praised God for revealing his dream and its translation to Daniel, yet he resorted back to his prideful ways by erecting an enormous golden image and commanding the people to worship it. Then, Nebuchadnezzar seemed to have taken another turn toward the "Most High God" because of the incredible miracle that he witnessed at the fiery furnace.

Nebuchadnezzar's lack of spiritual steadiness is not unlike that of many people today who feast upon religious smorgasbords. The world is full of "spiritualites," individuals who sample a little bit of this religion and a little bit of another one, mix it together, and label it "truth." Some even claim to be Christians, and although they may intellectually believe in the existence of a Supreme Being—and may even call it a "belief in God"—they have never experienced an authentic conversion of the heart. They have never admitted that they are sinners in need of the saving redemption that only the Lord Jesus Christ has the power and authority to give. Naturally, when seemingly spiritual people are ungrounded in their faith, they will ultimately return to a worldly lifestyle, which appeals to human desires. *"These proverbs have come true for them: 'A dog goes back to its vomit,' and 'A sow that has been washed goes back to roll around in the mud'"* (2 Peter 2:22).

There is a vast difference between knowing about God and Christ's teachings, even between witnessing miraculous signs and wonders firsthand, and accepting the truth that Jesus Christ, God's Son, is the only way to eternal life in heaven. Have we partaken of the bread of life and accepted His living water?

"I am the living bread that came from heaven. Whoever eats this bread will live forever. The bread I will give to bring life to the world is my flesh" (John 6:51b).

[13]Jesus answered her, "Everyone who drinks this water will become thirsty again. [14]But those who drink the water that I will give them will never become thirsty again. In fact, the water I will give them will become in them a spring that gushes up to eternal life." (John 4:13–14)

Feast on the living bread today.

DANIEL 4

Daniel 4:1–7

4:1 *From King Nebuchadnezzar. To the people of every province, nation, and language in the world. I wish you peace and prosperity.*

Thus far, Daniel recorded his account of Nebuchadnezzar's reign in the third person narrative voice, but in chapter four, a distinct shift in the point of view occurs. Verse four leaves little doubt that King Nebuchadnezzar narrated this chapter as his own personal experience. The reason that Daniel chose to include this account instead of his own version is unknown, though conclusions may be drawn from reading other chapters of Daniel. The most logical conclusion might be that it was such a rarity for an absolute monarch to recognize his own character flaws, to confess the error of his ways, and to surrender his own authority to a higher one.[1] Therefore, Nebuchadnezzar's testimonial account strengthens the impact of this story's lesson in humility. To open this narration, the king delivered a general greeting in which he wished peace to the inhabitants of the entire world.

4:2 *I am pleased to write to you about the miraculous signs and amazing things the Most High God did for me.*

Nebuchadnezzar explained that he chose to tell his version of this story because he wanted to attest to Almighty God's marvelous works in his life.

4:3 *His miraculous signs are impressive. He uses his power to do amazing things. His kingdom is an eternal kingdom. His power lasts from one generation to the next.*

The king testified of God's miraculous signs and power. Nebuchadnezzar had obviously been influenced by the living example of Daniel, Shadrach, Meshach, and Abednego and especially by the appearance of the Son of God in the fiery furnace. In essence, the king had witnessed God's complete control over creation and human experience. As a result, he had obtained at least some understanding of Jehovah and His attributes. (Unfortunately, the evidence of the king's actions recorded in later verses reveals an incomplete comprehension of Almighty God as the highest authority.) Sixteenth-century theologian John Calvin states, "He [Nebuchadnezzar] seemed to receive with the greatest modesty what God had manifested by his dream through Daniel's interpretation of it, yet he professed with his mouth what he did not really possess."[2]

4:4 *I, Nebuchadnezzar, was living comfortably at home. I was prosperous while living in my palace.*

Nebuchadnezzar expressed the contentment and peacefulness he felt within the security of his home. He currently prospered in material wealth, and his mind was clear of any anxieties.

4:5 *I had a dream that terrified me. The visions I had while I was asleep frightened me.*

Similar to a previous episode, Nebuchadnezzar experienced another dream. This second recorded vision abruptly interrupted the king's serenity and shattered his self-confidence. In addition, the king was not merely disturbed by this dream as he had been by the first dream but was also reduced to a state of uncharacteristic trembling and fear.

4:6 *So I ordered all the wise advisers in Babylon to be brought to me to tell me the dream's meaning.*

Unlike his first vision, Nebuchadnezzar remembered the events of this dream; he did not understand their meaning, however, so he still needed someone to interpret it. He apparently had not learned from his earlier mistake, for he repeated it. Without first consulting Daniel individually, Nebuchadnezzar again summoned Babylon's wise men to appear before him and venture an interpretation.

4:7 *The magicians, psychics, astrologers, and fortunetellers came to me. I told them the dream, but they couldn't tell me its meaning.*

We are told which groups of the king's wise men came to help him. When Nebuchadnezzar previously needed their assistance, they assured him that if he told them his dream they could then interpret its meaning for him. This time, however, the king was fully able to recount the details of his dream, yet the wise men could still not render an interpretation. The Lord prevented these worldly men from posing false explanations of the dream's meaning because He would once again fulfill His plan through His servant Daniel.

Notes/Applications
Although Daniel resolved the conflict of Nebuchadnezzar's first dream, Nebuchadnezzar again summoned the wise men of the kingdom before speaking to Daniel individually. The king obviously had not learned from his past experience of relying upon the magicians in his court to accomplish what only Almighty God could do.

Do we judge Nebuchadnezzar too harshly? Do we not also some-times commit the same sins time and time again? As Christians, those saved from sin's mire, why do we continue to make the same mistakes over and over before learning our lessons? Even the apostle Paul, whom many would label as the "ultimate Christian," struggled with this boggling question.

> [14]*I know that God's standards are spiritual, but I have a corrupt nature, sold as a slave to sin.* [15]*I don't realize what I'm doing. I don't do what I want to do. Instead, I do what I hate.* [16]*I don't do what I want to do, but I agree that God's standards are good.* [17]*So I am no longer the one who is doing the things I hate, but sin that lives in me is doing them.*
>
> [18]*I know that nothing good lives in me; that is, nothing good lives in my corrupt nature. Although I have the desire to do what is right, I don't do it.* [19]*I don't do the good I want to do. Instead, I do the evil that I don't want to do.* [20]*Now, when I do what I don't want to do, I am no longer the one who is doing it. Sin that lives in me is doing it.*
>
> [21]*So I've discovered this truth: Evil is present with me even when I want to do what God's standards say is good.* [22]*I take pleasure in God's standards in my inner being.* [23]*However, I see a different standard at work throughout my body. It is at war with the standards my mind sets and tries to take me captive to sin's standards which still exist throughout my body.* [24]*What a miserable person I am! Who will rescue me from my dying body?* [25]*I thank God that our Lord Jesus Christ rescues me! So I am obedient to God's standards with my mind, but I am obedient to sin's standards with my corrupt nature. (Romans 7:14–25)*

We must never forget that we are sinners saved by God's grace; His grace alone has pardoned us from the penalty of sin, which is eternal damnation in the lake of fire *(Matthew 25:41,46; Revelation 20:10,15)*. However, while on this earth, our spirit continues to battle against the innate desires of our sinful nature. Not only that, but our adversary, the devil, preys upon our vulnerabilities to keep us from being living examples of God's transforming grace. Ultimately, in our own strength, we have no human power over our sin nature. Our ability to resist temptation comes from the Holy Spirit that lives within us. Therefore, we must daily abide in the Holy Spirit in order to overcome sin.

> [16]*Let me explain further. Live your life as your spiritual nature directs you. Then you will never follow through on what your corrupt nature wants.* [17]*What your corrupt nature wants is contrary to what your spiritual nature wants, and what your spiritual nature wants is contrary to what your corrupt nature wants. They are opposed to each other. As a result, you don't always do what you intend to do. . . .*
>
> [25]*If we live by our spiritual nature, then our lives need to conform to our spiritual nature.* (Galatians 5:16–17, 25)

Since it seems that we constantly fail God by continually sinning, should we stop trying to live obediently? Of course not. He wants His children to have repentant hearts, to stop trying in our own strength, and to start trusting Him. *"*[6]*We know that the person we used to be was crucified with him to put an end to sin in our bodies. Because of this we are no longer slaves to sin.* [7]*The person who has died has been freed from sin"* (Romans 6:6–7).

Daniel 4:8–16

4:8 *Finally, Daniel came to me. (He had been renamed Belteshazzar after my god Bel.) The spirit of the holy gods is in him. I told him the dream:*

God allowed Nebuchadnezzar to exhaust his human resources before the king "finally" turned to Daniel, the only vehicle through which Nebuchadnezzar knew he could reach God. The king recognized that Daniel, whom he called Belteshazzar, possessed the Spirit of the Holy God. We continually see the progression of Nebuchadnezzar's spiritual awareness and understanding. He now recognized the Spirit of the Holy God, but we have no evidence that he had abandoned polytheism for sole devotion to Jehovah God. In fact, in this verse, Nebuchadnezzar's profession "after my God Bel" suggests a continued allegiance to the Babylonian patron god, Bel. Some biblical evidence indicates that Nebuchadnezzar later became a believer in Jehovah God, but again, at this point, the king probably did not fully commit himself to monotheism, the worship of one god.

4:9 *"Belteshazzar, head of the magicians, I know the spirit of the holy gods is in you. No secret is too hard for you to uncover. Tell me the meaning of the visions I had in my dream.*

As previously stated, the Babylonians worshipped many gods, but obviously, the king observed a difference in Daniel, which he only knew to refer to as "the spirit of the holy gods." At this point, Nebuchadnezzar expressed some awareness as to the scope and absolute power of the living God that Daniel served. Nebuchadnezzar, however, still held much pride in his heart, so he did not honor God's supremacy as it applied to his own life.

4:10–11 *¹⁰These are the visions I had while I was asleep: I was looking, and I saw an oak tree in the middle of the earth. It was very tall. ¹¹The tree grew, and it became strong enough and tall enough to reach the sky. It could be seen everywhere on earth.*

Nebuchadnezzar began recounting his dream. He first recollected a scene of an enormous tree that stood in the middle of the earth. Initially, the height of the tree was great, but nevertheless, it continued growing until it touched the heavens. This awesome tree could be seen from all over the world.

4:12 *It had beautiful leaves and plenty of fruit, enough to feed everyone. Wild animals found shade under it. Birds came to live in its branches. It fed every living creature.*

The king further stated that the tree's leaves were beautiful. In addition, this mammoth tree provided life and comfort to the entire earth's population. A vast supply of fruit that could adequately feed everyone and everything on earth flourished upon the tree, so no living being faced starvation. Also, various animals rested under the tree's shade while the birds of the air found their rest within the tree's branches.

4:13–14 *¹³"I was seeing these visions as I was asleep. I saw a guardian, a holy being, come down from heaven. ¹⁴He shouted loudly, 'Cut down the oak tree! Cut off its branches! Strip off its leaves! Scatter its fruit! Make the animals under it run away, and make the birds fly from its branches.*

The king continued. A guardian, also called "a holy being," descended from heaven. Most scholars identify this being as a heavenly angel sent by God to communicate a message.[3] The being sounded God's command to destroy the tree, cut off its limbs, shake off its leaves, and scatter its fruit. Consequently, the animals would no longer find shade beneath the tree, nor would the birds find shelter within its branches.

4:15 *But leave the stump and its roots in the ground. Secure it with an iron and bronze chain in the grass in the field. Let it get wet with the dew from the sky. And let it get its share of the plants on the ground with the animals.*

The tree's stump and roots were to remain untouched. The command required preservation of the stump by wrapping it with iron and brass in order to hold it together. This would ultimately ensure its potential for regeneration. Although the tree trunk and limbs were hewn down, the stump would remain rooted in the ground and receive refreshment from heaven's dew. Its existence would be like a beast in the grass of the fields.

4:16 *Let its human mind be changed, and give it the mind of an animal. Let it remain like this for seven time periods.*

The tree's heart would then be transformed from a man's heart to that of a beast. *Time periods* as used in this verse is translated from the Chaldean word *iddan*, which connotes one year, so this condition would last for seven years.[4]

Notes/Applications
King Nebuchadnezzar, ruler over the entire known world at this time, basked in his worldly achievements and considered himself untouchable in his position over creation. Nebuchadnezzar's exploits failed, however, in comparison to Almighty God's greatness. We may smugly criticize the king for placing his confidence in something so insecure as himself, but we, too, often hinge our security upon our personal prosperity.

On England's southern coastal shoreline stand the White Cliffs of Dover, which divide land and water. Seemingly, no amount of superhuman power could destroy these enormous fixtures—timeless, secure, and immovable. Reality greatly contradicts human perception, however. Fine sediments of granite, sandstone, and white chalk compose these stone walls, so each ocean wave, like a sculptor's chiseling tool, slowly but certainly erodes the face of these massive structures. With the naked eye, we may not see this occur, but it happens nonetheless. Therefore, what appears to be solid, eternal rock is actually constructed of many very fragile particles.

Our lives are much the same. We build our lives upon what we perceive to be solid foundations—our positions, possessions, and families. It only takes a culmination of the daily grind's recurring waves or one tidal wave of tragedy, however, and everything upon which we have placed our security washes away.

Nebuchadnezzar lost his possessions and also his humanity before realizing that the foundation upon which he had built his life paled in comparison to the constant, steadfast strength of Almighty God. Likewise, we may have to be stripped of our worldly layers in order to see the naked truth, which is that God, by His grace, makes us who we are and gives us what we have.

> *[24]If I put my confidence in gold*
> *or said to fine gold, "I trust you." . . .*
> *[25]If I enjoyed being very rich*
> *because my hand had found great wealth. . . .*
> *[26]If I saw the light shine*
> *or the moon move along in its splendor*
> *[27]so that my heart was secretly tempted,*
> *and I threw them a kiss with my hand,*
> *[28]then that, too, would be a criminal offense,*
> *and I would have denied God above. (Job 31:24–28)*

Daniel 4:17–24

4:17 *The guardians have announced this decision. The holy ones have announced this so that every living creature will know that the Most High has power over human kingdoms. He gives them to whomever he wishes. He can place the lowest of people in charge of them.'*

The messenger continued proclaiming the sentence. It was not a suggestion but a final, irrevocable command. Nebuchadnezzar understood the weight of such decrees, for he himself had often sanctioned them. God Almighty established this decree to proclaim to mankind that He alone reigns supremely over every being. Nothing on earth occurs without His permission. From the lowest servant to the highest king, God places and removes rulers from positions of authority according to His perfect will. He personally demonstrated this divine authority to Nebuchadnezzar through an experience the king would never forget.

> **DIG DEEPER:** *Earthly Authority*
>
> Throughout history, government leaders ascend to earthly power only by God's providence; although such leaders, generally speaking, rarely acknowledge the hand of God in their destinies (*Daniel 2:21; Romans 13:1; Colossians 1:16*). Almighty God is sovereign and supreme. Therefore, it is important that we never forget that our earthly rulers serve in their roles under the absolute sovereignty of God.

4:18 *I said, "This is the dream I, King Nebuchadnezzar, had. Now you, Belteshazzar, tell me its meaning because the wise advisers in my kingdom can't tell it to me. However, you can, because the spirit of the holy gods is in you."*

Nebuchadnezzar finished describing his dream. After reiterating that the other wise men had failed to interpret the dream, he asked for Daniel's explanation.

4:19 *Then Daniel (who had been renamed Belteshazzar) was momentarily stunned. What he was thinking frightened him. I told him, "Belteshazzar, don't let the dream and its meaning frighten you." Belteshazzar answered, "Sir, I wish that the dream were about those who hate you and its meaning were about your enemies.*

Daniel's thoughts deeply disturbed him. Perhaps, he realized that the dream's interpretation would displease the king and was briefly dumbfounded about what to say. He was not afraid for himself but, rather, for the king. In contrast, perhaps the king was already somewhat relieved by the prospect of knowing the dream's meaning. He told Daniel not to be so worried by the dream. It was as though he knew its interpretation could not be so dreadful. Daniel, almost thinking aloud, verbalized his wish that the judgment depicted in this dream would befall the king's enemies rather than the king himself.

4:20–21 *²⁰You saw an oak tree grow and become strong enough and tall enough to reach the sky. It could be seen everywhere on earth. ²¹It had beautiful leaves and plenty of fruit, enough to feed everyone. Wild animals lived under it, and birds made their homes in its branches.*

Daniel then began interpreting the king's dream. The towering tree, as previously stated, reached high into the heavens and could be seen from anywhere on the earth. He then repeated the idyllic scene—a tree clothed with beautiful leaves and enough fruit to feed all of creation. Also, beneath the shade of the tree, animals lounged, and the birds of the air rested within its branches.

4:22 *You are that tree, Your Majesty. You grew and became strong and mighty until you reached the sky. Your power reaches the most distant part of the world.*

Daniel interpreted the first part of the dream by explaining that the tree represented King Nebuchadnezzar. His kingdom was worldwide. As indicated by the dream, mankind and animals harmoniously coexisted during Nebuchadnezzar's reign, which meant that every aspect of creation prospered under his rule. Certainly at this point, the king must have been very pleased with the interpretation.

4:23 *You saw a guardian, a holy being, come down from heaven. He said, 'Cut down the oak tree! Destroy it! But leave the stump and its roots in the ground. Secure it with an iron and bronze chain in the grass in the field. Let it get wet with the dew from the sky. Let it get its share of the plants on the ground with the wild animals for seven time periods.'*

We now understand why Daniel had become so troubled. He repeated the scene in which the king saw a holy messenger descend from heaven, cut down and destroy the tree, yet protect the stump with bands of iron and brass. *Guardian* as used in this verse stems from the Chaldean word *iyr*, which means an "angel" or "guardian." *Holy being* translates from the Chaldean word *qaddiysh*, which means "saint."[5] This being, therefore, was an angel sent directly from God to Nebuchadnezzar.

Notice that the tree's roots remained in the ground to maintain the life of the stump. Although this preservation of the tree's roots would sustain only a minimal amount of life, the essence of life, nonetheless, would endure. Daniel then repeated that the stump became wet with the night's dew and dwelled as a beast in the grassy field for seven years.

4:24 *"This is the meaning, Your Majesty. The Most High has decided to apply it to you, Your Majesty.*

Daniel was charged with the difficult task of relaying the interpretation of this last sequence of Nebuchadnezzar's dream. He prefaced this portion of the interpretation by reemphasizing that it was a message from Almighty God and not of human concoction. Daniel was reminding the king that while the news was sobering, it was from a higher power and beyond his control. This was God's message for Nebuchadnezzar, not Daniel's.

Notes/Applications

Daniel was a man of integrity. Perhaps, he somewhat feared the king's response to the dream's dismal interpretation, but Daniel ultimately knew that God would protect him and bless his honesty. *"My shield is God above, who saves those whose motives are decent"* *(Psalm 7:10).*

Integrity is a lost commodity in today's marketplace. Unfortunately, many people underestimate its worth. At one time, a person's word legally and (more importantly) morally bound him, but today the world is complicated by legalities. Although it is wise for people to protect their agreements in writing, just think how different society would be if we knew that another person's word was trustworthy. Think how different it would be if that person knew the same about our word.

How do we respond to situations when proclaiming truth may not win us favor? When proclaiming truth may even endanger our lives? No matter the cost, we Christians are to be like Daniel, a people of integrity before our Holy God. May each of us be able to say confidently as the psalmist David said, "Judge me favorably, O Lord, because I have walked with integrity and I have trusted you without wavering" *(Psalm 26:1).*

Daniel 4:25–30

4:25 *You will be forced away from people and live with the wild animals. You will eat grass like cattle. The dew from the sky will make you wet. And seven time periods will pass until you realize that the Most High has power over human kingdoms and that he gives them to whomever he wishes.*

Daniel further explained that Nebuchadnezzar would eventually be removed from his palace and exiled into the fields to live among the animals as one of them. As the oxen and cattle, he would partake of the field's grasses for his nourishment. The degradation of his condition would humiliate him because even an animal would seek shelter in the dampness of the night. For seven years, the king would dwell outdoors day and night and wake up saturated with the morning dew. This is a picture of the dominant world leader being humbled into submission to God's authority because Nebuchadnezzar refused to recognize that it was God that granted him his position and power.

4:26 *Since I said that the stump and the tree's roots were to be left, your kingdom will be restored to you as soon as you realize that heaven rules.*

Daniel offered the king some encouraging news as well: a tree can grow again if the stump is protected. The tree's main trunk cannot grow again, but a new shoot can sprout from the stump. Therefore, God offered a promise that Nebuchadnezzar would not lose his life and that restoration would follow God's judgment, which perfectly illustrates God's mercy and grace. Daniel assured Nebuchadnezzar that once he honored God as divine ruler over all creation, including his own life, he would return to the throne as a changed, humbled king.

4:27 *"That is why, Your Majesty, my best advice is that you stop sinning, and do what is right. Stop committing the same errors, and have pity on the poor. Maybe you can prolong your prosperity."*

Daniel fervently warned Nebuchadnezzar that this sentence would transpire because of the king's stubbornness and pride. He counseled the king to repent of his sin so that judgment might be avoided. Although most citizens of Babylon prospered under Nebuchadnezzar's rule, Daniel suggested that Nebuchadnezzar might demonstrate a change of heart by extending mercy to the poor. This benevolent deed in and of itself could never earn Nebuchadnezzar God's gift of grace, but this act of humility could outwardly display the king's sincerity. If the king heeded this warning, he might have continued living peacefully in his accustomed manner.

4:28 *All this happened to King Nebuchadnezzar.*

This is a transition verse in the text. The king obviously did not heed Daniel's advice, so the fulfillment of the prophecy eventually came to pass.

4:29 *Twelve months later, he was walking around the royal palace in Babylon.*

Apparently, God extended the king a grace period of twelve months to consider what Daniel had told him and to repent of his ways, which illustrates for us God's patience and forbearance with sinful man. God first warned Nebuchadnezzar, then He gave the king ample time to heed the warning.

4:30 *The king thought, "Look how great Babylon is! I built the royal palace by my own impressive power and for my glorious honor."*

Obviously, the king did not embrace Daniel's warnings. If anything, Nebuchadnezzar reveled even more in his own accomplishments.

While walking in his palace, he arrogantly boasted, "I built the royal
palace by my own impressive power and for my glorious honor."
Undoubtedly, the king had accomplished many great things during
his reign, but none of these things had been done to glorify God.
Nebuchadnezzar ignored God's warning and became even more
obsessed with his own magnificence, so God fulfilled the fate prophesied by his servant Daniel.

Notes/Applications

Daniel predicted the tumultuous times ahead for King Nebuchadnezzar and urged the king to acknowledge God's supremacy.
The king, however, arrogantly ignored Daniel's wise counsel, refused
to humble himself, and credited himself with the prosperity of the
empire.

Humility requires the lowering or lessening of oneself, but very
few of us want to be lowered and lessened. The reason is because
humility goes against our prideful nature. Despite God's blessings
upon us, we expect more. In fact, most of us think that we deserve
more—more happiness, financial prosperity, and freedom—when in
fact, the attainment of such things is not our right but our privilege.

A prideful heart is a form of idolatry because it places the individual on a pedestal glorifying self without recognizing God's authority over everything and everyone. *"Before destruction a person's heart is
arrogant, but humility comes before honor"* (Proverbs 18:12). God gives
us the opportunity to humble ourselves, but we can be assured that
if we, like Nebuchadnezzar, continue in our stubborn self-absorp-
tion, either through direct or indirect circumstances, God Himself
will humble us, even if that means removing the pedestal out from
under us.

> [3]*"Your arrogance has deceived you.*
>   *You live on rocky cliffs.*
>   *You make your home up high.*
>   *You say to yourself,*
>   *'No one can bring me down to earth.'*

> *⁴Even though you fly high like an eagle*
> *and build your nest among the stars,*
> *I will bring you down from there,"* declares the Lord.
> *(Obadiah 1:3–4)*

What will it take to bring our hearts under submission to Almighty God? What must we lose before we are humbled? Are we seeking a spirit of humility? We can begin acquiring a humbled spirit by recognizing and thanking God for His blessings. *"A person's pride will humiliate him, but a humble spirit gains honor"* (Proverbs 29:23).

Daniel 4:31–37

4:31 *Before the words came out of his mouth, a voice said from heaven, "King Nebuchadnezzar, listen to this: The kingdom has been taken from you.*

The prophecy foretold in the dream finally happened. As the king reveled in his own achievements, even as the words of the previous verse departed from his lips, the audible voice of God Almighty spoke to him. God told Nebuchadnezzar that as of that very moment the kingdom had been taken away from him.

4:32 *You will be forced away from people and live with the wild animals. You will eat grass like cattle. And seven time periods will pass until you realize that the Most High has power over human kingdoms and that he gives them to whomever he wishes."*

The Lord then reminded Nebuchadnezzar of Daniel's exact words concerning the prophetic vision. Certainly, this reminder haunted Nebuchadnezzar because he realized that he had been cautioned yet had ignored the warnings.

4:33 *Just then the prediction about Nebuchadnezzar came true. He was forced away from people and ate grass like cattle. Dew from the sky made his body wet until his hair grew as long as eagles' feathers and his nails grew as long as birds' claws.*

Within the same hour that the Lord had spoken to the king, the prophecy became reality. The king's associates banished him from his palace when insanity overtook him.[6] Nebuchadnezzar's deranged condition was a result of his disobedience to a direct command from the Lord God. However, as Daniel predicted, the people of the king's court did not attempt to kill the king because God's hand still protected Nebuchadnezzar's life.

As also predicted, while in the fields, Nebuchadnezzar ate grass like the animals. The hair on his body became long like the feathers of an eagle, and his fingernails grew like the claws of a bird. In every other way, he became more like a beast than a human. At this point, Nebuchadnezzar lived among the creatures over which he had once ruled. He actually became lower than these beasts because he could not even survive by instinct. His survival was based entirely upon God's grace and provision for him. Notice and ponder the stark contrast between what this man had once been and his current existence.

We might wonder if thoughts of his past prominence tormented the king, but evidently, he did not even have the rationale to reason in such a manner. This, in itself, exemplifies God's grace even in the midst of His judgment. If God had allowed Nebuchadnezzar to continue in his prideful ways, like a time bomb, the king would have surely self-destructed. However, our just and compassionate God sentenced Nebuchadnezzar to this seven-year exile to ultimately break through Nebuchadnezzar's prideful will. Through this experience, God transformed Nebuchadnezzar into the king and person that God wanted him to be.

4:34 *At the end of the seven time periods, I, Nebuchadnezzar, looked up to heaven, and my mind came back to me. I thanked the Most High, and I praised and honored the one who lives forever, because his power lasts forever and his kingdom lasts from one generation to the next.*

The progression of Nebuchadnezzar's spiritual journey moved to the forefront. Seven years of dismal existence served as a milestone. God lowered Nebuchadnezzar until the king accepted rather than just acknowledged God's supremacy. At the end of the seven years, the period of God's judgment was fulfilled. Nebuchadnezzar lifted his eyes to God, whereupon God immediately restored the king's rationale. Just as prophesied, the king finally, wholeheartedly confessed Jehovah as the only true eternal God. More specifically, he blessed and praised God as the one Who personifies supremacy and sovereign control over everyone and everything.

4:35 *Everyone who lives on earth is nothing compared to him. He does whatever he wishes with the army of heaven and with those who live on earth. There is no one who can oppose him or ask him, "What are you doing?"*

Nebuchadnezzar learned that every person on earth, from servant to king, lives under subjection to God's sovereign will. No one ever has or ever will gain power that is not ordained by the Lord. The king also admitted that God accomplishes His plan in heaven and earth regardless of man's approval or disapproval. As the apostle Paul observed:

> [20]*Who do you think you are to talk back to God like that? Can an object that was made say to its maker, "Why did you make me like this?" [21]A potter has the right to do whatever he wants with his clay. He can make something for a special occasion or something for everyday use from the same lump of clay.*
>
> [22]*If God wants to demonstrate his anger and reveal his power, he can do it. But can't he be extremely patient with people who are objects of his anger because they are headed for destruction? [23]Can't God also reveal the riches of his glory to people who are objects of his mercy and who he had already prepared for glory? [24]This is what God did for us whom he called—whether we are Jews or not.* (Romans 9:20–24)

4:36 *Just then my mind came back to me. My royal honor and glory were also given back to me. My advisers and nobles wanted to meet with me again. I was given back my kingdom and made extraordinarily great.*

As soon as Nebuchadnezzar humbly surrendered himself to the truth, God returned his humanity to him. The king had certainly experienced torment too horrific to imagine. Babylon's imperial monarch had been reduced to a terrible existence for seven years. His repentance, however, served as a catalyst to restore him in the eyes of God and in the eyes of man. God returned unto Nebuchadnezzar his sanity, his position, his honor, and his splendor. The leaders of his government again looked to him as the king of Babylon, their leader.[7] God in His graciousness not only returned everything that the king had prior to these seven years of judgment, but He also added unto Nebuchadnezzar more blessings and majesty than the king had ever possessed.

4:37 *Now I, Nebuchadnezzar, will praise, honor, and give glory to the King of Heaven. Everything he does is true, his ways are right, and he can humiliate those who act arrogantly.*

For the first time in his life, Nebuchadnezzar sincerely worshipped the living God. He paid God the respect that only God deserves. This offering of praise surely carried a tone of humility, sincerity, repentance, and thankfulness! At the end of this verse, Nebuchadnezzar even personally testified to what he considered the life lesson of this experience: God humbles those who are full of pride. Though Nebuchadnezzar had not attained perfection, he had awakened spiritually. He now sought the guidance of Jehovah, the one, true, holy, and living Lord God.

Notes/Applications
Ironically, an attitude of self-promotion consumes pride-filled people, yet these prideful attitudes ultimately lead to destruction. Nebuchadnezzar's seven years of tribulation were God's judgment upon this king's prideful heart. Many times, our hearts must also be subjected to the refining fires of God's judgment to further transform us into His image.

When a metal such as gold or silver is subjected to fire, the physical properties of the metal change. Not only are the metal's elements purified, the metal's structure is strengthened as well. Likewise, in order to bring our unrepentant, proud hearts into submission, we too must pass through the refining fires of judgment and chastisement guided by the hand of our Holy Father. God may allow tribulation,

such as personal loss, abuse, financial pressure, or illness, to occur
in our lives and to test us in every way imaginable. As the intensity
of the trial increases, we may question God's plan. At times, we may
even doubt His love for us. However, God's purpose for each trial is
not to make our lives miserable. Our gracious God uses adversity to
correct us, to restore us, and to strengthen our faith in Him. For the
child of God, a seemingly dismal situation can actually be a blessing
because it ultimately deepens his relationship with God.

> ¹⁰*I have refined you,*
> *but not like silver.*
> *I have tested you in the furnace of suffering.*
> ¹¹*I am doing this for myself, only for myself.*
> *Why should my name be dishonored?*
> *I will not give my glory to anyone else. (Isaiah 48:10–11)*

After God cleanses the impurities of our sinful nature from our
lives with His refining fire, Father God then lovingly draws us, as He
did Nebuchadnezzar, into a dynamic, intimate fellowship-relation-
ship with Him. We emerge from these fires tried, toughened, and
true as God's precious treasure. *"The Lord disciplines everyone he loves.
He severely disciplines everyone he accepts as his child"* (Hebrews 12:6).

Do we desire to know God intimately enough to accept the refining process that is sometimes necessary?

DANIEL 5

Daniel 5:1-8

5:1 *King Belshazzar threw a large banquet for 1,000 nobles and drank wine with them.*

The events recorded here in chapter five happened about twenty years after the events of described in chapter four. Traditionally, biblical historians estimate the year to be 538–539 B.C. Approximately seventy years had passed since Nebuchadnezzar initially besieged Jerusalem and brought the Israelite captives to Babylon, so at this point Daniel would probably have been in his mid-eighties.[1]

The events recorded in this chapter characterize Belshazzar as a corrupt, self-absorbed, and abusive ruler. Months earlier, the armies of the Medes and Persians had captured and imprisoned his father, Nabonidus, king of the Babylonian Empire.[2] Belshazzar, the ruler over the city of Babylon, hosted this great feast and did not concern himself with the welfare of his father. The king invited a thousand of his lords, who were men of great prominence in the city. In a display of arrogance and blatant contempt, Belshazzar drank wine in their presence, which for a king was strongly discouraged since excessive wine compromised mental capacities. A king needed to remain alert against the threat of invasion.

> [4]"*It is not for kings, Lemuel.*
> *It is not for kings to drink wine*
>   *or for rulers to crave liquor.*
>   [5]*Otherwise, they drink*
>   *and forget what they have decreed*
>   *and change the standard of justice*
>   *for all oppressed people.*" *(Proverbs 31:4–5)*

The presence of women *(verse 2)* at this feast also indicates that this gathering was purely hedonistic. Belshazzar planned the event strictly as a social banquet and not for any official purposes. Sadly, the carousing sacrilege performed at this feast serves as Belshazzar's only claim to notoriety.[3]

5:2 **As they were tasting the wine, Belshazzar ordered that the gold and silver utensils which his grandfather Nebuchadnezzar had taken from the temple in Jerusalem be brought to him. He wanted to drink from them with his nobles, his wives, and his concubines.**

Apparently Belshazzar felt lightheaded and, as a result, behaved recklessly. As was standard military practice, when Nebuchadnezzar overtook the city of Jerusalem, he confiscated the gold and silver vessels from the Jewish temple and placed them within the temples of the Babylonian pagan gods.[4] Years later, unlike his forefather Nebuchadnezzar, Belshazzar's command to have these vessels brought to him for such unthinkable intentions aroused the wrath of Holy God.

The foolishness of Belshazzar's pagan acts is compounded by the fact that the armies of the Medes and the Persians, which had already captured King Nabonidus, were enclosing upon the city gates while these sacrilegious festivities occurred within the palace.[5]

Belshazzar's disregard for this imposing threat further magnified his pompous sense of invincibility.

5:3 *So the servants brought the gold utensils that had been taken from God's temple in Jerusalem. The king, his nobles, wives, and concubines drank from them.*

As commanded, servants fetched the vessels for the king so that he and his entourage could drink from them. This verse emphasizes again that these vessels originated from God's temple in Jerusalem. Although the vessels held no intrinsic holy value, they had been designed for exclusive use by the Jewish priests in the temple of the Holy God and had been dedicated to Him, thereby making them sanctified vessels.

5:4 *They drank the wine and praised their gods made of gold, silver, bronze, iron, wood, or stone.*

The partiers performed extensive sacrilegious acts with these vessels. In addition, Belshazzar's drunken guests probably competed to exceed each other's flagrantly sacrilegious displays. When Belshazzar took Jehovah's vessels and toasted the Babylonian idols, he promoted pagan practices that were an affront to God. Sadly, despite the personal witness of Nebuchadnezzar, Belshazzar arrogantly showed no reverence for Daniel's God, and in fact, his outward behavior displayed internal rebellion against this Most High God.

5:5 *Suddenly, the fingers of a person's hand appeared and wrote on the plaster wall opposite the lamp stand of the royal palace. The king watched as the hand wrote.*

God did not allow this sacrilege to continue for long. As the king and his court binged and caroused, a man's fingers suddenly appeared and wrote on the wall. These fingers inscribed a section of the wall that was illuminated by a light, so its message could be clearly seen. Historically, common practice warranted the writing of a king's past titles, victories, and exploits upon a wall at such feasts for the purpose of paying tribute to the king.[6] Therefore, the presence of a message on this wall was not unusual, but the means by which the message appeared there was unprecedented. Certainly, all eyes fell upon the ghostly fingers writing on the wall.

5:6 *Then the king turned pale, and his thoughts frightened him. His hip joints became loose, and his knees knocked against each other.*

When the king saw this marvel, he quickly became somber. In fact, the experience frightened him to the point of physical debilitation. His legs buckled and shook so badly that his knees quivered. Perhaps, the king's countenance dropped, or maybe, the blood drained from his face until he was completely pale. Regardless, Belshazzar's facial expressions displayed the amazing, horrifying effect of this wonder. He was physically and emotionally weakened from witnessing this phenomenon.

5:7 *The king screamed for the psychics, astrologers, and fortune-tellers to be brought to him. He told these wise advisers of Babylon, "Whoever reads this writing and tells me its meaning will be dressed in purple, wear a gold chain on his neck, and become the third-highest ruler in the kingdom."*

Belshazzar then summoned the Babylonian wise men, whose faith rested in false gods that were unable to assist the king in matters beyond the realm of human reason. In doing so, Belshazzar repeated the same mistake made by Nebuchadnezzar. We may safely presume, based upon the history of oral tradition, that the unique events surrounding Nebuchadnezzar's dreams and Daniel's interpretations of those dreams had been communicated from one generation to the next.[7] Therefore, we might conclude that Belshazzar would have learned from his grandfather's experiences. However, Belshazzar, like Nebuchadnezzar before him, attempted to entice the wise men with material rewards. Whoever could interpret the writing on the wall would be rewarded with a purple robe and a gold necklace and would receive a position as the third ruler in Babylon.

This promise of authority as the third ruler in the kingdom reveals that Belshazzar did not recognize the approaching armies of the Medes and Persians as a serious threat. Therefore, this great feast was not, a suicidal fling, as some scholars have theorized. It was not a feast thrown in the abandonment of hope. The king's behavior in this and other verses indicates the contrary.[8] He was simply partying and oblivious to reality.

5:8 *All the king's wise advisers came, but they couldn't read the writing or tell the king its meaning.*

God would not allow the wise men of Babylon to render an interpretation. God wanted Belshazzar and those with him to know that this marvel, though seemingly unbelievable, was very real. God blocked their understanding, so none could interpret this mysterious secret written upon the wall.

> **DIG DEEPER:** *Divine Knowledge*
>
> As his grandfather Nebuchadnezzar had done, Belshazzar sought the help of the wise men, but none of them could interpret the meaning of the writing on the wall. This was because they relied upon their pagan gods for such knowledge. Satan might be the god of this world, but he is not all-knowing nor does he have any powers except those temporarily granted to him by God. Real truth and wisdom come from God alone (*1 Corinthians 4:5; 1 John 4:4–6; Psalm 94:7–15*).

Notes/Applications

Although Belshazzar repeated some of the same sins that his grandfather Nebuchadnezzar had committed, Belshazzar progressed even deeper into the pits of idolatry. After demanding that the temple's golden vessels be brought to him, he and his guests worshipped their pagan gods and sacrilegiously drank wine from these vessels.

"God is a jealous God" means that He does not share His rightful glory as the only true, living God with false gods. *"The Lord your God is a raging fire, a God who does not tolerate rivals" (Deuteronomy 4:24)*. But how does His jealousy differ from ours?

Our human jealousy originates from our insecurities or from the idea that we deserve something more or better than what we have. God's jealousy, however, is based upon His supremacy—His holiness, perfection, goodness, justice, mercy, and grace. Essentially, we commit infidelity when we place ourselves, other things, or other people above Him. *"I'm as protective of you as God is" (2 Corinthians 11:2a)*. God alone deserves all of our honor and praise because He alone is worthy of it. Therefore, we express our sincere love for Him when we honor Him as the exclusive, sole object of our worship. God is long-suffering, but He will tolerate our irreverence for only so long before His judgment will follow.

> *³Never have any other god. ⁴Never make your own carved idols or statues that represent any creature in the sky, on the earth, or in the water. ⁵Never worship them or serve them, because I, the Lord your God, am a God who does not tolerate rivals. I punish children for their parents' sins to the third and fourth generation of those who hate me. (Exodus 20:3–5)*

What has been the object of our worship—people, family, material wealth, work, religion, pleasure, or selfish desires? Anyone or anything that we seek more than we seek Him becomes the focus of what we worship and serve.

Daniel 5:9-16

5:9 *King Belshazzar was terrified, and his face turned pale. His nobles didn't know what to do.*

The king's condition worsened because he was greatly terrified. The word *face* (also translated "countenance" in some versions) in this verse comes from the Chaldean word *ziyv*, which means "brightness or cheerfulness."[9] Belshazzar's cheerfulness, his disposition, changed so remarkably that it amazed and alarmed those in his midst.

5:10 *The discussion between the king and his nobles brought the queen herself into the banquet hall. The queen said, "Your Majesty, may you live forever! Don't let your thoughts frighten you, and don't turn pale.*

The queen, after hearing about the incident, lent her assistance. Most evidence suggests that this was not Belshazzar's wife, but a queen mother, perhaps the wife of Nabonidus or an earlier king. The strongest evidence that this queen was not a bride of Belshazzar is that she came to the banquet hall. She was evidently not counted among his wives who, according to verse three, were already gathered at the great feast. Furthermore, whatever her identity and relationship to Belshazzar, her words in the following verses indicate that she was personally acquainted with Nebuchadnezzar.[10] After addressing Belshazzar with the customary greeting, the queen attempted to comfort him by encouraging him not to let this experience burden him.

5:11 *There's a man in your kingdom who has the spirit of the holy gods. In the days of your grandfather, he was found to have insight, good judgment, and wisdom like the wisdom of the gods. Your grandfather, King Nebuchadnezzar, made him head of the magicians, psychics, astrologers, and fortunetellers.*

The queen assured Belshazzar that one man in the kingdom possessed the "spirit of the holy gods" and could help the king. The queen's description of this man did not necessarily mean, however, that she worshipped this man's God. Though noting the unique power of this man's God, she probably did not acknowledge this Holy God as the only true God. She also recalled that, in the days of Nebuchadnezzar, this man displayed supernatural wisdom unlike that of the wise men currently in the king's presence. This man possessed so much wisdom, in fact, that Nebuchadnezzar had appointed him as chief over the kingdom.

5:12 *This Daniel (who had been renamed Belteshazzar) was found to have knowledge, judgment, and an extraordinary spirit. He has the ability to interpret dreams, solve riddles, and untangle problems. Now, call Daniel, and he will tell you what it means."*

The queen described the ways in which this person surpassed the other wise men in the kingdom. She finally revealed this man's identity as Daniel, whom Nebuchadnezzar had renamed Belteshazzar. After reminding Belshazzar of Daniel's accomplishments for Nebuchadnezzar, she convinced Belshazzar to beckon Daniel to interpret these writings. Whatever the religion this woman practiced, she credited Daniel as a truly godly man.

5:13 *So Daniel was taken to the king. The king asked him, "Are you Daniel, one of the captives that my grandfather brought from Judah?*

As the queen advised, Belshazzar finally summoned Daniel to appear before him. The king confirmed Daniel's identity as a captive Jew, seemingly "to keep Daniel in servile obedience."[11] Again, Belshazzar's reference to his father Nebuchadnezzar indicates an ancestral link and not a direct father-son relationship.

5:14 *I've heard that you have the spirit of the gods and that you have insight, good judgment, and extraordinary wisdom.*

Belshazzar repeated what the queen told him about Daniel. Again, Daniel's close relationship to God characterized him. These compliments, however, did not spark haughtiness in Daniel because he had observed firsthand what pride could do in a man's life. He remained focused upon the source of his blessings.

5:15 *The wise advisers and the psychics were brought to me to read this writing and tell me its meaning. But they couldn't tell me its meaning.*

Belshazzar told Daniel, almost in the form of a challenge, that the other wise men in Babylon had already appeared before the king, but none of them successfully deciphered the meaning of the writing on the wall.

5:16 *I have heard that you can interpret such things and untangle problems. If you can read the writing and tell me its meaning, you will be dressed in purple, wear a gold chain on your neck, and become the third-highest ruler in the kingdom."*

Belshazzar expressed that his particular interest in Daniel resulted from the queen's comments about Daniel's gift for interpretations. The king then offered Daniel the same rewards that he previously promised to the other wise men. If Daniel could decode the writing, he would receive a purple robe, a golden necklace, and the third-highest position in Babylon directly under Belshazzar. These offerings did not tempt Daniel, however. He had already enjoyed the greatest levels of worldly material wealth and positions of authority. Such earthly commendations meant nothing to him, especially coming from such a heretical ruler as Belshazzar.

Notes/Applications

It is obvious from this passage that Daniel lived such a God-centered life that he was remembered for it even generations after his years of active service in Nebuchadnezzar's court. He left a legacy in the kingdom of Babylon that testified of God's character as a supreme yet personal God.

What do we want others to remember us for years after we are gone? Far greater than the wealth that we have acquired or the accomplishments that we have achieved, we should strive to leave a legacy of godly servitude. Only those things that we do for the kingdom of God will be of any eternal value in heaven. They are also likely the only things worth remembering on earth. *"Instead, store up treasures for yourselves in heaven, where moths and rust don't destroy and thieves don't break in and steal"* (Matthew 6:20).

Daniel 5:17–24

5:17 *Daniel told the king, "Keep your gifts. Give your gifts and awards to someone else. I'll still read the writing for you and tell you its meaning.*

Daniel politely declined Belshazzar's gifts and told the king to give the rewards to someone else. Daniel recognized the temporal value of these gifts, especially from such a wicked king whose reign neared its end. He did agree to read the writing and to decipher its meaning for Belshazzar, though not out of obligation as one of the king's subjects but because he understood his role as God's instrument.[12]

5:18–19 *18"Your Majesty, the Most High God gave your grandfather Nebuchadnezzar a kingdom, might, honor, and glory. 19People from every province, nation, and language trembled and were terrified by him, because God gave him power. Nebuchadnezzar killed whomever he wanted to kill, and he kept alive whomever he wanted to keep alive. He promoted whomever he wanted to promote, and he demoted whomever he wanted to demote.*

Before rendering the interpretation, Daniel reminded Belshazzar that Almighty God gave the kingdom of Babylon to Nebuchadnezzar, Belshazzar's forefather, and with this position came prestige, wealth, and power, but also much responsibility. The sovereign source of Nebuchadnezzar's great status was the Most High God Who determines all things, including the beginning and end of every king's reign.

5:20 *But when he became so arrogant and conceited that he became overconfident, he was removed from the royal throne. His honor was taken away from him.*

Daniel further explained how Nebuchadnezzar's pride had blinded him to Almighty God's omnipotence. King Nebuchadnezzar had become so filled with haughtiness that God dethroned him for

a time. The throne, however, was not the greatest treasure that
Nebuchadnezzar had lost; his greatest forfeiture was his identity as
a human being.

5:21 *He was chased away from people, and his mind was
changed into an animal's mind. He lived with wild donkeys, ate
grass like cattle, and his body became wet with dew from the
sky. This happened until he realized that the Most High God has
power over human kingdoms. God puts whomever he wishes in
charge of them.*

Daniel thoroughly recapped Nebuchadnezzar's condition as an
insane, scavenging wild animal. The king remained in this state for
seven years until he professed God as the ultimate ruler over everything and everyone, including all earthly leaders.

5:22 *"Belshazzar, you are one of Nebuchadnezzar's successors.
You didn't remain humble, even though you knew all this.*

Daniel brazenly pointed out that Belshazzar displayed the same
prideful tendencies that had destroyed his predecessor. In addition, Daniel reprimanded Belshazzar for refusing to humble himself
despite knowing the history of his grandfather's reign.

5:23 *But you made yourself greater than the Lord of heaven.
You had the utensils from his temple brought to you. You, your
nobles, wives, and concubines drank wine from them. You praised
your gods made of silver, gold, bronze, iron, wood, or stone. These
gods can't see, hear, or know anything. You didn't honor God,
who has power over your life and everything you do.*

Daniel then admonished the king for his deliberate disregard of
God's supremacy, holiness, and righteousness. Rather than leading
the nation with integrity and dignity, Belshazzar passed the temple
vessels among his guests, who toasted their false gods. They dishonored the only true, all-seeing, all-hearing, and all-knowing God upon

Whose mercy their every breath solely depended. Daniel stressed that the Lord God, who Belshazzar so recklessly dishonored with contemptuous irreverence, actually determined every second of Belshazzar's life and directed his every step. Furthermore, God held Belshazzar accountable for defaming the temple goods but, more importantly, for what this disgrace revealed—a defiant heart. Just as the gavel of divine justice fell upon Nebuchadnezzar, it would also fall upon Belshazzar to a far greater extent because he did not heed the lessons of the past.

5:24 *So he sent the hand to write this inscription.*

After rebuking the king for his wicked behavior, Daniel prepared to give the literal interpretation of the wall's writing. Unlike past writings that might have adorned the king's wall, the Lord's fingers wrote this message.

Notes/Applications

Whether positively or negatively, history does repeat itself. Unfortunately, instead of learning from past mistakes, one generation often duplicates the iniquities of its forefathers. Belshazzar refused to humble his heart before Almighty God despite knowing the events of his grandfather's reign. His lewdness, therefore, ultimately surpassed Nebuchadnezzar's foolishness because Belshazzar ignored the testimony of his grandfather.

> [20]*From the creation of the world, God's invisible qualities, his eternal power and divine nature, have been clearly observed in what he made. As a result, people have no excuse.* [21]*They knew God but did not praise and thank him for being God. Instead, their thoughts were pointless, and their misguided minds were plunged into darkness.* [22]*While claiming to be wise, they became fools (Romans 1:20–22).*

We, too, are individually accountable for what we do with Christ. If we come from an anti-God or atheistic background, we must break the cycle of our parents' sins and become the Christian seed planted in our family and society.

> [5]*He gave his teachings to Israel.*
> *He commanded our ancestors to make them known to their children*
> > [6]*so that the next generation would know them.*
> > *Children yet to be born would learn them.*
> > *They will grow up and tell their children*
> > > [7]*to trust God, to remember what he has done,*
> > > *and to obey his commands.*
> > [8]*Then they will not be like their ancestors,*
> > *a stubborn and rebellious generation.*
> > > *Their hearts were not loyal.*
> > > *Their spirits were not faithful to God.*
> > > (Psalm 78:5–8)

If we come from a rich Christian heritage, we should be thankful, but we must not depend upon the accomplishments of previous generations. We ourselves must move forward in our faith. Let us not be slaves to the sins or achievements of our forefathers. Let us be pioneers and break new ground in our spiritual journey.

Daniel 5:25–31

5:25 *This is what has been written: Numbered, Numbered, Weighed, and Divided.*

Though interpreted here, the inscription was actually comprised of the Chaldean words *"Mene, Mene, Tekel, Upharsin,"* which causes us to wonder why the king's wise men were unable to interpret the message.[13] Apparently, they could read the words but were unable to comprehend their implications. Despite the knowledge and intellect of the king's "wisest" men, the Lord blocked their understanding of what these words meant. The writing probably appeared to be nothing more than a word jumble.

5:26 *This is its meaning: Numbered—God has numbered the days of your kingdom and will bring it to an end.*

Mene is a Chaldean word that means "numbered." As Daniel stated, God numbered the days of the Babylonian Empire, and more specifically of Belshazzar's reign, and He now declared it finished. Ironically, the same wall that generally featured flattering legends of the king's magnificence now publicized this mysterious inscription, which foretold his fall. Furthermore, a monarch's death historically marked the end of his reign, thereby "finishing" his kingdom. This message not only predicted the end of Belshazzar's reign but the end of his life as well.

5:27 *Weighed—you have been weighed on a scale and found to be too light.*

The Chaldean word *tekel* means "weighed." Daniel explained that God had deliberated and deemed that Belshazzar failed to measure up to God's standards. Belshazzar, too immature or too consumed by worldliness to deal with such weighty matters, lacked the character traits necessary to be a good leader. It's already been established that no other historical contributions highlighted Belshazzar's ruling record other than this account of the blasphemous feast. In addition, although his father had been a prisoner for several months, Belshazzar evidently made little or no attempt to rescue him. Therefore, God rendered Belshazzar as spiritually bereft as a person and irresponsible as a king.

5:28 *Divided—your kingdom will be divided and given to the Medes and Persians."*

The word *upharsin* (also translated as *peres*) means "to divide." So, in summary, the wall's inscription actually said, "numbered, numbered [again], weighed, and divided." This statement meant nothing to most people, including the king's men, especially since God confounded their understanding. Daniel, however, knew that God had prescribed this message to alert Belshazzar that his kingdom was quickly nearing its end. Although this king had been given many resources, he had recklessly squandered them. He ruled so poorly, in fact, that God ultimately divided the Babylonian kingdom and gave it to a different race of people, the Persians and the Medes.

5:29 *Then Belshazzar ordered that Daniel be dressed in purple and wear a gold chain on his neck. He made Daniel the third-highest ruler in the kingdom.*

Belshazzar fulfilled his promise to Daniel. The king's servants clothed Daniel in a purple robe, placed a golden chain around his neck to signify his authority and leadership and appointed him as third ruler over Babylon.

Daniel ascended to prominent positions early in his life when he first came to Babylon under Nebuchadnezzar, and now in his later years, Daniel was promoted to a high position. He evidently retained this position throughout the Medo-Persian Empire. Daniel, however, must have tasted the bittersweet reality of knowing the imminent end of the Babylonian Empire.

5:30 *That night King Belshazzar of Babylon was killed.*

As predicted, during that same night, King Cyrus' armies attacked and murdered Belshazzar.

> [22]*The noise of battle and great destruction fills the land.*
> [23]*The hammer of the whole earth is broken and shattered.*
> *See how desolate Babylon is of all the nations!*
> [24]*I will set traps for you, Babylon.*
>> *You will be caught, but you won't know it.*
>> *You will be found and captured*
>>> *because you have opposed the Lord.*
> [25]*The Lord will open his armory*
>> *and bring out the weapons of his fury,*
>>> *because the Almighty Lord of Armies*
>>>> *has a job to do in the land of the Babylonians*
>>>> *(Jeremiah 50:22–25).*

> [40]*I will take them to be slaughtered like lambs, rams, and male goats.*
> [41]*Sheshach has been captured.*
> *Babylon, the city that the whole world praised, has been taken captive. (Jeremiah 51:40–41)*

5:31 *Darius the Mede took over the kingdom. He was 62 years old.*

God closed the curtain on the Babylonian Empire and instituted the next great kingdom—the Medo-Persian Empire. Darius the Mede succeeded Belshazzar as viceroy of Babylon. Few historians doubt his identity as the same Darius mentioned in chapters six, nine, and eleven of Daniel.[14] Darius was sixty-two years old when King Cyrus the Persian granted him jurisdiction as governor over the district previously known as the Babylonian Empire.

Notes/Applications

When God surveyed the spiritual condition of Belshazzar's heart, he found that instead of having a heart filled with humility, Belshazzar's heart was puffed up with pride. Therefore, in God's eyes, Belshazzar was found lacking. But how did Belshazzar fall short? When people looked at him, they probably saw a man that had everything a person could desire—kingship, money, friends, food, wine, and pleasure. However, when God looked at this king, He found a spirit void of His Holy Spirit.

Unlike a human judge who may be swayed by his own opinions, biases, or emotions, God is a righteous, holy, and perfect judge. *"Honest balances and scales belong to the Lord. He made the entire set of weights" (Proverbs 16:11).* When we look at others, we may draw conclusions based upon their appearance or accomplishments, but when God judges each of us, He does not consider anyone's house, job, financial status, educational level, or family name. The Lord looks internally to the core of our being. *"But the Lord told Samuel, 'Don't look at his appearance or how tall he is, because I have rejected him. God does not see as humans see. Humans look at outward appearances, but the Lord looks into the heart'" (1 Samuel 16:7).* God judges us based upon the condition of our heart and motives. He welcomes us when we approach Him with a broken spirit, a spirit fully surrendered to Him, acknowledging Him for Who He truly is. *"The sacrifice pleasing to God is a broken spirit. O God, you do not despise a broken and sorrowful heart" (Psalm 51:17).*

If we take a personal inventory of ourselves, what do we see? Do we see what God sees when He looks at us?

> Lord, thank You for the righteousness of Jesus Christ by which my spiritual lacking or wanting no longer condemns me. When You look at me, may You find a humbled spirit and a repentant heart that are pleasing in Your sight.

DANIEL 6

Daniel 6:1–7

6:1 *Darius decided it would be good to appoint 120 satraps to rule throughout the kingdom.*

Historical evidence indicates that Darius the Mede was not the conqueror of Babylon but was appointed as ruler over the kingdom by King Cyrus the Persian.[1] Though this chapter refers to Darius as "king," his job description resembled that of Belshazzar, who presided over Babylon under the authority of Nabonidus.

Darius established a ruling counsel in Babylon, which consisted of 120 satraps who governed the various regions of Babylon's kingdom. As in chapter three, *satrap* is an archaic Persian word that refers to a provincial governor who ruled over a distinct region, either a small prominent city or a larger territorial district.[2] In essence, the Medo-Persian government structure diluted the monarch's authority, fostered greater differences in opinions, decisions, styles, and ideas and, as a result, created the perfect atmosphere for political corruption where one group or person struggled for power over another.

6:2 *Over these satraps were three officials. Daniel was one of these officials. The satraps were to report to these three officials so that the king wouldn't be cheated.*

Three presidents supervised the 120 satraps to oversee the financial management of the king's assets. Darius established this chain of command to avoid involvement with the routine, menial problems associated with leading a great dominion and also as a means to protect his monetary interests. Basically, he delegated many of his financial tasks to these three presidents and then along to the 120 satraps, so Darius served more as an administrator than as an absolute monarch.[3] Daniel, chosen to be one of these three presidents, likely gained this position because of his honest, trustworthy, and godly character, whereas many of the king's subjects took advantage of their positions of authority by robbing the king and then hiding their actions with altered records.

6:3 *This man, Daniel, distinguished himself among the other officials and satraps because there was an extraordinary spirit in him. The king thought about putting him in charge of the whole kingdom.*

Daniel's godliness permeated his every word and action, which kept him unspoiled by the wealth and position he had gained. Darius favored Daniel over the other two presidents because Daniel had proven himself to be trustworthy. To reward Daniel for his honorable stewardship, Darius considered promoting him to an even higher position of authority.

6:4 *So the other officials and satraps tried to find something to accuse Daniel of in his duties for the kingdom. But they couldn't find anything wrong because he was trustworthy. No error or fault could be found.*

Whenever one person or group is esteemed above others, it often leads to jealousy among the less favored. Likewise, the other two presidents and the satraps probably despised Daniel because Darius so greatly respected him. Certainly, Daniel's ethnic heritage as a captive Israelite must have further fueled their resentment. These men searched for some justifiable reason to discredit Daniel's impeccable reputation as a fit ruler, but they found none. This does not imply that Daniel was perfect. It simply means that these conspirators found no suitable reason to disqualify Daniel from the position. Because Daniel gave God total control of his life, his sins—at least in the sight of the worldly eyes that sought to judge him—were insignificant, so he was beyond human reproach.

6:5 *These men said, "We won't find anything to accuse this man, Daniel, unless we find it in his religious practices."*

Since they were unable to find justifiable reasons to discredit Daniel, these resentful rulers concocted a scheme to incriminate Daniel and to provoke his dismissal. They maliciously fabricated a charge by targeting Daniel's greatest attribute: his relationship with God. They knew that Daniel prayed three times a day in his room as he sought God's guidance for his life, so they decided to entrap him by creating legislation that would conflict with the laws of Daniel's God.

6:6–7 *⁶So these officials and satraps went to the king as a group. They said to him, "May King Darius live forever! ⁷All the officials, governors, satraps, advisers, and mayors agree that the king should make a statute and enforce a decree. The decree should state that for the next 30 days whoever asks for anything from any god or person except you, Your Majesty, will be thrown into a lions' den.*

A representative group of the conspirators, possibly even just a minority of the court who had access to the king, assembled before Darius. After addressing the king with the customary greeting, these men claimed that every official throughout the kingdom had conferred on the matter when, in actuality, they likely misrepresented the true number of officials that had concurred. Even if all 122 of the other rulers had agreed on the matter, they had not consulted Daniel, Darius' most esteemed ruler, and so it was with deception that these conspirators approached the king.[4]

Once before the king, they explained their proposal for a new decree, which prohibited anyone from petitioning any god or person other than the king for thirty days, seemingly ample time to entrap Daniel. The conspirators then announced their prescribed punishment for breaking their proposed law. Anyone found guilty of violating this law would be thrown into the lion's den, a common method of execution during this era.[5] The king's men wished to execute this law and its punishment immediately.

Obviously, these men cleverly devised this recommendation to manipulate the king with flattery. Such a decree certainly inflated Darius' ego. Scripture does not emphasize that Darius was an egotistical king, as were Nebuchadnezzar and Belshazzar, but to varying measures, all people succumb to the sin of pride, and these men obviously preyed upon Darius' natural prideful inclinations. Furthermore, Darius probably viewed the proposal as a gesture of respect and honor since the decree had been formulated by his appointed leaders and not by him.

Notes/Applications

Many souls hunger for the living hope that they see in the lives of believers. However, like the conspirators who sought to entrap Daniel, there are others in this world: perhaps strangers, coworkers, peers, or even family members: who vehemently oppress those who claim the name of Christ.

> [2]*Rescue me from troublemakers.*
> *Save me from bloodthirsty people.*
> [3]*They lie in ambush for me right here!*
> *Fierce men attack me, O Lord,*
> *but not because of any disobedience. (Psalm 59:2–3)*

Corrie ten Boom, a committed Christian, suffered imprisonment in a German concentration camp for hiding Jews in her home during World War II. Ms ten Boom states, "In countries where Christians suffer great tribulation, even persecution, I have seen how the Lord used weak people and children as channels of streams of living water. Their own strength was not enough, but they trusted Him who filled them with the Spirit: not of fear, 'but of power, and of love, and of a sound mind.'"[6]

As Christians, no matter our age or level of spiritual maturity, the attacks of others wound us. However, we need to change our focus and perception, so we can perceive these struggles for what they truly are—moments that demand our total dependency upon God.

We do not have to fear persecution because, although none of us desire to be incriminated by others, what better charge could be laid to our account than to be identified as a follower of the Lord Jesus Christ? *"[28]So don't let your opponents intimidate you in any way. This is God's way of showing them that they will be destroyed and that you will be saved. [29]God has given you the privilege not only to believe in Christ but also to suffer for him"* (Philippians 1:28–29). The only area of Daniel's life that incriminated him was his intimate relationship with his heavenly Father. Can the same be said of us? *"Christ means everything to me in this life, and when I die I'll have even more"* (Philippians 1:21).

Daniel 6:8–14

6:8 *Your Majesty, issue this decree, and sign it. According to the law of the Medes and Persians no one could change it or repeal it."*

The presidents and satraps then asked the king to sign the recommendation into law, making it legally binding. The conspirators knew that the decree could not be overturned once the king signed it, but they also cunningly made the decree short-term (thirty days) since Medo-Persian laws were otherwise irreversible. James M. Freeman, author of *Manners and Customs of the Bible*, explains the confining nature of Medo-Persian law: "The strict etiquette of the Persian court obliged the king never to revoke an order once given, however much he might regret it, because in so doing he would contradict himself, and, according to Persian notions, the law could not contradict itself."[7] *"If it pleases you, Your Majesty, issue a royal decree. It should be recorded in the decrees of the Persians and Medes, never to be repealed"* (Esther 1:19). A law, however, could be "neutralized" by executing another decree that stated the opposite of the previous one.

6:9 *So Darius signed the written decree.*

Darius, upon the urging of his officials and with a heightened sense of importance, signed the decree into law without considering the ramifications of his actions.

6:10 *When Daniel learned that the document had been signed, he went to his house. An upper room in his house had windows that opened in the direction of Jerusalem. Three times each day he got down on his knees and prayed to his God. He had always praised God this way.*

It did not take long for news of the decree to reach Daniel. Perhaps, the conspirators even sent men to notify Daniel as soon as the decree was sealed. However, despite the decree's deadly ramifications, Daniel did not evade the issue or change his practice. Peering through his window toward Jerusalem, Daniel continued praying to Jehovah three times a day. He proved his commitment and faithfulness to God by praying openly and boldly according to Jewish custom.[8] *"I will bow toward your holy temple. I will give thanks to your name because of your mercy and truth. You have made your name and your promise greater than everything"* (Psalm 138:2).

6:11 *One of those times the men came in as a group and found Daniel praying and pleading to his God.*

Some of the satraps, maybe even the presidents themselves, arrived outside Daniel's window and saw him praying just as expected. In this way, they collected their witnesses and evidence against Daniel.

6:12 *Then they went and spoke to the king about his decree. They asked, "Didn't you sign a decree which stated that for 30 days whoever asks for anything from any god or person except you, Your Majesty, will be thrown into a lions' den?" The king answered, "That's true. According to the law of the Medes and Persians the decree can't be repealed."*

The conspirators approached Darius, yet before they informed him of their findings, they repeated to him the decree because they knew that he highly favored Daniel. The men again clarified the king's obligation to execute the punishment. Darius not only confirmed the validity of the decree but also reaffirmed that "according to the law of the Medes and Persians" neither this law nor its punishment could be rescinded.

6:13 *They replied, "Your Majesty, Daniel, one of the captives from Judah, refuses to obey your order or the decree that you signed. He prays three times each day."*

The conspirators finally disclosed Daniel's identity as one who had transgressed the law, and not just once but three times a day. They also undermined Daniel by referring to him as "one of the captives from Judah." They further alleged that Daniel had disregarded the king and his decrees by breaking this law.

6:14 *The king was very displeased when he heard this. He tried every way he could think of to save Daniel. Until sundown he did everything he could to rescue him.*

After hearing from his officials, Darius realized the impact of his rash decision and his helplessness to postpone enforcement of the penalty. Although he knew he had been swindled, he could not annul the matter, so he spent the rest of his day trying to circumvent the law, hoping to spare Daniel's life.

Notes/Applications
Daniel did not wait until the crisis, the signing of the decree, to begin his prayer life. Even before the crisis, his prayers were perpetually lifted to the God that he so intimately knew, and despite the bleak circumstances, Daniel faithfully prayed expectantly. *"Be happy in your confidence, be patient in trouble, and pray continually" (Romans 12:12).* Certainly, if Daniel thought that God would not hear his prayers and answer them, this wise man would not have squandered his time. Daniel, however, knew that omnipotent God would act in a mighty way. Therefore, the frequency of Daniel's petitions did not demonstrate a lack of faith. On the contrary, Daniel's earnest prayers displayed his obedience to the Lord and his faith that Almighty God answers the prayers of His people. *"Prayers offered by those who have God's approval are effective" (James 5:16).*

Perhaps, we yearn for a meaningful and dynamic prayer life but think that we do not know where to begin. Some situations completely baffle us, and we are unsure how to approach God, so we cease praying altogether. This is the wrong course of action. Even when heaven seems silent, we must faithfully converse with God. When we approach Him in sincerity, even when we cannot eloquently communicate our needs, His Holy Spirit intervenes and does this for us:

²⁶The Spirit also helps us in our weakness, because we don't know how to pray for what we need. But the Spirit intercedes along with our groans that cannot be expressed in words. ²⁷The one who searches our hearts knows what the Spirit has in mind. The Spirit intercedes for God's people the way God wants him to. (Romans 8:26–27)

God not only hears our mouths speaking; He hears our hearts as well. So if for nothing else, we can go before His throne and simply express our loss for words.

Is prayer our immediate response or our last resort to the situations that we face? Have we faithfully spent time in prayer with the King of Kings on a daily basis? Do we fervently pray believing that God will work mightily according to His will? *"Have faith that you will receive whatever you ask for in prayer"* (Matthew 21:22).

Daniel 6:15–22

6:15 *Then Daniel's accusers gathered in front of the king. They said to him, "Remember, Your Majesty, the Medes and Persians have a law that no decree or statute the king makes can be changed."*

The conspirators assembled before King Darius and reminded him about the mandatory punishment for violators of the decree. Although they sensed the king's resentment, they, nonetheless, pressured him to enforce the sentence against Daniel.

6:16 *So the king gave the order, and Daniel was brought to him and thrown into the lions' den. The king told Daniel, "May your God, whom you always worship, save you!"*

Darius had Daniel thrown into the lion's den. Notice Darius' statement at the end of this verse: "May your God, whom you always worship, save you!." Could it be that Darius recognized a difference between his idol gods that could not see, hear, move, or think and the one, true God that Daniel served? Based upon Daniel's example, Darius evidently believed in the capability of Daniel's God to extend mercy and deliverance to this servant. What an influence Daniel's consistent prayer life and spiritual walk must have been to convey the Lord's power and strength so clearly even to a king who did not serve Jehovah as his God!

6:17 *A stone was brought and placed over the opening of the den. The king put his seal on the stone, using his ring and the rings of his nobles, so that Daniel's situation could not be changed.*

The king's men placed a stone over the mouth of the den to prohibit any attempt of escape, and then the king sealed the stone with his own signet, as did the lords of his court. A signet was an engraved seal that marked the identity of the sealer. The seal authenticated official documents, so in effect the king's official seal of approval marked this stone to discourage anyone from attempting to free Daniel.[9]

6:18 *Then the king went to his palace and spent the night without food or company. He couldn't get to sleep.*

After closing the den, Darius returned to his quarters for an atypical night. The king spent the night in isolation. He did not partake of food or have his musicians play for him. According to this verse, he did not sleep at all that night.

6:19 *At dawn, as soon as it was light, the king got up and quickly went to the lions' den.*

Notice that this verse does not state that the king awoke from sleep, only that he got up from bed. As the previous verse stated, Darius had never gone to sleep throughout the night. The king arose early the next morning and hurried to the lion's den, implying that he hoped Daniel was still alive.

6:20 *As he came near the den where Daniel was, the king called to Daniel with anguish in his voice, "Daniel, servant of the living God! Was God, whom you always worship, able to save you from the lions?"*

We can only speculate whether Darius truly believed that Daniel had survived the night. When the king called out with anguish in his voice, his disposition seemed to be one of defeat. As he called into the pit, Darius referred to Daniel as a "servant of the living God." He then asked if Daniel's God had been able to deliver His servant from death.

6:21–22 ²¹*Daniel said to the king, "Your Majesty, may you live forever! ²²My God sent his angel and shut the lions' mouths so that they couldn't hurt me. He did this because he considered me innocent. Your Majesty, I haven't committed any crime."*

Although the king most likely did not expect a response, from the depths of the lion's den an answer emerged. What an enormous relief it must have been for Darius to hear Daniel's voice! Daniel responded, "Your Majesty, may you live forever," in the same respectful way he greeted all the kings he had served. Daniel answered Darius by testifying that God had "sent His angel" to shut the mouths of the lions. Remarkably, Daniel was not just alive but was altogether unharmed! It was, without doubt, God's awesome power protecting Daniel's life.

Daniel also assured the king of his own innocence. Although Daniel failed to abide by the king's law, the conspirators manipulated Darius into establishing this decree, which disobeyed the greater law of God. Therefore, if Daniel obeyed Darius' law, he transgressed the laws of God.

Notes/Applications

King Darius allowed his governors and satraps to flatter him and manipulate him into hurriedly signing the decree. Obviously, the king could have avoided much anguish if he had evaluated the situation before taking action.

A heart and mind yielded to the will of God will make deliberate decisions rather than hasty ones. *"The thoughts of righteous people are fair. The advice of wicked people is treacherous"* (Proverbs 12:5). We may recognize the need to commit the "big" things to the Lord but think that we can handle the "small" things ourselves. But how do we know the impact that any decision has upon our lives? Truthfully, if we do not seek God in the seemingly trivial matters, we probably do not search for His wisdom in the important decisions either. Yielding to the Holy Spirit is not a one-time event in the Christian journey.

We are so easily distracted by the temporal cares of this fast-paced world that we must begin taking every matter before the throne of God, thereby seeking His will and direction in every situation and listening for His voice. We must then not impart on a different course until we know that we have heard His voice—not the world's and not our own. Simply stated, we must surrender our will to His.

> [5]*Trust the Lord with all your heart,*
> *and do not rely on your own understanding.*
> [6]*In all your ways acknowledge him,*
> *and he will make your paths smooth. (Proverbs 3:5–6)*

Hasty decisions have consequences, and the impact of any decision endures far beyond the present. However, if we wait for God's direction before we act, we will spare ourselves of the consequential guilt and unrest that accompany trying to do the impossible, which is running ahead of God.

> [8] *"My thoughts are not your thoughts,*
> *and my ways are not your ways," declares the Lord.*
> [9]*"Just as the heavens are higher than the earth,*
> *so my ways are higher than your ways,*
> *and my thoughts are higher than your thoughts.*
> *(Isaiah 55:8–9)*

Daniel 6:23–28

6:23 *The king was overjoyed and had Daniel taken out of the den. When Daniel was taken out of the den, people saw that he was completely unharmed because he trusted his God.*

The king rejoiced because Daniel survived. Violation of the decree required that a sentence be served in the lions' den but failed to stipulate the duration of time spent there, so Darius ordered his men to remove Daniel from the pit. Although Daniel was checked for injuries, not a single scratch was found on him. Certainly, Daniel's accusers never comprehended that he would survive a single hour in the den, let alone emerge completely unscathed after spending an entire night there. The only reason for this related to Daniel's unreserved conviction in the power of Almighty God. Daniel's release, therefore, marvelously testified of God's care for those that sincerely love and faithfully obey Him.

> **DIG DEEPER:** *Deliverance*
>
> Because of Daniel's uncompromising commitment to God, his captors cast him into a lions' den to die for his "crimes." Once again, however, the Lord directed Daniel's course and miraculously spared his life. Throughout the Scriptures, Almighty God has demonstrated His faithfulness toward His children who remain obedient to Him despite trying circumstances (*Exodus 14; Acts 16*).

6:24 *The king ordered those men who had brought charges against Daniel to be brought to him. They, their wives, and their children were thrown into the lions' den. Before they reached the bottom of the den, the lions attacked them and crushed all their bones.*

Finally—justice! Ironically, Darius sentenced Daniel's accusers, their wives, and their children to the lions' den: the same execution they had designed for Daniel. This proclamation likely did not include all 120 satraps because the absence of several ruling authorities would have caused considerable upheaval, leaving the kingdom militarily vulnerable. Surely though, the group thrown to the lions included the most determined of the conspirators—probably the same people who first approached Darius regarding the decree.

This verse has other scriptural implications. It may seem unjust to punish the immediate families of these men, but the king felt justified in responding this way. This, in essence, illustrates the domino effect that an individual's sin has on others. Since these men extended no mercy toward the servant of God, King Darius demonstrated no mercy toward Daniel's accusers or toward their families. Without a doubt, the lions thrived as hungry, vicious beasts, which were ready, willing, and able to satisfy their voracious appetites because, before the conspirators even reached the bottom of the den, the lions completely ravished them.

6:25–26 *²⁵Then King Darius wrote to the people of every province, nation, and language all over the world: I wish you peace and prosperity. ²⁶I decree that in every part of my kingdom people should tremble with terror in front of Daniel's God, the living God who continues forever. His kingdom will never be destroyed. His power lasts to the end of time.*

Darius issued a new decree and forwarded it with a greeting of peace to every citizen throughout the Medo-Persian Empire. To avoid any misunderstanding, it reached every person of every nation and language and required them to revere the God of Daniel because, as Darius restated, He was "the living God." Darius declared that God was steadfast and immovable forever and that His kingdom would never be destroyed.

The forging of this decree by Darius after witnessing a miracle of God parallels Nebuchadnezzar's declaration after Shadrach, Meshach, and Abednego had been wondrously spared from the fiery furnace. *"So I order that people from every province, nation, or lan-*

guage who say anything slanderous about the God of Shadrach, Meshach, and Abednego will be torn limb from limb. Their houses will be turned into piles of rubble. No other god can rescue like this" (Daniel 3:29). Just like Nebuchadnezzar many years before him, Darius acknowledged that God holds ultimate power over the entire earth and that His dominion will eternally prevail.

6:27 *He saves, rescues, and does miraculous signs and amazing things in heaven and on earth. He saved Daniel from the lions.*

Whether or not Darius entrusted his life to God is unknown, but he testified of God's awesome, powerful works to the entire known world. In the decree, Darius explained that God continually presides over all matters in the universe as displayed by His deliverance of His servant Daniel.

6:28 *This man, Daniel, prospered during the reign of Darius and the reign of Cyrus the Persian.*

Daniel, well into his eighties at this point, lived a healthy life and prospered during the reign of King Cyrus the Persian. He lived and worked directly under the authority of Darius the Mede. Because Daniel continued in his spiritual walk of faithful service to Almighty God, he prospered!

Notes/Applications

Some people pose the argument that Daniel survived the lions' lair because the lions were sick or were not hungry. However, Scripture explains that an angel shut the mouths of the lions. Daniel once again experienced the miraculous power of God, thereby testifying to an earthly king the transforming, miraculous power of the heavenly King.

Whether our lions' den consists of emotional, familial, financial, physical, or spiritual strife, we can know that in the midst of the spiritual warfare, our God can shut the lions' mouths. We may not always be spared from the lions' lair, but God will perform a miracle within us that glorifies Himself and strengthens us during our spiritual journey. Like Daniel, we will be a living testament of Almighty God's immeasurable, miracle-working power. *"Almighty Lord, you made heaven and earth by your great strength and powerful arm. Nothing is too hard for you"* (Jeremiah 32:17). With God Almighty, the impossible is possible. *"It is impossible for people to save themselves, but everything is possible for God"* (Matthew 19:26b). *"But nothing is impossible for God"* (Luke 1:37).

DANIEL 7

Daniel 7:1–7

7:1 *In Belshazzar's first year as king of Babylon, Daniel had a dream. He saw a vision while he was asleep. He wrote down the main parts of the dream.*

The first six chapters in the book of Daniel recount Daniel's intervention in the lives of kings and God's intervention in the lives of Daniel and his fellow captives. While studying these passages, we are awed by the miracles of our loving, sovereign God expressed through the testimony of His obedient and faithful servant Daniel.

During the last half of the book of Daniel, beginning with this chapter, a much different tone surfaces. The separation in the text is clear, almost as though the book were written in two sections, one which could be entitled "History" and the other "Prophesies." Whereas chapters one through six describe Daniel's interpretations of the visions and dreams of Babylon's leaders, chapters seven through twelve recount specific prophetic visions that God revealed directly to Daniel. In the first year of Belshazzar's reign, between 556 B.C. and 553 B.C., God sent a vision to Daniel.[1] Placed within the chronological sequence outlined in the first six chapters of the book, this vision happened sometime between the events recorded in chapter four and chapter five. That means at the conclusion of chapter six, we take a fourteen-year step backwards to examine Daniel's prophetic vision concerning the end-time events awaiting the Jewish race and the entire world.

God had formerly used Daniel to interpret the dreams of the kings he had served, but this chapter features the first recorded account of Daniel himself having a dream or a vision. This vision appeared to Daniel in the form of a dream, so when he awoke, Daniel recorded the details of the vision because he wanted to accurately document what God had revealed through these prophetic visions.

7:2 *In my visions at night I, Daniel, saw the four winds of heaven stirring up the Mediterranean Sea.*

Daniel conveyed his dream by describing the four winds of heaven that rushed upon a great sea. Many interpretations regarding the symbolism of the "four winds of heaven" exist, but the most logical explanation suggests that the four winds represent nothing more than actual gusts of wind. The description of four specific winds also suggests that these opposing winds converged upon the sea from different directional origins, most likely the four major orientations of the earth—north, east, south, and west. The emphasis on these winds being "of heaven" implies that they were both created and guided by Almighty God Himself to fulfill His providential, sovereign will. This imagery of winds used to accomplish God's purposes appears in other scriptural texts as well, and usually signals God's approaching judgment upon wayward people.

> *I'll bring the four winds*
> > *from the four corners of heaven against Elam*
> > *and scatter its people in every direction.*
> *There won't be a nation*
> > *where Elam's refugees won't go. (Jeremiah 49:36)*

This is what the Lord says:
I will stir up a destructive wind against Babylon
and against the people who live in Leb Kamai.
(Jeremiah 51:1)

The Lord sent a violent wind over the sea. The storm was so
powerful that the ship was in danger of breaking up. (Jonah 1:4)

Many expositors contend that the "Mediterranean Sea" (translated "Great Sea" in other versions) in this verse represents the entire population of mankind on a grand scale.[2] The literal Hebrew translation of this word, however, means "sea" or "ocean" as we commonly understand it today.[3] Therefore, this sea likely refers specifically to the Mediterranean Sea, and the region to which this prophetic vision pertains.[4]

[6]The western border is the coastline of the Mediterranean Sea.
[7]The northern border extends from the Mediterranean Sea to
Mount Hor. (Numbers 34:6–7)

Your borders will be the desert on the south, nearby Lebanon to the
Euphrates River (the country of the Hittites) on the north, and the
Mediterranean Sea on the west. (Joshua 1:4)

Whether or not the four winds and the Mediterranean sea hold any greater figurative significance remains uncertain, but to strongly infer that such is the case would be, at best, speculation and could, at worst, diminish the pertinence of the beasts.

7:3 Four large animals, each one different from the others, came out of the sea.

Four great beasts arose from the sea, though they were great only in the eyes of man. These beasts resembled mythological creatures in their appearance. We know that they were not actual animals but were images that symbolized a deeper message. Each beast varied from the others, and the following verses reveal their appearances became progressively more grotesque.

7:4 *The first animal was like a lion, but it had wings like an eagle. I watched until its wings were plucked off and it was lifted off the ground. It was made to stand on two feet like a human and was given a human mind.*

Generally, a lion connotes strength, and the eagle represents speed. Lions tear at their prey with their sharp claws and powerful jaws, and their teeth can slice through the toughest meat. The lion is the king of all beasts, and the eagle is the king of all birds. Since ancient times, the eagle has symbolized courage and power. It possesses superb aerial skills. The bird's wings give it the ability to flee danger but also to swiftly attack its prey.

This first beast, which looked like a lion with the wings of an eagle, had four feet, yet stood upon its hind legs as a human stands upon his feet. Daniel's observations of this beast indicated that it had been weakened by some stronger force. First, the feathers of its wings were "plucked off," thereby stripping the beast of its swiftness. Second, this beast was forced to "stand on two feet like a human," so it was unable to utilize its full potential of power. Finally, it no longer had the strong, courageous heart of a lion. Instead, it was given the weak, timid, and fearful heart of man.

7:5 *I saw a second animal. It looked like a bear. It was raised on one side and had three ribs in its mouth between its teeth. It was told, "Get up, and eat as much meat as you want."*

The predatory agility of a bear lacks in comparison to a lion's coordination. A bear moves awkwardly; therefore, it must conquer with its crushing brute strength. This profound strength can literally obliterate anything in its path, so the bear's presence poses a threat and must never be underestimated. When a bear attacks, it mauls and rips the flesh of its prey.

This bear-like beast appeared to be raised up on one side, clenching between its teeth three ribs of an unidentified being. While Daniel observed this spectacle, a voice commanded the beast to eat as much as it wanted. Scholars debate the source of those instructions. Many good arguments support each interpretation. Since the answer does not appear to play an integral role in the overall interpretation of the vision, perhaps it is wisest to conclude that the source of this voice is the Lord Himself. This interpretation encompasses all other interpretations, as John Calvin expresses, not because "God was the author of cruelty, but since He governs by His secret counsel the events which men carry on without method."[5] Ultimately, regardless of who spoke to the beast, the fulfillment of God's providential plan was enacted by the command.

7:6 *After this, I saw another animal. It looked like a leopard. On its back it had four wings, like the wings of a bird. The animal also had four heads. It was given power to rule.*

A leopard is a graceful creature—slim and swift yet strong and fierce. Noted as an agile climber and stalker of its prey, the leopard, a nocturnal creature, hunts at night when its prey may be less alert and when natural conditions allow it to surprise its victim. Although the leopard cunningly calculates an attack, once it does attack, its movements are swift and sure, leaving its prey no time to react.

This beast resembled a leopard because it typified rapid conquests, yet this beast differed from a leopard because it was four-headed with four wings on its back. While similar to the first beast, this beast's wings were somehow inferior since they compared to the wings of a common bird rather than those of an eagle. Daniel explained that it was given dominion, which revealed the first hint of the figurative significance of the beasts.

7:7 *After this, I saw a fourth animal in my vision during the night. It was terrifying, dreadful, extraordinarily strong, and had large iron teeth. It devoured and crushed its victims and trampled whatever was left. It acted differently from all the other animals that I had seen before. It had ten horns.*

The fourth beast contrasts the others as well as any beast that has ever lived. The fourth beast is perhaps the most intriguing beast to study because its significance has not yet been completely fulfilled. In addition, this beast's horrible appearance and great power paint a fearful image. It had iron teeth, representing the fierceness with which it consumed everything in its path and trampled inferior beings beneath its feet in order to bring all creation, both man and beast, under its subjection. Most significant were the ten horns upon its head.

Notes/Applications

Daniel's dream in this chapter somewhat parallels the dream in chapter two that he interpreted for Nebuchadnezzar. God used the earlier experience to increase Daniel's understanding for what he now faced. Likewise, God also uses our present situations to prepare us for the future that He has planned.

It is sometimes difficult to acknowledge God's hand in every aspect of our lives because this principle challenges our theology. We gladly accept the good times as gifts from God, but we question how He could allow the bad things to happen. Is it realistic to praise God for our fiery furnace or lions' den experiences that come in the form of losing a loved one, a job, our health, or our hope? How can we be thankful for these things? Thankfulness prevails in seeing things from God's perspective, the big picture, and knowing that God never ceases being Who He is—the Sovereign God Who equips us to persevere through today's momentary troubles. *"We know that all things work together for the good of those who love God—those whom he has called according to his plan"* (Romans 8:28).

Everything in our lives, whether jewel or junk, is either procured by God or permitted by Him. Therefore, when we intimately know Him, we can find something in every situation for which to be thankful. *"Whatever happens, give thanks, because it is God's will in Christ Jesus that you do this"* (1 Thessalonians 5:18). Nothing that happens to us today is without purpose because today prepares us for tomorrow as we "hold firmly to the word of life. Then I can brag on the day of Christ that my effort was not wasted and that my work produced results" *(Philippians 2:16).*

"I will bless you every day.
I will praise your name forever and ever" (Psalm 145:2).

Daniel 7:8–14

7:8 *While I was thinking about the horns, another horn, a little horn, came up among them. It uprooted three of the other horns. This horn had eyes like human eyes and a mouth that spoke impressive things.*

As Daniel examined the ten horns, a little horn arose from among them. Although these horns had grown for a time, three of the first ten horns were uprooted immediately, seemingly as a result of the emergence of this little horn.

This little horn possessed eyes like a man and a mouth that spoke arrogant propaganda. The message was of monumental importance because the little horn's "impressive" spoutings were actually horrible words blaspheming the name of God. *"⁵The beast was allowed to speak arrogant and insulting things. It was given authority to act for 42 months. ⁶It opened its mouth to insult God, to insult his name and his tent—those who are living in heaven"* (Revelation 13:5–6).

7:9 *I watched until thrones were set up and the Ancient One, who has lived for endless years, sat down. His clothes were as white as snow and the hair on his head was like pure wool. His throne was fiery flames, and its wheels were burning fire.*

Daniel watched this scene of the horrible beast with the ten horns and the little horn until the thrones—that is, the thrones of authority belonging to the kingdoms and empires represented by the beasts described in the previous verses and interpreted in verses to follow—were finally put in where they belong. God Almighty, the Ancient One, will ultimately subdue the existence of these great world empires.

This title, the Ancient One, expresses the infinitude of God the Father, and seems to be reserved specifically for the Father rather than the Son or the Spirit. Some readers may presume that the Ancient One mentioned in this verse refers to the Lord Jesus simply to collaborate an interpretation that this verse refers to His second coming before His millennial reign. However, verse thirteen clearly identifies Jesus as the "Son of Man," Who is brought before the Ancient One.

In addition, Daniel's physical description of God the Father is simple yet incomprehensible. God's pure, radiant white garments and His soft hair, white as wool, depict His wisdom, antiquity, glory, and authority. Certainly, the Holy God seated upon His throne in all of His beauty, majesty, and holiness must have been an incredible sight to behold.

7:10 *A river of fire flowed. It came from him. Thousands and thousands served him. Ten thousand times ten thousand were stationed in front of him. The court convened, and the books were opened.*

This fiery stream flowed from the throne of the Ancient One as a vast multitude waited upon the Lord. Ten thousand times ten thousand, a seemingly endless gathering, stood in awe before the holiness of the Lord God Almighty. *"Then I heard the voices of many angels, the four living creatures, and the leaders surrounding the throne. They numbered ten thousand times ten thousand and thousands times thousands"* (Revelation 5:11).

Daniel, discerning the significance of the scene, realized that the time of judgment was at hand. He saw what were apparently books of judgment opened before the Lord. *"I saw the dead, both important and unimportant people, standing in front of the throne. Books were opened, including the Book of Life. The dead were judged on the basis of what they had done, as recorded in the books"* (Revelation 20:12).

7:11 *I continued to watch because of the impressive words that the horn was speaking. I watched until the animal was killed. Its body was destroyed and put into a raging fire.*

Daniel then observed the little horn and heard all that it spouted until a blazing flame finally consumed the little horn, presumably as a specific result of the "impressive words" that it spoke.

7:12 *The power of the rest of the animals was taken away, but they were allowed to live for a period of time.*

Daniel then briefly mentioned the fates of the three lesser beasts. Unlike the final beast, these beasts did not meet destruction simultaneously but successively. Apparently, they lost their power and no longer posed a threat, so their lives continued for a while.

7:13 *In my visions during the night, I saw among the clouds in heaven someone like the Son of Man. He came to the Ancient One, who has lived for endless years, and was presented to him.*

Daniel continued explaining his visions, which should be understood to mean either the one and same vision described to this point or another vision related directly to the previous one and occurring that same night shortly after the first vision. Therefore, the plural use of the word visions in this verse likely indicates several parts of the same dream, and during the last segment of this vision, Daniel saw the Son of Man come "among the clouds of heaven" to the Ancient One. "*Then I looked, and there was a white cloud, and on the cloud sat someone who was like the Son of Man. He had a gold crown on his head and a sharp sickle in his hand*" (Revelation 14:14). Daniel watched as God the Son drew near to God the Father.

7:14 *He was given power, honor, and a kingdom. People from every province, nation, and language were to serve him. His power is an eternal power that will not be taken away. His kingdom will never be destroyed.*

The scene appeared to be a coronation. Jesus was ushered in before His Father where God would give His Son all power and dominion over the earth, not as a guiding hand that would control all manner of providence but as the direct and physically present authority. He would literally return as supreme ruler over mankind and would begin the reign of His "everlasting dominion." Further explanation of this kingdom is provided in the interpretation of this vision in later verses.

Notes/Applications

Every mighty roar of the sea applauds God's power; every thunderstorm announces His sovereign control over all life; every blossoming flower verifies that Almighty God personally and lovingly cares for even the smallest element of His creation. *"The heavens declare the glory of God, / and the sky displays what his hands have made" (Psalm 19:1).* Yes, the beauty of God's creation reflects to us only a fraction of His glory, but Daniel's vision of the Ancient One, Almighty God, seated upon His heavenly throne and arrayed in His eternal glory is unequaled in nature. Walters Chalmers Smith, lyricist of the classic hymn, "Immortal, Invisible," somewhat captures the magnificence of Holy God upon His eternal throne:

> Immortal, invisible God only wise,
> In light inaccessible hid from our eyes,
> Most blessed, most glorious, the Ancient of Days,
> Almighty, victorious, Thy great name we praise.
>
> Unresting, unhasting, and silent as light,
> Nor wanting, nor wasting, Thou rulest in might;
> Thy justice, like mountains, high soaring above;
> Thy clouds, which are fountains of goodness and love.
>
> To all, life Thou givest, to both great and small;
> In all life Thou livest, the true life of all;
> We blossom and flourish as leaves on the tree,
> And wither and perish—but naught changeth Thee.
>
> Great Father of glory, pure Father of light,
> Thine angels adore Thee, all veiling their sight;

All praise we would render; O help us to see
'Tis only the splendor of light hideth Thee!⁶

Trying to imagine the beauty of the brightness that emanates from our Father God makes us anxious for our eternal home with Him. As believers, one day, we will see our heavenly Father and His Son, face-to-face in the fullness of their eternal glory. Then this life, its questions and disappointments, will make sense yet will no longer matter. *"Now we see a blurred image in a mirror. Then we will see very clearly. Now my knowledge is incomplete. Then I will have complete knowledge as God has complete knowledge of me"* (1 Corinthians 13:12). Thank You, heavenly Father, for the promise that we have of one day seeing You face-to-face in all of Your glory. *"No eye has seen, no ear has heard, and no mind has imagined the things that God has prepared for those who love him"* (1 Corinthians 2:9).

Daniel 7:15–20

7:15 *I, Daniel, was deeply troubled, and my visions frightened me.*

Seeing the Son of Man and the Ancient One did not trouble Daniel. Rather, Daniel's distress resulted from his uncertainty regarding the significance of the beasts, specifically the last beast and the little horn. Though Daniel did not fully comprehend the symbolic meaning of the beasts, he understood that they were of grave importance, which is why, as described in the verses that follow, he sought to know the interpretation of the vision.

7:16 *I went to someone who was standing there and asked him to tell me the truth about all this. So he told me what all this meant.*

Daniel approached someone standing nearby, apparently within the vision itself, and asked the meaning of the things he observed. It is a possibility that Daniel understood some of the vision since God had instilled in him the gift of interpretation and understanding. *"God gave these four men knowledge, wisdom, and the ability to understand all kinds of literature. Daniel could also understand all kinds of visions and dreams" (Daniel 1:17).* Regardless, Daniel refrained from relying upon his own judgment because he hungered for God's truth by way of this "one who was standing there." Daniel desired truth and wisdom, so all was made known to him.

7:17 *He said, "These four large animals are four kingdoms that will rise to power on the earth.*

This vision, given first to Daniel then consequently to us, was disclosed in "capsule" form, meaning that a large amount of information appeared in a condensed presentation. The being that Daniel approached explained that these beasts represented four great kings or kingdoms that would emerge from within the earth.

Of the many varied interpretations available, and within the context and relevance of the other events recorded by Daniel, these beasts seem to correlate most closely with the same four kingdoms presented in Nebuchadnezzar's dreams and visions, and they parallel the governmental system types that these kingdoms exemplified. From that point of reference, the next two verses depict a panorama of the entire time span from the start of the Babylonian Empire to the return of the Lord Jesus Christ as King of kings.

The golden head in the image of Nebuchadnezzar's dream and the lion-like beast with eagle wings in Daniel's vision represent the first type of governmental system, the absolute monarchy of the Babylonian Empire. The silver breast and arms of Nebuchadnezzar's image and the bear-like beast in Daniel's vision represent the second form of government instituted by the Medo-Persian Empire. In addition, many historians conclude that the three ribs clenched between the bear's teeth represent the kingdoms that had been devoured by the Medes and Persians—Babylon, Egypt, and Lydia.[7] The brass thigh in the image of Nebuchadnezzar's dream and the leopard-like beast in Daniel's vision represent the third government system of the Greco-Macedonian Empire. The four heads of this beast likely signify the four kingdoms into which the Greco-Macedonian Empire was eventually separated—Greece, Macedonia, Syria, and Egypt. After Alexander the Great's death, the kingdom was divided between four contending successors—Lysimachus, Cassander, Seleucus, and Ptolemy.[8] The iron-and-clay feet of the image in Nebuchadnezzar's dream and the final, dreadful, iron-toothed beast in Daniel's vision represent a futuristic empire that has yet to occur.

Though many arguments may be developed regarding the similarities of these visions, at least one major difference between these accounts exists. The image in Nebuchadnezzar's dream illustrates the sequential deterioration of these forms of authoritative power from a human perspective. The vision given to Daniel, however, apparently reveals God's view of this dilution of power because each beast seemed to lessen in power and grace but increase in grotesqueness and abnormality from the one before it.

7:18 *But the holy people of the Most High will take possession of the kingdom and keep it forever and ever."*

The saints, those throughout the ages who are redeemed through the atonement of Jesus Christ and faith in Almighty God, "the Most High," will inherit the final kingdom, which is the eternal, heavenly kingdom of God. What a great promise that we are given in this verse: the assurance of every believer's inheritance of God's everlasting kingdom, a world without end.

7:19 *Then I wanted to know the truth about the fourth animal, which was so different from all the others. It was very terrifying and had iron teeth and bronze claws. It devoured and crushed its victims, and trampled whatever was left.*

Having resolved the matter of the previous three beasts rather expediently and realizing that the significance of the vision relied more heavily upon the interpretation of the last beast than upon the first three, Daniel sought to understand the meaning of the fourth beast. This beast represents the fourth major kingdom of the world, the Roman Empire, which philosophically continues as a model for present-day governmental systems.

7:20 *I also wanted to know about the ten horns on its head and about the other horn that had come up and made three of the horns fall out. That horn had eyes and a mouth that spoke impressive things. It appeared to be bigger than the others.*

Ten horns protruded from the head of the fourth beast. Three of the ten horns fell when "the other," the little horn with the eyes of a man, arose. This resembles an account in Revelation that equates these ten horns with ten kings. *"The ten horns that you saw are ten kings who have not yet started to rule. They will receive authority to rule as kings with the beast for one hour" (Revelation 17:12).* It is possible that these ten kings or kingdoms represent the division of the end-time world under ten primary global powers that will control the earth's population. This little horn spoke blasphemous things, had much influence with his words, and appeared greater than the other horns.

Notes/Applications

Despite knowing the depravity of mankind's ever-increasing wickedness, Daniel still grieved because he viewed the fate awaiting those who refuse to submit to Almighty God.

There are no new sins. *"Whatever has happened before will happen again. Whatever has been done before will be done again. There is nothing new under the sun" (Ecclesiastes 1:9).* However, due to technological advances, fulfillment of man's evil desires is more easily accessible today than in Daniel's day. The sinful desires innate in all of us are aroused at an earlier age by vulgar and violent images. People are no longer naïve about sin. They are simply callous about it and caustic toward those who preach against it.

It is easy to give up on people and to forget that they need a Savior. However, when our Lord and Savior Jesus Christ looked upon the crowd of people, compassion filled His heart, and he referred to them as "sheep without a shepherd" *(Matthew 9:36).* Are we also moved with compassion for lost sheep? How grieved are we by the moral, ethical, or spiritual deterioration of our world, nation, state, community, and home?

The multitudes around us near damnation in hell. How much does this truth burden our hearts? Enough to pray for them and tell them about the Good Shepherd? Enough to abandon our sins and to live in a way that points them to the Savior?

Daniel 7:21–28

7:21 *I saw that horn making war against the holy people and defeating them.*

As Daniel's vision continued, the messenger specifically told him that the little horn would attack the saints and overpower them for a period of time. *"It was allowed to wage war against God's holy people and to conquer them. It was also given authority over every tribe, people, language, and nation" (Revelation 13:7).* Therefore, the description of this little horn confirms that this figure will be a prominent charismatic leader with worldwide appeal, as the antichrist discussed in greater detail in the book of Revelation. This, however, does not necessitate that the little horn will have global power of a political nature, though he will have enormous influence over those who are in authority—those represented by the ten horns of the fourth beast.

7:22 *It did this until the Ancient One, who has lived for endless years, came and judged in favor of the holy people of the Most High. The time came when the holy people took possession of the kingdom.*

In the previous verse the saints were defeated by the little horn and depicted as victims, yet in this verse the saints ruled as victorious conquerors because God's judgment had vindicated their suffering. This sudden and absolute turn of events did not come to pass due to an innovative military strategy of the saints but, as clearly explained by this verse, because of the judgment of God Almighty, the Ancient One, Who will ultimately give His saints possession of the earth. The eternal kingdom of God will manifest itself at that point with the reign of the Lord Jesus Christ.

7:23 *He said, "The fourth animal will be the fourth of these kingdoms on earth. It will be different from all other kingdoms. It will devour, trample, and crush the whole world.*

Again, we return to the interpretation of the fourth beast or the fourth kingdom, which differed from the preceding three beasts because it was much more dreadful and much more powerful.

This beast does not represent any king or kingdom that ruled during Daniel's lifetime, but one that will preside shortly before God allows His great and final judgment to fall upon the earth. The dominating power of this kingdom will emerge as a global figure that will influence all authorities of the world. This ruler will care for no one, will be loyal to no one and will be honest with no one. He will be indwelled with and controlled by Satan. *"They worshiped the serpent because it had given authority to the beast. They also worshiped the beast and said, 'Who is like the beast? Who can fight a war with it?'"* (Revelation 13:4)

7:24 *The ten horns are ten kings that will rise to power from that kingdom. Another king will rise to power after them. He will be different from the kings who came before him, and he will humble three kings.*

This verse, as with its parallel Scripture in Revelation, confirms the notion that the ten horns of this beast represent ten kings. *"The ten horns that you saw are ten kings who have not yet started to rule. They will receive authority to rule as kings with the beast for one hour"* (Revelation 17:12). These ten kings will obtain power, but from within their midst, another one will rise to power. This ruler will differ from the others because this ruler will exercise spiritual influence in addition to the secular, political power possessed by the ten kings.

7:25 *He will speak against the Most High God, oppress the holy people of the Most High, and plan to change the appointed times and laws. The holy people will be handed over to him for a time, times, and half of a time.*

The little horn will spout a terrible, heretical message. His words will flagrantly blaspheme God, but his eloquent, powerful delivery will influence many. His charisma will attract the multitudes to him, even though his anti-God campaign will ignite unspeakable abominations in the temple in Jerusalem. *"³Don't let anyone deceive you about this in any way. That day cannot come unless a revolt takes place first, and the man of sin, the man of destruction, is revealed. ⁴He opposes every so-called god or anything that is worshiped and places himself above them, sitting in God's temple and claiming to be God"* (2 Thessalonians 2:3–4).

Almighty God will allow the little horn to reign for a predetermined period of time, which is commonly believed to be three and a half years. *"The beast was allowed to speak arrogant and insulting things. It was given authority to act for 42 months"* (Revelation 13:5). During that timeframe, this blasphemer will murder numerous saints through wars and executions in his efforts to rid the whole earth of godly people. He will also rebel against any established tradition, institution, or custom, and he will demand worship of his position and worldly accomplishments.

7:26 *But judgment will be handed down, his power will be taken away, and he will be completely and permanently destroyed.*

The "little horn" figure will seemingly control every facet of life because of the transcendent power he will possess. However, judgment is inevitable. God will ultimately consume the little horn's power and destroy him. God's verdict will then stand final. Furthermore, this sequence of events will demonstrate to the world that the one Who creates and decides all things is not the little horn but is, in fact, the supreme and all-powerful God of creation.

7:27 *The kingdom, along with the power and greatness of all the kingdoms under heaven, will be given to the holy people of the Most High. Their kingdom is eternal. All other powers will serve and obey them."*

God offers assurance that the awesome dominion of the kingdom of heaven will be granted to His saints. After judging the little horn, God will present the earth to His faithful followers, and all creation will dwell under the perfect authority of Christ Jesus, the King of kings and Lord of lords.

Again, this kingdom bestowed upon the Son of Man is an ever-lasting dominion. As other verses confirm, Christ's reign over the earth will mark the end of time, as the world now exists, and will precede the final judgment of mankind, which begins the new earth and the new heaven prepared by God as the eternal dwelling of all believers. *"I saw a new heaven and a new earth, because the first heaven and earth had disappeared" (Revelation 21:1). "There will no longer be any curse. The throne of God and the lamb will be in the city. His servants will worship him" (Revelation 22:3).*

7:28 *Here is the end of the matter. I, Daniel, was terrified by my thoughts, and I turned pale. I kept this to myself.*

Daniel concluded his account by conveying all that needed to be said on the matter. As he considered these things laid before him in the vision, Daniel's outward appearance changed because he felt burdened by knowing such momentous events. Daniel literally saw the devastation that awaited mankind. Nevertheless, he "kept the matters in his heart." He did not tell anyone about his vision or its interpretation.

Notes/Applications

Daniel had a panoramic view of the end of the world. He witnessed the turmoil that would befall mankind, but He also saw the glorious outcome. Fortunately, the persecution of God's people will only last for a time, and then every ruler and dominion will bow to the Most High. God's saints will finally unite with Him to abide forever in His heavenly kingdom.

God's kingdom has not ended in the past, nor will it begin sometime in the future. Just as God is infinite, His kingdom always has been and always will be. *"Your kingdom is an everlasting kingdom. Your empire endures throughout every generation" (Psalm 145:13).* God

Almighty ordains the beginning and ending of earthly rulers, so ulti-mately, all of creation will bow to the authority of its Creator.

27All the ends of the earth will remember and return to the Lord.
All the families from all the nations will worship you
28because the kingdom belongs to the Lord
and he rules the nations. (Psalm 22:27–28)

God rules justly and absolutely, so nothing, including persecu-tion, that He allows to happen to His creation is without significance. *"Your throne, O God, is forever and ever. The scepter in your kingdom is a scepter for justice" (Psalm 45:6).*

As a result of understanding Daniel's vision, we may grow uncomfortable in realizing the peril that may come upon us because we are children of God. However, we should also rest confidently in the knowledge that we worship the true, victorious God, who is the Most High. *"The Lord has set his throne in heaven. His kingdom rules everything" (Psalm 103:19).*

DANIEL 8

Daniel 8:1–7

At the conclusion of chapter seven, Daniel changed his writings from Aramaic to Hebrew, his native language. This is an interesting note, considering the remainder of the chapters in the book of Daniel deal more specifically with his people, the nation of Israel.

8:1 *In Belshazzar's third year as king, I, Daniel, saw a vision. This vision came after the one I saw earlier.*

Belshazzar, as we studied in chapter five, ruled over the city of Babylon for about fourteen years. He did so under the authority granted to him by Nabonidus, the king of the Babylonian Empire. This chapter presents a prophecy that further describes the rise of the Medo-Persian and Greco-Macedonian Empires, which eventually succeeded the Babylonian Empire. Daniel recorded this as his second vision, which occurred around 552–551 B.C. in the third year of Belshazzar's reign, two years after the vision recorded in chapter seven.

8:2 *In my vision I saw myself in the fortress of Susa in the province of Elam. In my vision I saw myself at Ulai Gate.*

Daniel's vision revealed that the capital city would be moved from Babylon to Susa, one of the Babylonian Empire's major cities after the rise of the Medo-Persian Empire. Daniel saw himself in the fortress at Susa when he received this vision. This city was located in the province of Elam by the River Ulai. The dream appears to be prophetic in nature; therefore, we may conclude that Daniel was probably unfamiliar with the fortress mentioned in this verse.[1]

8:3 *I looked up and saw a single ram standing beside the gate. The ram had two long horns, one longer than the other, though the longer one had grown up later.*

Daniel looked up and beheld a ram by the river. Two horns were perched upon the ram's head, and the second horn eventually grew to be taller than the first, thereby defying normal expectations.

8:4 *I saw the ram charging west, north, and south. No other animal could stand in front of it, and no one could escape from its power. It did anything it pleased and continued to grow.*

The ram moved away from his position by the River Ulai in westward, northward, and southward directions, trampling every other beast in his path. No animals could successfully oppose the ram's campaign or hinder his capacity to subjugate any territory that he desired.

Later verses discuss the interpretation of this vision more specifically. However, for the purpose of clarifying details that appear here, though not within the subsequent interpretation, it is important to mention that this ram symbolizes the Medo-Persian Empire: "The ram which you saw, having the two horns—they are the kings of Media and Persia" *(Daniel 8:20, NKJV).* This segment of Daniel's vision historically corresponds with the military excursions of Cyrus, King of Persia (represented by the larger of the two horns), whose conquered territories extended west into Babylon, Syria, and Asia; north into Albania, Armenia, and Iberia; and south into Arabia, Ethiopia, and Egypt.[2] Therefore, the animals mentioned in this verse evidently represent the territories conquered by King Cyrus.

8:5 *As I was watching closely, I saw a male goat coming from the west. It crossed the whole earth without touching it. This goat had a prominent horn between its eyes.*

Daniel reflected upon his vision to this point. As he pondered, something else unfolded in the vision. A male goat with a sizable horn between its eyes approached from the west. In describing the great speed and power with which the goat advanced, Daniel noted that the goat did not touch the ground.

8:6–7 *⁶The goat was coming toward the two-horned ram that I had seen standing beside the gate. It furiously ran at the ram. ⁷I saw it come closer to the ram. The goat was extremely angry with the ram, so it attacked the ram. It broke both of the ram's horns. The ram didn't have the strength to stand up against the goat. So the ram was thrown down on the ground and trampled. No one could rescue the ram from the goat's power.*

Charging with fierce power, the goat swiftly overtook the ram and broke its horns. A ram's protection depends upon the strength of its horns so this rendered the ram defenseless. The goat then tossed the ram to the ground and crushed it. As this verse indicates, no person or group of persons could aid or rescue the ram because of the goat's overpowering strength and speed.

Notes/Applications

Comparable to the goat in this passage, Satan seeks to kill and to destroy us, both physically and spiritually, and he preys upon the areas in which we are most vulnerable. *"Keep your mind clear, and be* alert. Your opponent the devil is prowling around like a roaring lion as he looks for someone to devour" (1 Peter 5:8).

What do we rely on as our primary defense weapon against his attacks? If we rely on our own strength to overcome him, we will certainly meet defeat. Therefore, we must daily arm ourselves with prayer and Bible study to prepare for the spiritual battles before us.

> *¹³For this reason, take up all the armor that God supplies. Then you will be able to take a stand during these evil days. Once you have overcome all obstacles, you will be able to stand your ground.*
>
> *¹⁴So then, take your stand! Fasten truth around your waist like a belt. Put on God's approval as your breastplate. ¹⁵Put on your shoes so that you are ready to spread the Good News that gives peace. ¹⁶In addition to all these, take the Christian faith as your shield. With it you can put out all the flaming arrows of the evil one. ¹⁷Also take salvation as your helmet and the word of God as the sword that the Spirit supplies.*
>
> *¹⁸Pray in the Spirit in every situation. Use every kind of prayer and request there is. For the same reason be alert. Use every kind of effort and make every kind of request for all of God's people. (Ephesians 6:13–18)*

We must recognize that we are involved in spiritual warfare and that Satan desires to ruin our Christian influence upon others. However, we do not have to fight this battle alone. We can firmly stand knowing we may suffer external injury, but nothing can rob the victory from us. "Thank God that he gives us the victory through our Lord Jesus Christ" (1 Corinthians 15:57). Are we prepared daily for the battle before us? Through our Lord Jesus Christ, the source of our strength, we are more than conquerors.

> *⁷The Lord is my strength and my shield.*
> *My heart trusted him, so I received help.*
> *My heart is triumphant; I give thanks to him with my song.*
> *⁸The Lord is the strength of his people*
> *   and a fortress for the victory of his Messiah. (Psalm 28:7–8)*

Daniel 8:8–14

8:8 *The male goat became very important. But when the goat became powerful, his large horn broke off. In its place grew four horns. They corresponded to the four winds of heaven.*

The goat attained military power. Its horn was destroyed, but four more replaced it. The description of these horns corresponding "to the four winds of heaven" probably refers to the four main directions of the earth, describing a territory that exceeded the ram's victories. Apparently, the four horns arose after the large horn expanded the prosperity of the male goat.

8:9 *Out of one of the horns came a small horn. It gained power over the south, the east, and the beautiful land.*

The horn mentioned in this verse is described as "small," but this does not suggest insignificance. Rather, this description simply compares its power to that of the "large horn" that preceded it. Even so, this small horn proved to have a vast dominion that reached toward the south and east and, more relevantly, into the "beautiful land," the land of Israel, which God had prepared for the habitation of His people.

As in chapter seven, this verse speaks of the rise of a "small horn" among the other horns. However, this small horn does not represent the same figure as the little horn mentioned in the previous chapter. How do we know this to be true? Notice that this horn arose from among four horns, not ten. Furthermore, we can ascertain that the prophecies of this vision and Daniel's first vision refer to different time periods. Both little horns, however, have proven and will prove to be extremely hostile toward the children of God.

8:10 *It continued to gain power until it reached the army of heaven. It threw some of the army of heaven, the stars, down on the ground and trampled them.*

This small horn achieved greatness. The word *army* in this verse comes from the Hebrew word *tsaba*, which means "a mass of persons, especially organized for war."[3] With this in mind, this verse most likely depicts the brutal persecution that this small horn would inflict upon the Jews, God's people, called "the army of heaven." It does not stand to reason that this host signifies angels, as some expositors have suggested, for the interpretation of this prophecy, which is given in later verses, discusses an actual, physical series of events versus a spiritual one (except in the figurative sense of the spiritual refinement that takes place as a result of persecution.)[4]

8:11 *Then it attacked the commander of the army so that it took the daily burnt offering from him and wrecked his holy place.*

The small horn would magnify himself as God, would seize control over the holy temple in Jerusalem, and would then forbid the daily sacrifices that took place there. By these actions, he would prohibit the Jews from practicing the religious ordinances that distinguished them as a people. He would also cleverly coerce their allegiance to him.

8:12 *In its rebelliousness it was given an army to put a stop to the daily burnt offering. It threw truth on the ground. The horn was successful in everything it did.*

The truth was cast down and ungodliness prevailed as the small horn was permitted to continue his horrible acts against God's people. Furthermore, he was given "an army" to enforce these policies that forbade the Jews from worshipping in the temple and mandated its desecration. Considering the list of atrocities committed by this horn, perhaps most disturbing is the last statement: "The horn was successful in everything it did." What a horrifying thought were it not for the providential hand of God over all things!

8:13 *Then I heard a holy one speaking. Another holy one said to the one who was speaking, "How long will the things in this vision—the daily burnt offering, the destructive rebellion, the surrender of the holy place, and the trampling of the army—take place?"*

In Daniel's vision, apparently several others, each referred to as a holy one, witnessed the events taking place. The term *holy one* does not necessarily identify these beings as angels, though this seems to be the most likely case. Daniel heard one of these beings question how long the dreadful reign of the small horn would last. In other words, this holy one wanted to know the duration of the temple's desecration and this persecution of the Jews.

8:14 *He told me, "For 2,300 evenings and mornings. Then the holy place will be made acceptable to God."*

The holy one rendered an answer—2300 days. Though some scholars have interpreted the 2300 days in this verse as 2300 years, meaning a week of years rather than a week of days *(see commentary on Daniel 9:24)*, the accurate translation of the time period indicated in this verse is a twenty-four hour day.[5] This conclusion is supported by the fulfillment of this prophecy in verse twenty-six of this chapter, which renders these days as "evening and mornings." Therefore, the "destructive rebellion" described in verse thirteen would last for 2300 days or 6.3 years.

Notes/Applications
In Daniel's second vision, the evil ruler prohibited people from worshipping God Almighty. It is difficult to understand why God would allow the desolation of His temple and the persecution of His servants to occur.

Why does a good God allow bad things to happen to "good" people? This is a natural, timeless question that has universally stumped every person at one time or another. However, there is a fallacy in this question. This question is unanswerable because our finite, imperfect minds can never fully understand all of God's ways.

> You said, "Who is this that belittles my advice
> without having any knowledge about it?"
> Yes, I have stated things I didn't understand,
> things too mysterious for me to know. (Job 42:3)

Rather than focusing on the "why," we must focus on the "Who." It is important to understand, as fully as possible, Who God is, which begins by recognizing that God is both sovereign and good.

The sovereignty of God refers to His supremacy. God is the Potter, the Creator, and we are the clay, the creation that he lovingly molds. Whether we accept or reject God's supremacy does not alter His position as the Most High. God is sovereign, so He does not need a reason for doing anything that He chooses to do because all of His actions are, by His very nature, perfect.

Almighty God, in His goodness, coupled with His great love for us and His great hatred for sin, allows and even causes affliction to happen, even to His very own if that will further mold them into His image. Many situations that appear to be dreadful are actually God's hand working in our spiritual, physical, and emotional best interest. In his book, *The Attributes of God*, A. W. Tozer, author and twentieth-century theologian, simply yet accurately describes our Lord's goodness in simple, human terms:

> When I say that God is good, that God has a kind heart, I mean that He has a heart infinitely kind and that there is no boundary to it. . . .God is not only infinitely good, He is perfectly good. God is never part-way anything . . . . If you don't feel that way about it, it's unbelief that makes you feel otherwise; it's preoccupation with this world. If you would believe God, you would know this to be true.[6]

Since we can never fully comprehend or define the perfect sovereignty or goodness of Almighty God, our Christian growth comes in learning to praise the Lord simply because of Who He is and to trust in His constant goodness.

> *But now, Lord, you are our Father.*
>> *We are the clay, and you are our potter.*
>>> *We are the work of your hands. (Isaiah 64:8)*

Has unbelief clouded our focus upon and acceptance of God's sovereign control and perfect goodness? Are we willing to accept both triumphs and trials as blessings from God?

Daniel 8:15–22

8:15 *Now as I, Daniel, watched the vision and tried to understand it, I saw someone who looked like a man standing in front of me.*

By man's standards, Daniel's abilities qualified him as an expert dream and vision interpreter. However, Daniel sought his answers from the all-knowing God. When Daniel searched, God responded by sending a messenger. It was not a man but, as stated in the verse, "the appearance of a man." Through this being, God revealed to Daniel the interpretation of this prophetic vision, just as Daniel had previously made known the interpretation of others' visions and dreams.

8:16 *I heard a man in Ulai Gate call loudly, "Gabriel, explain the vision to this man."*

A voice called to this man and identified him as Gabriel, whose name means "man of God."[7] Other biblical accounts describe later episodes when Gabriel was again sent to Daniel to interpret the prophecy of the seventy sets of time periods *(Daniel 9)*, to Jerusalem to announce the birth of John the Baptist to Zacharias *(Luke 1:19)*, and also to Nazareth to announce to the Virgin Mary that she would give birth to the Messiah *(Luke 1:26)*.

In this verse, however, Daniel was by the River Ulai when he heard a man's voice sounding from between the banks of the river. This was not the voice of the one described in the previous verse as one "who looked like a man." The voice instructed Gabriel to tell Daniel the interpretation of the vision in its entirety, so the voice apparently came from the very mouth of God, Who has command over all of the angels.[8]

8:17 *Gabriel came up beside me, and when he came, I was terrified and immediately knelt down. He said to me, "Son of man, understand that the vision is about the end times."*

Gabriel then moved closer to Daniel, and as he did, Daniel fell prostrate in fear before him. The angel preempted a detailed interpretation of the vision by explaining that it concerned the "end times." How this phrase is interpreted depends upon how the vision as a whole is interpreted. A few expositors contend that this refers to the end of the world and the time of the final antichrist.[9] Most scholars agree, however, that the "end" here refers to the promised completion of the 2300 days (explained in verse fourteen) that conclude the destructive rebellion to which this entire vision relates.[10] The latter interpretation is more easily defendable, as further explained in verse nineteen.

8:18 *As he spoke to me, I fainted facedown on the ground, but he touched me and made me stand up.*

While Daniel lay facedown on the ground, he fell into a deep sleep. He did not slumber due to boredom but from physical and emotional exhaustion. Then, Gabriel touched Daniel, lifted him upright, and restored his consciousness.

8:19 *He said, "I will tell you what will happen in the last days, the time of God's anger, because the end time has been determined.*

Gabriel announced that he would proclaim the meaning of the vision, and surely, Daniel yearned to understand the mystery. Perhaps, he realized the urgency and magnitude of this vision. Gabriel assured Daniel that the time had been determined for the end of the persecution inflicted upon the Jews by the small horn.

8:20 *"The two-horned ram that you saw represents the kingdoms of Media and Persia.*

Gabriel first explained the symbolic meaning of the ram and its two horns. Darius ruled as the king of Media, and Cyrus ruled as the king of Persia. Though rising to prominence shortly after the Median dominion and ultimately ruling concurrently with it, Cyrus the Persian, would prove to be the greater of the two powers. Therefore, in Daniel's vision, the larger horn that came up after the smaller horn symbolizes Cyrus. The ram in the vision represents the union of these two kingdoms into the Medo-Persian Empire, which was depicted as the silver portion of the image in Nebuchadnezzar's first dream *(Daniel 2:39)* and the bear-like beast in Daniel's first vision *(Daniel 7:5)*.

8:21 *The hairy male goat is the kingdom of Greece, and the large horn between its eyes is its first king.*

The male goat represents the Greco-Macedonian Empire, and the horn between its eyes symbolizes the first king of that empire. This king and kingdom correspond with the bronze portion of the image in Nebuchadnezzar's first dream *(Daniel 2:39)* and with the four-winged, four-headed leopard in Daniel's first recorded vision *(Daniel 7:6)*. Most scholars conclude that the large horn on this goat represents Alexander the Great, a very distinguished world leader that ascended to power and devised swift military conquests.[11]

8:22 *The horn broke off, and four horns replaced it. Four kingdoms will come out of that nation, but they won't be as strong as the first king was.*

The breaking of the horn describes the downfall of Alexander, who died in 323 B.C. at only thirty-three years of age at the height of his power and conquest.[12]

Gabriel foretold the events surrounding the division of Alexander's kingdom into four parts. Where there had once been a single king leading a single kingdom, there would now be four kings

and four separate kingdoms. Historically, these four horns represent the following kings and kingdoms that succeeded Alexander:[13]
• Ptolemy (Egypt in the south)
• Seleucus (Syria in the east)
• Cassander (Macedonia in the northwest)
• Lysimachus (Asia Minor in the northeast)
  None of these kings ever received the notoriety for conquering as many nations as Alexander the Great, and none of their kingdoms ever prospered as Alexander's kingdom had.

Notes/Applications
Josephus, the renowned first-century historian, discussed in his book, *Antiquities of the Jews*, Alexander the Great's reaction to the prophecies written in the book of Daniel. According to Josephus, Alexander sent orders to Jaddua, the high priest in Jerusalem, offering the priest his allegiance as well as supplies for the Persian armies. Jaddua, however, refused Alexander's aid because, as a priest, his loyalty belonged to the Persian king. Infuriated, Alexander then decided to march into Jerusalem himself. Despite the Jews' surmounting fear as Alexander and his army approached the city, the high priests of Jerusalem dressed in their priestly robes and garments, threw open the city gates, and prepared to meet Alexander the Great face-to-face, as God, through a dream, had directed Jaddua to do.

When Alexander arrived in Jerusalem, however, he refused to allow any harm to come upon the people because he also had a dream in which he had seen these priests dressed identically to what they now wore. As a result, Alexander offered sacrifices to Almighty God, granted the Jews the right to enjoy the laws of their forefathers, and left their city unharmed.[14] Because Jaddua the priest acted in faith by responding according to God's leading, even when these actions seemed contrary to human logic, God divinely intervened.

Do we desire God's divine intervention to transform our circumstances? Do we long to experience God in a unique way, unexplainable by human logic? When we respond to pressing situations in the

manner that the Holy Spirit leads us, God will intervene. He generally responds to our cries by changing the situation, our perspective
of it, or both. However, when we plan our own escape route according to our own way and timing, we will become entangled in a web
of undesirable consequences.

Most of us have allowed our circumstances to defeat us,
and as a result, we do not think that we are daily experienc-
ing God. However, God miraculously proves Himself every day,
but to see God working in our lives, we must stop dwelling
upon the circumstances and redirect our attention upon the
one who commands the circumstances. *"My eyes look to you,
Lord Almighty. I have taken refuge in you. Do not leave me defenseless"*
(Psalm 141:8).

Daniel 8:23-27

8:23 *"In the last days of those kingdoms, when rebellions are finished, a stern-looking king who understands mysterious things will rise to power.*

Some expositors explain the phrase "when rebellions are finished" as a reference to the apostate Jews who had forsaken their faith and embraced the manners of the heathen during the reign of Alexander and his four successors.[15] After these four generals ruled for some time, a new king emerged—a vicious, greedy king who stubbornly disregarded Almighty God. Aside from his imposing demeanor, this king possessed great power with which he carried out his sinister schemes.

As we have already studied, the goat in this chapter symbolizes the Greco-Macedonian Empire, whose kingdom, though in the future at the time Daniel had this vision, has now long since ceased. Therefore, this little horn does not symbolize the end-times antichrist figure that is also depicted as a little horn in the previous chapter. The small horn in this chapter most likely represents Antiochus IV, also called Antiochus Epiphanes, the notoriously wicked king of the Seleucus dynasty in Syria.[16]

Antiochus Epiphanes was the son of Antiochus III the Great, ruler over Syria from 176 B.C. to 164 B.C. The younger Antiochus proved to be brutally tyrannical, one of the most bloodthirsty enemies of the Jewish Nation. He called himself Antiochus the Illustrious, though others considered him to be a madman. In his youth, his father surrendered him as a hostage to the Romans, but he was eventually recaptured by his brother, Seleucus IV, who reigned as leader at the time and who sent his own son as Antiochus' replacement. Later that same year, Seleucus IV was murdered, so Antiochus Epiphanes seized the throne. When his sister Cleopatra, queen of Egypt, died, Antiochus laid claim to Palestine and battled against Egypt. It was during this war against the Egyptians that he perpetrated unspeakable cruelties against the Jews, as prophesied in later verses.[17]

8:24 *He will become very strong, but not by his own strength. He will cause astounding destruction and will be successful in everything he does. He will destroy those who are powerful along with some holy people.*

Satan controlled this king. Antiochus singled out and destroyed those who posed a threat to his plans. In other words, he did not kill simply for the sake of killing. He had an agenda. He targeted specific people: the powerful, who were the politically motivated; the holy people, who were the spiritually motivated; and any other people groups that opposed him. God allowed this man of unspeakable wickedness to prosper until God's sovereign will was accomplished in this empire.

8:25 *He will cleverly use his power to deceive others success-fully. He will consider himself to be great and destroy many people when they don't expect it. He will oppose the Commander of Commanders, but he will be defeated, though not by any human power.*

Deception flourished under this man's administration. He exalted himself in his own prideful heart. This man rebelled against the high priest in God's holy temple, against God's chosen people, and even against the great Commander, God Almighty Himself.[18]

Many of those that Antiochus killed were slain when they didn't expect it, or "in their prosperity" (*NKJV*). This meant they lived under a false pretense of peace, a typical ploy of the spirit of antichrist both in this leader and in the end-times figure. We see an example of this deception when Antiochus acquired Syria from his nephew under the pretense of uniting their forces to fortify a defense against their common enemies.[19]

As foretold in this verse, Antiochus' death was obviously dictated by an act of God. Antiochus marched into Persia and robbed the temple at Elymais and was finally driven away by a tumultuous resistance. He then received news of the defeat of his armies against the Jews and of the restoration of their temple services. The emotional quandary in which he found himself quickly took its toll on his physical health, and he died shortly thereafter. This prompted the belief that the cause of his death was directly related to Antiochus' unmerciful atrocities against the Jews and to his blatant irreverence for Almighty God.[20]

According to Josephus, the Jewish temple was then cleansed, and the sacrifice ritual was reinstated on the twenty-fifth day of the ninth month in the one hundred forty-eighth year of Seleucus.[21] Therefore, the calculation of the duration of Antiochus IV's desecration of the temple until it was restored and proper sacrifices reconvened was exactly 2300 days, which corresponds with the prophesy in verse fourteen. This also confirms that this small horn personified Antiochus and not the future antichrist figure discussed in Revelation and other Scriptures, though strong similarities clearly exist between the two types of antichrist.

8:26 *The vision about the 2,300 evenings and mornings that was explained to you is true. Seal the vision, because it is about things that will happen in the distant future."*

Gabriel concluded by stating that this vision was prophetic, true, and unalterable. He was also specific about the duration of these events lasting 2300 days. Now that the vision and its interpretation were unveiled, Gabriel told Daniel to "seal" or conceal this message since the events of the prophecy were still many years away.

8:27 *I, Daniel, was exhausted and sick for days. Then I got up and worked for the king. The vision horrified me because I couldn't understand it.*

Evidently, Daniel retained some official capacity in the Babylonian court after the death of Nebuchadnezzar. Daniel was so intensely disturbed by the ramifications of this vision that he fell ill for several days. Nevertheless, after a short while, he regained his strength and returned to his routine. The vision, however, remained emblazoned in his mind and in his thoughts.

Notes/Applications
At the completion of this vision, Gabriel, God's messenger, told Daniel two things. First, Gabriel emphasized that the vision was true and unalterable, and second, he admonished Daniel to seal the vision along with Daniel's other writings until a later time. The idea that the vision was unalterable reaffirms that God does not merely react to mankind. His predesigned master plan will be accomplished without any deviation, regardless of the seemingly reckless actions of His creation. However, God's instruction for Daniel to seal up the message required action on Daniel's part and proved that God employs His creation in accomplishing His will. Although Daniel lacked a detailed understanding of the vision's interpretation, he still obediently followed the angel's instructions.

What excuse do we have for disobeying the voice of our God? We either have not learned how to discern His voice, or we have chosen to disobey it. We contend that if God would only send His message to us via an angel, as He did with Daniel, we, too, would obey Him. However, God reveals His instructions to us in a myriad of ways, though. He speaks to us through His Holy Word, yet we neglect to study it. He speaks to us through others, such as godly ministers and teachers, yet we ignore their counsel. *"Obey the Lord your God and follow his commands and laws which I'm giving you today"* (Deuteronomy 27:10).

God expects our obedience even though He rarely divulges comprehension of His plan. Nevertheless, our lack of full understanding does not nullify our responsibility to obey. God speaks, but we must begin to listen and to obey.

> *[11]God said, "Go out and stand in front of the Lord on the mountain." As the Lord was passing by, a fierce wind tore mountains and shattered rocks ahead of the Lord. But the Lord was not in the wind. After the wind came an earthquake. But the Lord wasn't in the earthquake. [12]After the earthquake there was a fire. But the Lord wasn't in the fire. And after the fire there was a quiet, whispering voice. (1 Kings 19:11–12)*

Are we intimately familiar with the manner in which God speaks to us? Do we easily recognize His voice? Do we readily obey God despite uncertainty concerning His plan?

DANIEL 9

Daniel 9:1–7

9:1–2 *¹Xerxes' son Darius, who was a Mede by birth, was made ruler of the kingdom of Babylon. ²In the first year of his reign, I, Daniel, learned from the Scriptures the number of years that Jerusalem would remain in ruins. The Lord had told the prophet Jeremiah that Jerusalem would remain in ruins for 70 years.*

The sixty-eighth year of the Jewish captivity would have been approximately 538 B.C. In that year Darius, the son of Ahasuerus the Mede, was appointed as ruler of Babylon by Cyrus the Persian.[1] Darius presided over the immediate region of Babylonia, which included the captive Israelites.

In the first year of Darius' reign, Daniel, who had familiarized himself with the writings of his contemporaries, concluded through the prophecies of Jeremiah that the Jewish people were to remain captives for seventy years. The Jews had disobeyed God's laws given to them through the prophet Moses concerning reverence for God's Sabbath. *"¹¹This whole land will be ruined and become a wasteland. These nations will serve the king of Babylon for 70 years. ¹²When the 70 years* are over, I will punish the king of Babylon and that nation for their crimes, declares the Lord. I will turn Babylon into a permanent wasteland" (Jeremiah 25:11–12). God required the Hebrew nation to observe a time of rest for the land every seven years:

> ³Then, for six years you may plant crops in your fields, prune your vineyards, and gather what they produce. ⁴However, the seventh year will be a festival year for the land. It will be a year to honor the Lord. Don't plant crops in your fields or prune your vineyards. ⁵Don't harvest what grows by itself or harvest grapes from your vines. That year will be a festival for the land. (Leviticus 25:3–5)

If this were not observed, God would still ensure the observation of His Sabbath by sending His people into captivity, thereby allowing, by His intervention, the land to rest.

> ³³I will scatter you among the nations. War will follow you. Your country will be in ruins. Your cities will be deserted.
> ³⁴Then the land will enjoy its time to honor the Lord while it lies deserted and you are in your enemies' land. Then the land will joyfully celebrate its time to honor the Lord. (Leviticus 26:33–34)

The disobedient people did not observe the Sabbath for the land. Consequently, God's judgment fell upon them, and they were taken captive by the Babylonians.

> ⁸This is what the Lord of Armies says: You did not listen to my words, ⁹so I'm going to send for all the families from the north. I will also send for my servant King Nebuchadnezzar of Babylon, declares the Lord. I will bring the families from the north to attack this land, its people, and all these surrounding nations. I'm going to destroy them and turn them into something terrible, something ridiculed, and something permanently ruined. ¹⁰I will take from them the sounds of joy and happiness, the sounds of brides and grooms, the sound of mills, and the light of lamps. ¹¹This whole land will be ruined and become a wasteland. These nations will serve the king of Babylon for 70 years. (Jeremiah 25:8–11)

9:3 *So I turned to the Lord God and looked to him for help. I prayed, pleaded, and fasted in sackcloth and ashes.*

Daniel committed himself to interceding on behalf of his nation. He turned his face to God. Perhaps this meant he knelt at his window facing Jerusalem. Daniel fervently sought the Lord without false pretense or wrongful motivation. He wore sackcloth, which was usually made of dark and generally shapeless goat's hair.² Daniel was a man of high political stature who would have typically worn royal robes. This gesture demonstrated his deep sorrow and repentance for his own sins and for those of his people. It outwardly expressed his inward earnestness and utter humility before Holy God.

9:4 *I prayed to the Lord my God. I confessed and said, "Lord, you are great and deserve respect as the only God. You keep your promise and show mercy to those who love you and obey your commandments.*

As preparation to meet God, Daniel cast aside all of his worldly concerns. Although Daniel's daily, personal relationship with God was unencumbered, he took extra measures for an intimate and uninterrupted communion with the heavenly Father. After preparing himself to approach God, Daniel prayed fervently.

Daniel first confessed his own iniquities. Before he asked God for anything, he praised God for Who He is—the great and awesome God—and then for what He does—keeps His promises.

DIG DEEPER: *Mercy*

Daniel acknowledged the Lord as one Who is merciful toward those who love Him and keep His commandments. Mercy is compassionate leniency that is demonstrated toward some undeserving person. Although no one deserves the love and compassion of a holy and perfect God, the Lord abundantly bestows His mercies upon His children (*Ephesians 2:4–5; 1 Peter 1:3; Psalm 25:6–10; Psalm 89*).

9:5 *We have sinned, done wrong, acted wickedly, rebelled, and turned away from your commandments and laws.*

In Daniel's confession, he admitted first and foremost that we have sinned, thereby including himself among the transgressors. Despite his close relationship with God, he still counted himself as a sinner in need of forgiveness. Daniel said, "We have sinned, done wrong," acknowledging that they, the Israelites, had turned away from God's principles.

9:6 *We haven't listened to your servants the prophets, who spoke in your name to our kings, leaders, ancestors, and all the common people.*

Daniel confessed further acts of disobedience. He admitted that the Israelites, God's chosen people, had not listened to God's servants, the prophets. The Lord spoke directly to His people through these men and had forewarned their kings, princes, fathers, and elders of His judgment. However, the Israelites stubbornly disregarded and rejected the things that they did not want to hear.

9:7 *You, Lord, are righteous. But we—the men of Judah, the citizens of Jerusalem, and all the Israelites whom you scattered in countries near and far—are still ashamed because we have been unfaithful to you.*

Daniel attributed righteousness to God alone. He contended that his people deserved their fateful captivity in a foreign land and the destruction of their homeland as judgment for their disobedience. They had all sinned and were guilty of willful disobedience, which was compounded by their unrepentant attitude.

Notes/Applications
Daniel fervently sought the Lord through prayer and fasting. He did not do this selfishly based upon his own desires, but after realizing

the spiritual transgressions of his Israelite brethren, he petitioned God on the entire nation's behalf.

Fasting is a voluntary abstinence from food for one or more meals. Scriptural fasting, however, does not merely refrain from eating but replaces physical food with spiritual food, such as prayer and Bible study. Therefore, this abstinence from physical food must be a conscious, strategic effort made by a Christian for spiritual reasons. Physically, fasting cleanses an individual's blood, thereby allowing one's mind and body to function more healthily. Spiritually, fasting focuses one's attention upon God's will for his life.

The discipline of fasting is not a magic genie bottle that we, as Christians, rub in order to get our wishes fulfilled. In God's eyes, an acceptable fast does not seek fulfillment of selfish desires, as the prophet Isaiah states:

> ³*Don't you see that on the days you fast,*
> *you do what you want to do?*
> *You mistreat all your workers.*
> ⁴*Don't you see that when you fast,*
> *you quarrel and fight and beat your workers?*
> *The way you fast today keeps you from being heard in*
> *heaven.*
> ⁵*Is this the kind of fasting I have chosen?*
> *Should people humble themselves for only a day?*
> *Is fasting just bowing your head like a cattail*
> *and making your bed from sackcloth and ashes?*
> *Is this what you call fasting?*
> *Is this an acceptable day to the Lord?* (Isaiah 58:3–5)

The main purpose of an acceptable fast is to tune out the world and to tune into the voice of God. However, we may also fast in order to repent of our sins, to humble ourselves, to worship God, to intercede for others, to grieve a loss, to obtain power and deliverance, to seek God's guidance, and to petition for our needs:

> *⁶This is the kind of fasting I have chosen:*
> *Loosen the chains of wickedness,*
> *untie the straps of the yoke,*
> *let the oppressed go free,*
> *and break every yoke.*
> *⁷Share your food with the hungry,*
> *take the poor and homeless into your house,*
> *and cover them with clothes when you see them naked.*
> *Don't refuse to help your relatives. (Isaiah 58:6–7)*

A fast should be an intimate time between the individual believer and Almighty God. Therefore, it should be conducted as privately as possible. We should not broadcast to everyone when we are fasting. In truth, we are to do our best to conceal the fact that we are fasting. Jesus said:

> *¹⁶When you fast, stop looking sad like hypocrites. They put on sad faces to make it obvious that they're fasting. I can guarantee this truth: That will be their only reward. ¹⁷When you fast, wash your face and comb your hair. ¹⁸Then your fasting won't be obvious. Instead, it will be obvious to your Father who is with you in private. Your Father sees what you do in private. He will reward you. (Matthew 6:16–18)*

God rewards those who seek Him for the right reasons. In response to our fasting, God may choose to change our circumstances or to change us in the midst of them. Either way, He will move miraculously in our lives and in the lives of those around us.

Daniel 9:8–14

9:8 *We, our kings, leaders, and ancestors are ashamed because we have sinned against you, Lord.*

Daniel acted as a spokesman for the Israelites. He placed the blame for the spiritual condition of the Israelite nation upon his shoulders and upon the shoulders of his people. God does not move away from people; people move away from God. Without exception, human beings are always at fault.

Daniel first repented on behalf of the kings because they were the leaders. The kings' actions (either by decree or example) had affected whether the Israelites moved toward God or away from Him. Next, Daniel interceded for the princes and those in authority under the king. He then included the sins of the elders and fathers of the land. Finally, the rest of the people received blame because not a single person, Daniel included, was without fault to some degree.

9:9 *"But you, Lord our God, are compassionate and forgiving, although we have rebelled against you.*

Daniel acknowledged that God's mercy and forgiveness are never depleted despite mankind's disobedience. He again included himself among the transgressors when he said, "We have rebelled against You." Although the Jews rebelled, God was willing to forgive them if they sought His forgiveness.

9:10 *We never listened to you or lived by the teachings you gave us through your servants the prophets.*

The Jews disobeyed the voice of the Lord by not obeying His laws and by disregarding the forewarnings of the prophets, who were a direct mouthpiece of God. By his mention of these specific things, Daniel was admitting not to the passive disobedience of ignorance but to willful disobedience. God had given His laws directly to His people through their fellow man, and God had warned of judgment directly through their fellow man.

9:11 *All Israel has ignored your teachings and refused to listen to you. So you brought on us the curses you swore in an oath, the curses written in the Teachings of your servant Moses. We sinned against you.*

In addition to disobeying the Law given to Moses, the Israelites also turned away from God by attempting to leave Him out of their lives altogether.

> ⁵*The people of Jerusalem turned away from me without ever returning.*
>> *They still cling to deceit.*
>> *They refuse to return.*
> ⁶*I have paid attention and listened,*
>> *but they weren't honest.*
>> *They don't turn away from their wickedness and ask,*
>>> *"What have we done?"*
>> *They go their own ways like horses charging into battle.* (Jeremiah 8:5–6)

They gave God no consideration whatsoever. They had departed from God's ways so far that they could no longer discern His voice or recognize His prophets. Therefore, the curse that had been poured out upon them was the seventy years of desolation or captivity as prophesied in the Law of Moses.

9:12 *So you did what you said you would do to us and our rulers by bringing a great disaster on us. Nowhere in the world has anything ever happened like what has happened to Jerusalem.*

God kept His promise. He had spoken against Israel and judged it with a curse of captivity. One of their transgressions, as already mentioned, was in not allowing the land to rest every seventh year. There were many ways the Jews turned their back on God, but this particular reason was singled out. Furthermore, Daniel said that no other nation had ever endured the hardships that were placed upon Israel because it, as a nation, had been given so much from God.

There are definite consequences for those who disobey God's laws and commandments. When God speaks against us, He judges us for our disobedience. His laws and standards are not subject to situational ethics or to individual interpretation. They are absolute and final.

9:13 *This entire disaster happened to us, exactly as it was written in Moses' Teachings. Lord our God, we never tried to gain your favor by turning from our wrongs and dedicating ourselves to your truth.*

In the Law of Moses, God had outlined the physical and spiritual principles by which His people were to abide in order to live healthy and holy lives. The Israelites were, therefore, without excuse. Because they departed from God's ways and then refused to acknowledge their sinful condition, God disciplined them by allowing curses to befall them. Still, they did not repent. The Israelites, like a wayward child who willfully refuses to correct his behavior, rebelled more vehemently than before. The people had become so hard-hearted that they would not even pray to God their Father. If they had earnestly prayed and sought God's face, their sin would have been revealed to them, and they could have turned from their destructive and disobedient ways. However, Israel wallowed in her rebellion and, as a result, wandered further and further from God. God finally judged His people by ousting them from their homeland and transporting them to Babylon as captives.

9:14 *So you were prepared to bring this disaster on us. Lord our God, you are righteous in everything you do. But we never listened to you.*

God watched with great disappointment the evil disobedience of His people. Did God now hate the Israelites? No. God's disappointment and His displeasure are not synonymous with hate. In fact, God's deep love for His people motivated His severe judgment of them.

Daniel admitted that the Israelites deserved the consequences they received since they had disobeyed God, in essence, rejecting His love. Daniel further deemed this judgment from the Lord as both justifiable and righteous. God is immovable. He is the same yesterday, today, and forever. It is mankind that refuses to listen to His voice and consequently strays from His guidance.

Notes/Applications

When Daniel prayed, he first confessed the sins of his people before he petitioned for God's mercy. Confession, acknowledgement of sin, should be a crucial ingredient in every believer's prayer life. True confession, however, is not just saying apologetic words. The words must express a genuine remorse that is accompanied by an abandonment of sin.

To obtain everlasting life, we must embrace the naked truth about ourselves: We sin, therefore we are sinners in need of Christ's redemptive work on Calvary to bridge the gap between us, an imperfect people, and God, true perfection. *"⁹God is faithful and reliable. If we confess our sins, he forgives them and cleanses us from everything we've done wrong. ¹⁰If we say, 'We have never sinned,' we turn God into a liar and his Word is not in us"* (1 John 1:9–10). We must then accept, based upon a genuine conviction, Who Jesus Christ is, what He did and what He promises to do. There is no doubt that confession is the first step to repentance, a turning from sin; and true repentance promotes transformation and restoration with Holy God.

> *¹⁰In fact, to be distressed in a godly way causes people to change the way they think and act and leads them to be saved. No one can regret that. But the distress that the world causes brings only death.*

> [11]*When you became distressed in a godly way, look at how much devotion it caused you to have. You were ready to clear yourselves of the charges against you. You were disgusted with the wrong that had been done. You were afraid. You wanted to see us. You wanted to show your concern for us. You were ready to punish the wrong that had been done. In every way you have demonstrated that you are people who are innocent in this matter. (2 Corinthians 7:10–11)*

Once we have entered into this relationship with God, through the threshold of His Son, we should commit ourselves to the spiritual discipline of regularly confessing our sins. This post-conversion confession does not resave us. The God Who draws us to salvation also keeps us. However, what perpetual confession does accomplish is a close fellowship with our Redeemer. It shows that we do not make excuses for our sinful actions but seek to walk closer with God. *"Whoever covers over his sins does not prosper. Whoever confesses and abandons them receives compassion"* (Proverbs 28:13). *"You, O Lord, are good and forgiving, full of mercy toward everyone who calls out to you"* (Psalm 86:5).

Daniel 9:15–23

9:15 *"Lord our God, you brought your people out of Egypt with your strong hand and made yourself famous even today. We have sinned and done evil things.*

Daniel referenced the time of Moses but acknowledged that God was the one Who brought His children out of slavery in Egypt. No credit was given to Moses. Moses was the instrument that God used to accomplish His purposes. Daniel said that God had created a name for Himself when He delivered the Israelites out from under the bondage of Egypt. Daniel lauded God for His greatness and also admitted how sinful the Israelite people had become.

9:16 *Lord, since you are very righteous, turn your anger and fury away from your city, Jerusalem, your holy mountain. Jerusalem and your people are insulted by everyone around us because of our sins and the wicked things our ancestors did.*

Daniel made his request for forgiveness after confessing the Israelite nation's reproach against God and admitting that the Israelites deserved the punishment that they received. Daniel recognized that the Lord judged the Israelites according to His perfect and unchanging goodness. They had suffered the consequences of their sins, and according to the prophecies of Jeremiah, the period of judgment was almost over *(verse 2)*.

Daniel asked God to turn away His anger and fury from Jerusalem, the holy mountain, which is commonly interpreted as a reference to Mount Moriah.[3] Daniel asked God to turn away His fury from the Israelites and from the city of Jerusalem. He did this so they could once again inherit the land where God had intended for them to rebuild His temple, and so they would no longer be the object of mockery and scorn to neighboring nations. Eighteenth-century scholar John Gill depicts Daniel's petition as a heart's cry—a pouring out of this prophet's plea for God's mercy upon the Israelites and the city of Jerusalem. Gill states, "The prophet earnestly entreats, that the marks of divine displeasure, which were upon it, might be removed; that the punishments or judgments inflicted, as the effects of the anger and wrath of God, might cease, and the city be rebuilt, and restored to its former glory."[4] Simply stated, Daniel prayed that God would send His presence to dwell once again within the city of Jerusalem and within its temple.

9:17 *"Our God, listen to my prayer and request. For your own sake, Lord, look favorably on your holy place, which is lying in ruins.*

Throughout this prayer, Daniel used the plural pronoun *we* in order to address God on behalf of the nation of Israel. However, in this verse, he asked God to "listen to my prayer." Daniel referred to himself not as an enlightened teacher, great interpreter of visions, eloquent statesman, or faithful man of God. Shedding his earthly titles, Daniel humbly asked God to shine His glory once again upon the temple in Jerusalem.

9:18 *Open your ears and listen, my God. Open your eyes and look at our ruins and at the city called by your name. We are not requesting this from you because we are righteous, but because you are very compassionate.*

Daniel desired to sense God's presence in a genuine, intimate way. He implored the Lord to hear his petition. He wanted the Lord to see the desolation they were in as a nation and as a city because of their transgressions. God, of course, knew all of this, for He is sovereign over all things that happen to all nations. Daniel appealed in such a way, however, that did not petition God based upon the Israelites' righteousness but upon God's mercy.

9:19 *Listen to us, Lord. Forgive us, Lord. Pay attention, and act. Don't delay! Do this for your sake, my God, because your city and your people are called by your name. "*

Daniel appealed to God to listen, to forgive, but also to act without hesitation. He asked God not to defer allowing His chosen people to reoccupy their land. God, in His time, eventually reunited His people with their land just as Daniel requested. In 538 B.C, King Cyrus the Persian, shortly after conquering the Babylonian Empire, passed a decree releasing the Jews from their captivity to begin the rebuilding of the temple in Jerusalem.[5]

9:20–21 *[20]I continued to pray, confessing my sins and the sins of my people Israel. I humbly placed my request about my God's holy mountain in front of the Lord my God. [21]While I was praying, the man Gabriel, whom I had seen in the first vision, came to me about the time of the evening sacrifice. He was exhausted.*

Daniel was in a spirit of prayer and in a position for prayer. He focused his physical, emotion, mental, and spiritual energy upon this time before God's throne. As Daniel earnestly sought the Lord in confession and supplication, the angel Gabriel appeared. Daniel recognized Gabriel as the same messenger who had interpreted his first vision *(Daniel 8:16)*. Gabriel arrived around the time of the evening offering, which was generally the ninth hour of the day or about three o'clock in the afternoon.[6]

9:22–23 *[22]He informed me, "Daniel, this time I have come to give you insight. [23]As soon as you began to make your request, a reply was sent. I have come to give you the reply because you are highly respected. So study the message, and understand the vision.*

Gabriel explained that his mission was to give Daniel the insight to comprehend this vision. According to this explanation, God had commissioned Gabriel to help Daniel understand the vision as soon as Daniel first began praying. God knows what we need before we ask, but He still wants us to ask. *"Don't be like them. Your Father knows what you need before you ask him"* (Matthew 6:8). Daniel was also told that he was greatly respected, and then he was instructed to meditate upon the matter and to understand the vision.

Notes/Applications

Daniel deeply loved his fellow Israelites. How do we know this? Because Daniel prayerfully interceded on their behalf. He faithfully and passionately prayed for the spiritual, physical, and emotional healing of his people.

People all around us are collapsing under the weight of their sin and sorrow. If we think that we can do nothing to help them, we underestimate the power of intercessory prayer. Recognizing that the Lord Jesus Christ lovingly intercedes on our behalf should motivate us to pray for the needs of other people. *"That is why he is always able to save those who come to God through him. He can do this because he always lives and intercedes for them"* (Hebrews 7:25). Christ's love can be demonstrated through us in no better way than to reach out to others by selflessly praying for them while knowing that we may receive no direct benefit from doing so.

A godly intercessor not only prays for friends and loved ones but also for the "unlikable," those who are difficult to love. This person may be a temperamental neighbor, a fallen pastor or teacher, a hardened criminal, or a corrupt politician. Only God can equip us with the love to reach out in compassion to these individuals. Many times He does this through our prayers. By continually praying for them, God transforms our hearts and attitudes, so we can love the unlovable.

> ⁴*In return for my love, they accuse me,*
> *but I pray for them.*
> ⁵*They reward me with evil instead of good*
> *and with hatred instead of love. (Psalm 109:4–5)*

To make intercessory prayer a part of our prayer life requires heightened awareness to the spiritual, physical, and emotional needs around us. It requires us to see people as God sees them and to love them as He loves us. It requires us to commit ourselves to being more outwardly focused in our prayers instead of totally self-absorbed. *"Pray in the Spirit in every situation. Use every kind of prayer and request there is. For the same reason be alert. Use every kind of effort and make every kind of request for all of God's people"* (Ephesians 6:18). With Christ as our example, how faithful are we in praying for the needs of others?

Daniel 9:24–27

9:24 *"Seventy sets of seven time periods have been assigned for your people and your holy city. These time periods will serve to bring an end to rebellion, to stop sin, to forgive wrongs, to usher in everlasting righteousness, to put a seal on a prophet's vision, and to anoint the Most Holy One.*

The last four verses of this chapter have been called by some the most controversial passage in the entire Bible. They have been the subject of great debate among biblical scholars throughout the ages.[7] Only two major views, however, agree on certain issues that seem to be basic interpretative truths within this text. Therefore, only these two views warrant reasonable consideration. (Other views shift arbitrarily between figurative and literal meanings in certain segments of the text in order to make them "fit."[8]) Through the study of related Scripture passages, various esteemed commentators, and a balanced dose of prudence and reason, we will examine this passage in light of these two viewpoints and draw conclusions that seem most dependable and consistent.

For the most part, these views disagree on two major elements of the text: 1) the meaning of the phrase "seven time periods" in verse twenty-four, and 2) the eschatological rendering of verse twenty-seven. The first position, a first advent interpretation, considers the entire prophecy to be fulfilled in the birth, death, and resurrection of the Messiah, the Lord Jesus Christ. The second viewpoint, a second advent position, actually combines the first advent viewpoint with an indefinite interruption of time between the sixty-ninth and seventieth "seven time period," thereby projecting the eventual fulfillment of this prophecy to end times, specifically to the last seven years before Christ Jesus' Second Coming. Whereas the second advent position has gained widespread acceptance over the last hundred years or so, its dependency upon a series of future events for the ultimate fulfillment of this prophecy seems unnecessary since it can be more easily demonstrated how the prophecy was fulfilled in its entirety upon the resurrection of Jesus Christ.

One crucial matter that both positions agree upon is the meaning of the phrase "seven time periods." This phrase is derived from the Hebrew word *shabuwa* and denotes a general grouping of seven.[9] It does not in any way constitute a "week" of days, as some other translations interpret, at least as the word "week" is commonly understood by its modern English definition. This is comparable to the word *dozen*, which means a grouping of twelve. It does not by itself identify that group as eggs, doughnuts, or any other specific item. This group of seven could, therefore, consist of either days or years, depending on the situation. Historically, reference to a week of years was as common to Jewish tradition as was a week of days, as this passage shows: [27]"Finish the week of wedding festivities with this daughter. Then we will give you the other one too. But you'll have to work for me another seven years. [28]That's what Jacob did. He finished the week with Leah. Then Laban gave his daughter Rachel to him as his wife" (*Genesis 29:27–28*).

With this in mind, Gabriel seems to be responding to Daniel's heartfelt prayer quoted in verses four through nineteen. Though there have been many variations in the specific interpretation of this verse, it is generally agreed that the phrases found herein all refer to the first advent of the Messiah. This verse, in a sense, is the synopsis of God's message and could serve as a conclusion just as adequately as it serves as a preface.[10]

Daniel sought to know the fate of his people, the Jews, and of their city, Jerusalem. God's response was probably not what Daniel expected to hear. The relationship that the Jews had both enjoyed and neglected as God's chosen people, and as citizens of God's holy city, would not be the everlasting covenant they thought it would be. *"Only if these laws stop working, declares the Lord, will Israel's descendants stop being a nation in my presence"* (*Jeremiah 31:36*). Daniel was informed that in four hundred and ninety years, this exclusive relationship would be finished. After that duration had ended, the

Messiah would come to "bring an end to rebellion, to stop sin, to forgive wrongs, to usher in everlasting righteousness, to put a seal on a prophet's vision, and to anoint the Most Holy One." Christ's resurrection provided the atonement for the sins of the world. *"Through the blood of his Son, we are set free from our sins. God forgives our failures because of his overflowing kindness"* (Ephesians 1:7). Through His atonement, salvation would become obtainable to all who believe, both Jew and Gentile. *"If you declare that Jesus is Lord, and believe that God brought him back to life, you will be saved"* (Romans 10:9). Furthermore, the "prophet's vision" regarding the Messiah was fulfilled and vindicated with the advent of Christ Jesus, in Whom all prophecies, having been fulfilled, would cease or be "sealed." *"Jesus took the twelve apostles aside and said to them, 'We're going to Jerusalem. Everything that the prophets wrote about the Son of Man will come true'"* (Luke 18:31).

9:25 *Learn, then, and understand that from the time the command is given to restore and rebuild Jerusalem until the anointed prince comes, seven sets of seven time periods and sixty-two sets of seven time periods will pass. Jerusalem will be restored and rebuilt with a city square and a moat during the troubles of those times.*

God, through His messenger Gabriel, advised Daniel to ponder the significance of these events. The message was clear: the period of time that would elapse between the edict to rebuild Jerusalem until the time of the Messiah would be 483 years—seven sets of "seven time periods" of years (49 years) plus sixty-two sets of "seven time periods" (434 years). The difficulty, though, is in determining which king's decree was intended and also which event (birth, baptism, or resurrection) of the Messiah was meant. Some commentators argue that the beginning of the seventy "seven time periods" was marked with Cyrus' issuing of the decree to rebuild the temple in Jerusalem (587 B.C.), but this seems improbable since the time span between this decree and the Messiah is too long except with the permission of creative calculating[11] (*Ezra 1:1–2*). However, most scholars, regardless of their rendering of verse twenty-seven, agree that the beginning of this period more likely began with the decree issued by Artaxerxes I (Longimanus) during the seventh year of his reign in 457 B.C.[12] (*Ezra 7:8–28*). Forty-nine years after this decree was issued, in 408 B.C., the rebuilding of Jerusalem was completed.[13]

Using the aforementioned as the most defensible benchmark, a quick computation reveals that by adding sixty-nine weeks of years (483 years) to the issuing of this decree by Artaxerxes I in 457 B.C. we arrive at A.D. 27 (not 26, since there is no A.D. 0), which is generally agreed to be about the time that Jesus, the Messiah, began his public ministry.[14]

9:26 *But after the sixty-two sets of seven time periods, the Anointed One will be cut off and have nothing. The city and the holy place will be destroyed with the prince who is to come. His end will come with a flood until the end of the destructive war that has been determined.*

The purpose of the Messiah was clear. He did not come into the world for Himself but to fulfill the will of God for reconciling the sins of the world.

There is a bit of ambiguity surrounding the identity of the "prince who is to come." Many conclude that this is Satan, the prince of this world. Whereas Satan was certainly as persistent in his efforts against the people of God then as he is today, there is no reason to presume that this prophecy suddenly makes an abstract shift here from an earthly premise to a strictly spiritual one. These people were more likely the Romans who, under the leadership of their prince, Titus Vespasian, would destroy the city and the sanctuary.[15] This segment of the prophecy—the only segment that is clearly separated from its surrounding events as "to come"—was ultimately fulfilled in A.D. 70, when Jerusalem was destroyed by Titus. The destruction spoken of in this verse indicates that the end of Jerusalem, both as a city and a nation, would culminate in a flood (most likely a figurative word denoting the intensity of the event) and destructive wars.[16] Ultimately, the fulfillment of this prophecy was in the providential acts of God to complete His old covenant with the Jews and introduce the new covenant through the Messiah, as explained in the following verse.[17]

9:27 *He will confirm his promise with many for one set of seven time periods. In the middle of the seven time periods, he will stop the sacrifices and food offerings. This will happen along with disgusting things that cause destruction until those time periods come to an end. It has been determined that this will happen to those who destroy the city."*

This verse is where many otherwise like-minded theologians part ways. Many presume that the person mentioned here suddenly refers to the end-times antichrist figure and, therefore, they separate the seventieth week of this prophecy to apply to the last years before the second advent of the Lord Jesus Christ.[18] However, an eschatological leap at this verse seems more out of preference than necessity. Perhaps it is better reserved for chapter eleven, where prophetic descriptions are more difficult to reconcile with specific historical events and persons. On the other hand, all matters discussed within this verse can easily be shown to have been fulfilled not in the end-times antichrist but in the person of Christ Jesus Himself.

Though the elements described here sound like treacherous behavior in light of an antichrist interpretation, the very same elements seem much less threatening when viewed as Messianic prophecy. Indeed the things named in this verse are not cause for alarm but for celebration.

Jesus confirmed his "promise with many" through his public ministry in which he performed miracles and preached of a new covenant.[19] *"Jesus has been given a priestly work that is superior to the Levitical priests' work. He also brings a better promise from God that is based on better guarantees" (Hebrews 8:6). "My promise to them will be fulfilled when I take away their sins" (Romans 11:27).* In the middle of this last "seven time periods," a short three years into His ministry, the Lord brought an end to the old covenant of sacrifice and offering with His own sacrifice at Calvary.

> ⁹*The first part of the tent is an example for the present time. The gifts and sacrifices that were brought there could not give the worshiper a clear conscience.* ¹⁰*These gifts and sacrifices were meant to be food, drink, and items used in various purification ceremonies. These ceremonies were required for the body until God would establish a new way of doing things.*
>
> ¹¹*But Christ came as a chief priest of the good things that are now here. Christ went through a better, more perfect tent that was not made by human hands and that is not part of this created world.* ¹²*He used his own blood, not the blood of goats and bulls, for the sacrifice. He went into the most holy place and offered this sacrifice once and for all to free us forever.*
>
> ¹³*The blood of goats and bulls and the ashes of cows sprinkled on unclean people made their bodies holy and clean.* ¹⁴*The blood of Christ, who had no defect, does even more. Through the eternal Spirit he offered himself to God and cleansed our consciences from the useless things we had done. Now we can serve the living God.*
>
> ¹⁵*Because Christ offered himself to God, he is able to bring a new promise from God. Through his death he paid the price to set people free from the sins they committed under the first promise. He did this so that those who are called can be guaranteed an inheritance that will last forever. (Hebrews 9:9–15)*

With the resurrection of Christ, the offerings and sacrifices required under the Law became obsolete and unnecessary.[20] "*God made this new promise and showed that the first promise was outdated. What is outdated and aging will soon disappear*" *(Hebrews 8:13)*. Furthermore, those Jews who failed to recognize the one who stopped the sacrifices and food offerings would soon be forced to stop their futile ceremonies by God's providential hand in the destruction of the temple by Titus. It seems gratuitous to presume this final verse refers to an end-times antichrist who will cause sacrifice and offering to cease in the temple since these ceremonial acts as well as the temple itself have already long since been eliminated, in both a spiritual sense and a physical one, at the time of Christ.

In effect, the Jews who failed to recognize Jesus as the Messiah had actually become the ones who committed these disgusting things by their continued adherence to the old covenant and by their rejection of the new covenant of Christ Jesus. *"³They don't understand how to receive God's approval. So they try to set up their own way to get it, and they have not accepted God's way for receiving his approval. ⁴Christ is the fulfillment of Moses' Teachings so that everyone who has faith may receive God's approval"* (Romans 10:3–4).

Notes/Applications

In these verses, God revealed a portion of His plan for extending grace upon Israel and the rest of mankind. He would sacrifice His Son. It is difficult to comprehend why God would send His Son to suffer the penalty for the world's sins. And why would God's Son, this Messiah, leave heaven's splendor in order to die for such reprobate people? *"You know about the kindness of our Lord Jesus Christ. He was rich, yet for your sake he became poor in order to make you rich through his poverty"* (2 Corinthians 8:9).

Verse twenty-six in this passage states the "Anointed One will be cut off and have nothing." The Messiah did not come for Himself but for each one of us. *"Jesus was made a little lower than the angels, but we see him crowned with glory and honor because he suffered death. Through God's kindness he died on behalf of everyone"* (Hebrews 2:9). God did not need to save us. He did not need our companionship or our obedience. Certainly, our worship and ministry please the Lord, but He did not need them or any part of us. God graciously extended salvation to us because He loved us and because it pleased Him to do so. When we consider the cost of grace, we grasp, in small part, the value of this undeserved gift.

By His grace, we have been saved. *"⁸God saved you through faith as an act of kindness. You had nothing to do with it. Being saved is a gift from God. ⁹It's not the result of anything you've done, so no one can brag about it. ¹⁰God has made us what we are. He has created us in Christ Jesus to live lives filled with good works that he has prepared for us to do"* (Ephesians 2:8–10). By His grace, we live. *"So we can go confidently to the throne of God's kindness to receive mercy and find kindness, which will help us at the right time"* (Hebrews 4:16). And by His grace, we will one day die and enter eternity where we will praise Him face-to-face: *"¹⁰God, who shows you his kindness and who has called you through Christ Jesus to his eternal glory, will restore you, strengthen you, make you strong, and support you as you suffer for a little while. ¹¹Power belongs to him forever. Amen"* (1 Peter 5:10–11).

> Amazing grace! How sweet the sound, that saved a wretch like me! I once was lost, but now am found, was blind, but now I see.
>
> 'Twas grace that taught my heart to fear, and grace my fears relieved; How precious did that grace appear the hour I first believed!
>
> Thro' many dangers, toils, and snares, I have already come;' Tis grace hath bro't me safe thus far, and grace will lead me home.
>
> The Lord has promised good to me, His Word my hope secures; He will my shield and portion be as long as life endures.
>
> Yea, when this flesh and heart shall fail, and mortal life shall cease, I shall possess, within the veil, a life of joy and peace.
>
> The earth shall soon dissolve like snow, the sun forbear to shine; But God, Who called me here below, shall be forever mine.
>
> When we've been there ten thousand years, bright shining as the sun, We've no less days to sing God's praise than when we'd first begun.[21]

DANIEL 10

Daniel 10:1-7

10:1 *In Cyrus' third year as king of Persia, a message was revealed to Daniel (who had been renamed Belteshazzar). The message was true. It was about a great war. Daniel understood the message because he was given insight during the vision.*

Scholars have dated the year of this vision between 554 and 532 B.C., depending on their delineation of King Cyrus' third year as king. The strongest evidence suggests that this historical point of reference does not refer to Cyrus' initial rise to power over Persia (about 558 B.C.) but to the expansion of his dominion over the entire Medo-Persian territory (about 538 B.C.). As such, this vision probably occurred around 535–534 B.C.[1] Although the events of the vision would not be fulfilled for many years, Daniel was told that they would surely come to pass. He was also given full understanding of the vision's meaning. The final two chapters of the book of Daniel are the continuation and completion of the prophecy that begins in this chapter.

10:2 *During those days I, Daniel, mourned for three whole weeks.*

Much speculation has been focused upon the reason for Daniel's mourning. Some attribute his grief to the timing of the vision during the feasts of Passover and Unleavened Bread.[2] These, however, were celebrations to the Lord and, as such, scarcely seem reason for mourning. Others contend that Daniel was still grieving over the vision of the seventy weeks, as recorded in the previous chapter.[3] This, too, seems an unlikely reason since that vision had occurred at least two years earlier *(Daniel 9:1–2)*. Most likely, Daniel was grieved by the complacency of his people. Several years had passed since Cyrus had signed the decree that freed the Israelites from their captivity in Babylon, thereby allowing them the liberty to return to their homeland to restore the city and temple. Only a handful of the Israelites desired to leave the foreign land to which they had grown so accustomed.[4] Furthermore, according to chapters two and three of Ezra, Jerusalem and its temple were still in ruins at this time. When the Israelites were finally prepared to rebuild the temple, many of them, including the priestly tribe, had become corrupted from intermarriage with the Babylonians.

> *[1]After these things had been done, the leaders came to me and said, "The people of Israel, including the priests and Levites, have failed to keep themselves separate from the neighboring groups of people and from the disgusting practices of the Canaanites, Hittites, Perizzites, Jebusites, Ammonites, Moabites, Egyptians, and Amorites. [2]The Israelites and their sons have married some of these foreign women. They have mixed our holy race with the neighboring groups of people. Furthermore, the leaders and officials have led the way in being unfaithful." (Ezra 9:1–2)*

Any one or more of these explanations serve as possible reasons for Daniel's bereavement. Whatever the cause may be, Daniel mourned for three weeks. Unlike the use of the "seven time periods" (or *weeks*) in the previous chapter that referred to a grouping of seven years, the word for *weeks* here signifies a grouping of seven days, as confirmed by verse thirteen, which calls these three weeks a literal twenty-one days.

10:3 *I didn't eat any good-tasting food. No meat or wine entered my mouth. I didn't wash myself until the entire three weeks were over.*

Daniel mourned and fasted. He did not abstain from sustenance altogether; rather, he adhered to a strict discipline of foods that he deemed allowable. He ate no rich-tasting breads, meats, or wines, which was similar to the diet he maintained during the early years of his captivity. Simply stated, he deprived himself of any luxurious, highly seasoned foods that satisfied human desires. Neither did he tend to his hygiene. He did only the bare minimum required to survive. Daniel's physical deprivation mirrored his spiritual emptiness and searching. His plight was a private one of lamenting and fasting for three weeks over his sin and his people's sin against God.

10:4–5 *⁴On the twenty-fourth day of the first month, I was by the great Tigris River. ⁵When I looked up, I saw a man dressed in linen, and he had a belt made of gold from Uphaz around his waist.*

Daniel dated this last recorded vision by referencing the year of the king's reign (*verse 1*) and by specifying the date as the twenty-fourth day of Nisan, the first month of the Jewish year, which falls within our months of March and April.[5]

Daniel was along the shore of the great Tigris River, called Hiddekel in some translations, when he saw a man "dressed in linen, and he had a belt made of gold from Uphaz." Uphaz is commonly believed to be another name for the country of Ophir because of the similarity between the Hebrew spellings of the words.[6] This interpretation seems to be credible because the Bible refers to Ophir as a place renowned for its vast quantities of fine gold (*1 Kings 9:28; Job 22:24; Isaiah 13:12*).

10:6 *His body was like beryl. His face looked like lightning.*
His eyes were like flaming torches. His arms and legs looked like
polished bronze. When he spoke, his voice sounded like the roar
of a crowd.

The descriptions given in verses five and six warrant a conclusion
that this glorious being was most likely an appearance of a preincarnate Christ. His majesty here can only be described by Daniel as
an exquisite gemstone like beryl.[7] We can also assume that this was
a Christophany because of similarities with other biblical depictions
identified as Jesus Christ:

> [13]*There was someone like the Son of Man among the lamp stands. He*
> *was wearing a robe that reached his feet. He wore a gold belt around*
> *his waist.* [14]*His head and his hair were white like wool—like snow.*
> *His eyes were like flames of fire.* [15]*His feet were like glowing bronze*
> *refined in a furnace. His voice was like the sound of raging waters*
> *(Revelation 1:13–15).*

10:7 *I, Daniel, was the only one who saw the vision. The men*
with me didn't see the vision. Yet, they started to tremble vio-
lently, and they quickly hid themselves.

Only Daniel witnessed this vision. The other men with Daniel were
unable to view this appearance because they were stricken with fear
and, therefore, retreated.

Notes/Applications

None of us has ever actually seen God with our eyes. We have never
felt Him literally take us by the hand or heard Him call our names
audibly. However, as believers, we have certainly experienced God's
reality through His presence, especially during moments when, like
Daniel, we have desperately needed His peace and reassurance.

The presence of our Lord can be a place of quiet refreshment
where He rejuvenates us for the day's journey. *"So change the way*
you think and act, and turn to God to have your sins removed" (Acts 3:19).

Moments spent in His presence steadies us for the day by fixing His will upon our hearts, but when we neglect spending time in God's presence on a daily basis, the winds of chaos quickly blow us down.

As a testimony to the heavenly peace found only in the presence of God, hymnist Cleland Boyd McAfee penned the following lyrics after his two nieces died from diphtheria:

> There is a place of quiet rest near to the heart of God.
> A place where sin cannot molest, near to the heart of God.
>
> There is a place of comfort sweet near to the heart of God.
> A place where we our Savior meet, near to the heart of God.
>
> There is a place of full release near to the heart of God.
> A place where all is joy and peace, near to the heart of God.
>
> *Refrain:*
> O Jesus, blest Redeemer, sent from the heart of God,
> Hold us who wait before Thee near to the heart of God.[8]

Do we need the comfort and reassurance found in the Lord's presence? Have we entered today into that place near to the heart of God? May we come before Him and be assured that He will meet us in the quietness of this moment. "*Come close to God, and he will come close to you*" (*James 4:8a*).

Daniel 10:8–14

10:8 *So I was left alone to see this grand vision. I had no strength left in me. My face turned deathly pale, and I was helpless.*

Daniel reemphasized that he was alone during this vision since the others had gone to hide themselves. He was already weakened from three weeks of fasting, and what little energy might have remained in him was completely drained by this staggering vision. The overwhelming experience of standing in the presence of God affected his entire appearance.

10:9 *I heard the man speak, and as I listened to his words, I fainted facedown on the ground.*

Daniel collapsed as though dead as a result of being so completely overwhelmed by the vision; all of his faculties yielded to a state of temporary paralysis.[9] Despite this helpless condition, Daniel was still able to hear the words that were being spoken to him.

Daniel's response is similar to John's reaction to the appearance of the Son of Man in Revelation. *"When I saw him, I fell down at his feet like a dead man"* (Revelation 1:17a). In comparing the passage in Revelation chapter one and this passage in Daniel chapter ten, we see many parallels in both the vision of the Christophany and in the response of these two witnesses. However, there is one notable difference between these prophets' experiences. When the Christophany appeared to Daniel at a time long before the birth of Christ, He lacked something that was present with Him when He later appeared to the apostle John long after Christ's ascension—the keys of death and hell! *"I was dead, but now I am alive forever. I have the keys of death and hell"* (Revelation 1:18). What a wonderful assurance that Jesus has conquered death and hell and that He lives forevermore at the right hand of the Father as the glorified, risen Christ!

10:10 *Then a hand touched me and made my hands and knees shake.*

While Daniel was in this weakened condition, a hand reached down, touched him, and made him tremble on his hands and knees.

10:11 *The man said to me, "Daniel, you are highly respected. Pay attention to my words. Stand up, because I've been sent to you." When he said this to me, I stood up, trembling.*

Daniel assumed an upright position, though he still shuddered with fear, and found himself in the presence of a being different than the first.[10] Although the introduction of another being is not clearly described, we may conclude by the surrounding evidence that Daniel was visited by two separate beings. The description in verses five and six of the first being depicts an unmistakable and glorious appearance that is distinctive to the Son of God when compared to His similar appearances recorded in the Bible. Therefore, such a magnificent description within those verses likely characterizes a Being greater than an angel. Furthermore, the one who now stood before Daniel seems, by his own words, to be simply a messenger sent specifically to Daniel, which would indicate that this being was an angel of God. In verse thirteen, it will be explained how his efforts in response to Daniel's prayers were hampered by the "commander of the Persian kingdom." Nothing can ever impede the inclinations of the Lord, and it should be concluded, therefore, that these were two separate and unique beings that appeared to Daniel.[11]

The angel addressed Daniel as "highly respected." What a privilege it must have been loved and respected by God! As evidenced throughout his life, Daniel had truly cultivated a deep fellowship with God and commitment to prayer. He did not waiver in his convictions but firmly stood upon the principles and promises of God.

10:12 *He told me, "Don't be afraid, Daniel. God has heard everything that you said ever since the first day you decided to humble yourself in front of your God so that you could learn to understand things. I have come in response to your prayer.*

The messenger arrived at the appointed time to comfort and reassure Daniel. Daniel was told not to fear because his voice had been heard in heaven from the first moment he uttered his heartfelt prayer. The angel explained that he had been sent immediately in response to Daniel's prayers, but there had been a delay, as explained in the following verse.

10:13 *The commander of the Persian kingdom opposed me for 21 days. But then Michael, one of the chief commanders, came to help me because I was left alone with the kings of Persia.*

The angel contended that "the commander of the Persian kingdom opposed me for 21 days" until the archangel Michael came to his assistance. This commander should not be misinterpreted to mean either Cyrus, the king of Persia, or his son, Cambyses. Rather, this is a commander/prince of a spiritual realm, a principle agent among the vast forces of Satan.[12] This verse implies that God immediately sent the angel when Daniel first prayed, but then this angel was thwarted in spiritual battle along the way. This was the reason given for the delay when responding to Daniel's prayer. Nevertheless, this delay does not diminish the total sovereignty of Almighty God over all matters.

With all the significant visions, wonderful miracles, and valuable lessons packed within the book of Daniel, this verse in conjunction with others in this chapter offers us an amazing insight that is often understated or overlooked altogether. In a manner not found anywhere else in the Bible, we are given a firsthand account of the spiritual warfare that takes place all around us yet remains unseen by the human eye. *"This is not a wrestling match against a human opponent. We are wrestling with rulers, authorities, the powers who govern this world of darkness, and spiritual forces that control evil in the heavenly world"* (*Ephesians 6:12*).

10:14 *I have come to explain to you what will happen to your people in the last days, because the vision is about times still to come."*

The angel told Daniel that he could be stalled no longer from coming to make Daniel understand the future of the Israelites. Through the message given to him, Daniel was given spiritual insight of a prophetic nature because he had not sought God in a token, ritualistic way. He humbled, deprived, and prepared himself to talk to and to hear from Almighty God, and as we see in these verses, the Lord graciously answered Daniel's prayers.

Notes/Applications

According to the angel, the Lord answered Daniel's prayers from the very moment that Daniel completely surrendered himself to God. For our prayers to be effectual, we must be certain that we have not erected roadblocks that hinder our communication with God. *"The Lord is far from wicked people, but he hears the prayers of righteous people"* (*Proverbs 15:29*).

Sin obstructs our communication with God. When we clutter our minds and hearts with sin, our relationship with God will be strained due to our hardened hearts, and Holy God will not honor the prayers of those who live in disobedience to His commands. *"If I had thought about doing anything sinful, the Lord would not have listened to me"* (*Psalm 66:18*). *"Surely the prayer of someone who refuses to listen to God's teachings is disgusting"* (*Proverbs 28:9*). Our busy schedules, family obligations, and other worldly preoccupations can also detour us away from prayer because they drain our time and energy. Ironically, when these daily pressures become unbearable, we often neglect what should be our first priority. Therefore, we must learn to differentiate between what seems to be most urgent with what is most important—time spent in communion with God. *"Serve* the Lord *wholeheartedly and willingly because he searches every heart and understands every thought we have. If you dedicate your life to serving him, he will accept you. But if you abandon him, he will reject you from then on"* (1 Chronicles 28:9b).

The roadblocks to an effectual prayer life can be easily removed if we will set our hearts to loving and obeying God. When Daniel sought Him, God was easily found. God promises that if we wholeheartedly seek Him, we, too, will find Him. *"But if you look for the Lord your God when you are among those nations, you will find him whenever you search for him with all your heart and with all your soul"* (Deuteronomy 4:29). What roadblocks are hindering our intimacy with God? Have we focused our whole attention on seeking intimate conversation with God?

Daniel 10:15–21

10:15 *When he said this to me, I bowed down with my face touching the ground and was silent.*

Daniel, while utterly dumbfounded and unable to speak, again put his face to the ground. This being had come as a direct messenger of God, and he spoke truth. Daniel, perhaps beginning to understand the monumental importance of this angel's visit, was incapable of uttering even a single word.

10:16 *Then someone who looked like a human touched my lips. I opened my mouth and began to talk. I said to the person standing in front of me, "Sir, because of this vision, pain has overwhelmed me, and I'm helpless.*

This was likely the same being that had touched Daniel in verse ten and had been conversing with him since then. The first word Daniel uttered was, "Sir." We know from earlier verses that Daniel was not addressing the Lord God but was respectfully addressing this messenger. Daniel admitted that he was overwhelmed, deeply grieved and utterly weakened as a result of all he saw.

10:17–18 *[17]How can I talk to you, sir? I have no strength left, and the wind has been knocked out of me." [18]Again, the person who looked like a human touched me, and I became stronger.*

Daniel did not feel strong enough to speak with the angel that he again addressed as "sir." As previously stated, he was physically weakened from his fasting and emotionally drained from his mourning. When the angel again touched Daniel, his strength was instantaneously restored to him by the power of God through one simple touch from this messenger.

10:19 *He said, "Don't be afraid. You are highly respected. Everything is alright! Be strong! Be strong!" As he talked to me, I became stronger. I said, "Sir, tell me what you came to say. You have strengthened me."*

The messenger restated that Daniel was a man greatly respected by God, so Daniel was to combat his anxieties and rest in that assurance. To fully grasp what was occurring, Daniel had to release all of his fears and be willing to trust. The angel then proclaimed, "Don't be afraid," and when the angel spoke these things, Daniel immediately regained his strength. Daniel then encouraged the angel to deliver his message.

10:20 *He asked, "Do you know why I have come to you? Now I will return to fight the commander of Persia. When I go, the commander of Greece will come.*

It seems the angel answered Daniel's petition to know the message with a rhetorical question, almost as if to settle any uncertainty concerning Daniel's ability to grasp the magnitude of his current situation. Then the angel said that he had to return to fight with the prince of Persia, and when that empire had run its preordained course, the Grecian Empire would attain power, and the angel would then have to battle with the controlling demons of that empire.[13] By the angel's words, we again sense the ongoing spiritual warfare between good and evil. Satan and his angels are a powerful force that only God can conquer. Satan constantly tries to interfere with God's plan for creation and, more specifically, with those who seek the will of God, but he is only able to do that which is allowed by Sovereign God. Therefore, this warfare is not a war, at least as most people generally understand the term, because Almighty God has already won the victory.

10:21 *However, I will tell you what is inscribed in the true writings. No one will support me when I fight these commanders except your commander, Michael.*

The messenger told Daniel that he would reveal the truth. Then, the messenger claimed that no other angel except Michael, the watchman over the nation of Israel, could help him in this battle against Satan's forces and their relentless hostility toward the Jews.[14] *"The person who looked like a human continued, 'At that time Michael, the great commander, will stand up on behalf of the descendants of your people'"* (Daniel 12:1).

Notes/Applications

Daniel was physically exhausted from fasting and fervently praying. Despite Daniel's infirmity, God strengthened him, thereby empowering the prophet to withstand this test of his faith.

We are fragile pots, ceramic vessels. We appear to be strong enough to withstand any trial or temptation, but all of us have experienced or will experience a breaking point. When unexpected events turn tragic, we quickly find that we are not resilient and that we need more sustenance than we can muster. At that hour, when our spirit is utterly broken, God picks up the rubble of our lives and binds the pieces together by His miraculous power. In our weakness, God is made stronger because we realize, more then ever before, how much we need Him. *"⁹But he told me: 'My kindness is all you need. My power is strongest when you are weak.' So I will brag even more about my weaknesses in order that Christ's power will live in me. ¹⁰Therefore, I accept weakness, mistreatment, hardship, persecution, and difficulties suffered for Christ. It's clear that when I'm weak, I'm strong"* (2 Corinthians 12:9–10).

Times of weakness empty us and cleanse us of our pride, so we can be used for God's purposes. We become consecrated vessels, ready to be filled with His power and to pour forth a living testimony to other people who also need Him. *"Those who stop associating with dishonorable people will be honored. They will be set apart for the master's use, prepared to do good things"* (2 Timothy 2:21). Have we experienced our breaking point before the Lord? What has God accomplished both in us and through us as a result of our brokenness?

DANIEL 11

Daniel 11:1–8

11:1 *During Darius the Mede's first year as king, I strength-ened and defended Michael."*

The angel, not Daniel as some expositors have speculated, contin-ued speaking as evidenced in the obvious flow and continuation of this text from the previous chapter. As the angel had promised, he would now reveal to Daniel the fate of the nation of Israel in future times. *"I have come to explain to you what will happen to your people in the last days, because the vision is about times still to come"* (Daniel 10:14). Apparently, the Lord had also sent this angel to strengthen Darius the Mede, which suggests that God had used the king as an instru-ment in His divine plan.

11:2 *The person who looked like a human continued, "What I am about to tell you is the truth. Three more kings will rule Persia. Then there will be a fourth, who will become much richer than all the others. As he becomes strong through his wealth, he will turn everyone against the kingdom of Greece.*

Through this messenger, God first revealed to Daniel the truth about what would become of the Medo-Persian Empire. The angel explained that three kings would follow Darius the Mede and that a fourth king would be far richer than the previous kings. This passage arouses debate over the identity of these four kings, who ruled concurrently with Cyrus the Persian. The second king is likely Cambyses, sometimes referred to as Artaxerxes, who was the son and successor of Cyrus the Persian.[1] Because Cambyses perceived the strengthening of the Jews as a threat to his authority, he overturned his father's earlier decree and forbade the continuation of the rebuilding of Jerusalem for several years.[2] Cambyses died a mere six years into his reign. For seven months after that the ruler over the empire was Gaumata, who is often called Pseudo-Smerdis because he deceitfully obtained the throne by claiming to be Smerdis, son of Cyrus.[3] Afterwards, Darius I (not Darius the Mede, but the son of Hystaspes) became king.[4] The fourth king refers to Xerxes, also named Ahasuerus, who rose to power after the death of his father in 486 B.C. inheriting enormous wealth.[5] After amassing the largest army ever assembled to that point in history, Xerxes devoted himself to the conquest of Greece to avenge his father's death, which marked the beginning of the fall of the Persian Empire. In addition, historical records reveal that there were several other kings of the Persian Empire, but only these four are mentioned in this vision since the above-noted kings all had some influence over the affairs of the Jewish people, the restoration of their temple, or the rebuilding of Jerusalem.[6]

11:3 *"Then a warrior-king will come. He will rule a vast empire and do as he pleases.*

Since the kingdom of Persia was in a state of decline, this verse refers to the ruler of the kingdom that would follow, which was the Greco-Macedonian Empire. A powerful king would obtain great dominion and rule as he pleased. This king proved to be Alexander the Great, who became a world leader at a very young age. He withstood the battle against an experienced Persian army, defeated them, and thereby brought Greece onto the scene as the third great world empire.[7]

11:4 *But as soon as he is established, his kingdom will be broken into pieces and divided in the directions of the four winds of heaven. The empire will not be given to his descendants. It will no longer be like his empire, since it will be uprooted and given to others.*

Once Alexander the Great reached the pinnacle of his power, his kingdom was separated into four kingdoms according to the four basic directions of the earth—north, east, south, and west. The division of this kingdom and the dissolution of its ruling authority weakened its dominion. By the sovereignty of God Almighty, the death of Alexander the Great allowed less powerful rulers to share authority in his place. These emerged as four generals that individually ruled over the four divided nations, and this sharing of authority contributed to the decline of the Greco-Macedonian Empire.[8] Alexander lost his power and his empire's dominance because, as evident in verse three, he did all things according to his own will.

11:5 *"The southern king will be strong, but one of his officers will become stronger than he is and rule a vast empire.*

Ptolemy I (Soter), a strong leader who claimed the title King of Egypt, developed the southern kingdom into a great nation of commerce. The phrase "one of his officers" does not refer to the king of the South but to Alexander, whose kingdom was divided among four generals, one of which was the officer referred to in this verse. This officer was Seleucus I (Nicator), who became the king of the North over the region of Syria and who ultimately gained dominion over the king of the South.[9]

11:6 *After a few years the southern and northern kings will make an alliance. The southern king's daughter will go to the northern king to make peace. She won't hold on to her power, and the alliance won't last. She, those who came with her, and the one who fathered and protected her will be given away.*

After a number of years, there was a marriage between royal families of the kingdom of the South and the kingdom of the North. As was often the case, the union was strictly political. In an attempt to establish peace, such royal marriages were sometimes arranged so that warring kingdoms could settle their differences and unite their power.[10]

Berenice, the daughter of Ptolemy II (Philadelphus), was given to be married to the king of the North, Antiochus II (Theos), who had illegally divorced his wife, Laodice, and disinherited their son in order to marry Berenice.[11] As we will see, this scheme would fail on all fronts, primarily because Berenice would not remain queen for very long. "The one who fathered" seems to signify a parental reference, but this may not be the intention. According to some historical sources, Berenice's father, Ptolemy II, was already dead by this point. The phrase could more accurately be conveyed as "him who was begotten by her," referring to the child born to Berenice and Antiochus II.[12] Indeed, this prophecy seems to be more clearly fulfilled in their son. Upon his head, by virtue of this marriage, the crown would have ultimately fallen were it not for the intervention of Laodice, Antiochus' first wife. Though Berenice would eventually reconcile with Antiochus, Laodice contracted the murders of both Berenice and her infant son in Antioch, thereby assuring that they would not retain any authority. The crown would then be passed down to Laodice's own son, Seleucus II (Callinicus).[13] Furthermore, after reuniting with Antiochus, Laodice allegedly poisoned Antiochus to death, thereby eliminating any risk of future betrayal and any threat of surrendering her own son's inheritance.[14]

Consequently, both kingdoms were weakened instead of strengthened by the union of Berenice and Antiochus.

11:7 *"At that time a shoot will grow from her roots to replace her father. He will attack the northern army, enter the stronghold of the northern king, fight against them, and be victorious.*

The phrase "her roots" refers to Berenice's father, Ptolemy II, upon whose death Ptolemy III (Euergetes) ascended the throne as king of Egypt, the king of the South. Ptolemy III, accompanied by an enormous army, marched into the kingdom of the North to avenge the murder of his sister, Berenice. He fought the Seleucids and prevailed, killing Laodice in the process.[15] As a result, the king of the South dominated the king of the North.

11:8 *He will take the metal statues of their gods and their precious utensils of silver and gold back to Egypt. He will rule for more years than the northern king.*

Ptolemy III confiscated the idols of the northern kingdom and carried these precious golden and silver vessels back into Egypt. These vessels came out of the temples of the gods and the palaces of the kings.[16] According to this verse, the kingdom of the South lasted longer than the kingdom of the North.

Notes/Applications
When one kingdom crumbled under the weight of its own greed and pride, another kingdom eventually conquered it. Both the northern and southern kingdoms governed themselves according to man's shifting standards rather than by God's steadfast principles.

People live their lives, their own "kingdoms," in a number of ways. Our world embraces this collage of alternative lifestyles, and it spouts that we are all headed to the same place, just arriving by different roadmaps. However, as believers, we know that the Lord Jesus Christ is the only pathway to eternity in heaven and that all other roads lead to eternity in hell. *"13Enter through the narrow gate because the gate and road that lead to destruction are wide. Many enter through the wide gate. 14But the narrow gate and the road that lead to life are full of trouble. Only a few people find the narrow gate"* (Matthew 7:13–14).

Life's broad road, convenient and widely traveled, appears to be paved with pleasure and freedom, whereas the narrow road appears to be cluttered with potholes of rules. The broad road entices the multitudes because it accommodates every manifestation of individual expression, but eventually this one-lane fast track destines its traveler to self-destruction and separation from God. The narrow road leads to truly abundant life and freedom in Christ, a life that is not free from tribulation but is free from the penalty of sin. However, this road is less traveled. Although it is the highway to eternal life, few tread this path because they seek immediate gratification of their desires.

What path have we been traveling? The broad with the many or the narrow with the chosen few?

> *26Carefully walk a straight path,*
>   *and all your ways will be secure.*
> *27Do not lean to the right or to the left.*
> *Walk away from evil.* (Proverbs 4:26–27)

If we have been living the kingdom of our lives according to our own sense of direction, we must change our course and enter God's kingdom through His Gatekeeper, the Lord Jesus Christ.

Daniel 11:9–16

11:9 *He will invade the southern kingdom and return to his own country.*

Historical records contend that many years after the invasion of the Seleucid Kingdom by Ptolemy III, Laodice's son, Seleucus II (Callinicus), attempted an invasion of Egypt. This campaign of revenge failed, and the Seleucid armies were forced to retreat back to their own kingdom in defeat.[17]

11:10 *"Then his sons will prepare for war. They will assemble a large number of forces so that they can overwhelm the enemy and pass through its land. They will return and wage war all the way to the stronghold.*

Years later, the descendents of the king of the North again revolted against the king of the South, Ptolemy IV (Philopater). Soon, a great leader arose from among the kingdom of the North. This was Antiochus III, also known as Antiochus the Great, who assembled vast and powerful armies to rise against the southern kingdom.[18]

11:11 *The southern king will be outraged. He will go to fight the northern king, who will raise a large army that will fall into the southern king's hands.*

The king of the South, Ptolemy IV, became enraged with the threat of the northern kingdom's campaign against his armies. Therefore, Ptolemy gathered his armies to wage war against Antiochus III, who had amassed an army even larger than that of his foe. Nevertheless, by the providential hand of God, Ptolemy was victorious and Antiochus fell "into the southern king's hands."[19]

11:12 *When that army is captured, the southern king will become conceited. Although he will dominate tens of thousands of people, he will not always be strong.*

After defeating the great armies of Antiochus III the Great, Ptolemy IV was filled with pride and inflated confidence. Despite this extraordinary military victory, in which it is reported that his armies slaughtered seventeen thousand of Antiochus' soldiers, Ptolemy was content to reclaim the territories he had lost in earlier battles and to make peace with Antiochus.[20] Ultimately, his failure to take full advantage of the spoils of his triumph would backfire.

11:13 *"The northern king will return and raise an army larger than the first one. After a few years he will invade with a large army and a lot of equipment.*

Antiochus the Great, king of the North, had escaped from the hands of Ptolemy IV and had returned to the northern kingdom to recover his losses from the defeat. Through various military and political strategies, including the formation of an alliance with Philip V of Macedon, Antiochus the Great assembled a multitude that was much larger than his previous army. He spent many years and much money preparing for his second attack against the South.[21]

11:14 *In those times many people will rebel against the southern king, and violent men from your own people will rebel in keeping with this vision, but they will be defeated.*

The king of the North was not the only enemy that opposed the king of the South. By virtue of its geographical location, Israel had many natural enemies. The country was constantly being trampled and pillaged by the armies of the North and the South during their wars with each other. The order to rebuild Jerusalem and the temple had been given, but Israel still experienced obvious difficulties in fulfilling the tasks because of her warring neighbors.

Apparently, several Jewish renegades who ignored the laws of God participated in the spoils and plunder of their warring neighbors and contributed to the destruction of the southern kingdom. Nevertheless, as this verse indicates, those Israelites that forsook their roles as God's chosen people would neither progress nor profit from their actions but would suffer the consequences for their disobedience, as will be further described in the details of the verses to follow.[22]

11:15 *Then the northern king will come, build dirt attack ramps, and capture a fortified city. The southern forces will not be able to withstand him. Even their best troops will not be strong enough.*

The king of the North, Antiochus the Great, eventually overpowered the king of the South. With relative ease, Antiochus' armies brought even the most fortified cities of his enemy—seemingly the best-defended and most-protected cities—under the subjection of his authority.[23] As Antiochus' armies marched, they again had to go through Israel, and the resulting effects will be explained in the verse to follow.

The greatest efforts of the Egyptian armies could not withstand the invasion headed by Antiochus. The Egyptians simply had no strength against this crushing Seleucid army. God granted strength at the appointed time and withdrew strength when it was time to fall. As was true for these empires, all earthly powers rise and fall according to God's plan and God's timing.[24]

11:16 *The invader will do as he pleases, and no one will be able to withstand his attack. He will rise to power in the beautiful land and it will be completely under his control.*

Because of the certain destruction that awaited any who opposed Antiochus III, the Jews pledged their support to him and the Seleucid forces. Antiochus was afforded all of the provisions that Israel could make available and was warmly received into Jerusalem, "the beautiful land."[25]

Notes/Applications

Amazingly, king after king conquered the richest lands and people, yet these kings were still never satisfied. They warred with one another for more wealth, more land, and more power. This reveals mankind's true nature. The more we get, the more we want until the pursuit of worldly desires consumes us. *"¹⁵Don't love the world and what it offers. Those who love the world don't have the Father's love in them. ¹⁶Not everything that the world offers—physical gratification, greed, and extravagant lifestyles—comes from the Father. It comes from the world"* (1 John 2:15–16). As was the case for these kingdoms, any nation, community, church, home, or life built on greed eventually collapses.

A spirit of greed recklessly pursues its prize to the point of ignoring the spiritual, emotional, and physical needs of others.

> *These dogs have huge appetites.*
>   *They are never full.*
> *They are the shepherds,*
>   *but they don't understand.*
> *All of them have turned to go their own ways.*
>   *Each one seeks his own gain. (Isaiah 56:11)*

This sin, like all other sin, arouses a lustful desire that can never be satisfied no matter how much money, pleasure, success, or material goods are obtained. Like a dog that chases its own tail, a greedy person lives a vicious cycle of endless searching. The spiritual aspect of this problem is that the sin of greed usually progresses into other sinful appetites since this lust cannot be quenched. *"Certainly, the love of money is the root of all kinds of evil. Some people who have set their hearts on getting rich have wandered away from the Christian faith and have caused themselves a lot of grief"* (1 Timothy 6:10).

Have we succumbed to the sin of greed in our pursuit for more? Here are a few steps that we can take to find contentment in every area of our lives:

1. Recognize that nothing satisfies us except a relationship with our Lord and Savior Jesus Christ.

¹³Jesus answered her, "Everyone who drinks this water will become thirsty again. ¹⁴But those who drink the water that I will give them will never become thirsty again. In fact, the water I will give them will become in them a spring that gushes up to eternal life." (John 4:13–14)

2. Confess our pursuit of worldly things as greed.

> *²⁴If I put my confidence in gold*
> *or said to fine gold, "I trust you". . . .*
> *²⁵If I enjoyed being very rich*
> *because my hand had found great wealth. . . .*
> *²⁶If I saw the light shine*
> *or the moon move along in its splendor*
> > *²⁷so that my heart was secretly tempted,*
> > *and I threw them a kiss with my hand,*
> *²⁸then that, too, would be a criminal offense,*
> *and I would have denied God above.* (Job 31:24–28)

3. Recognize that the things of this world are temporal, and commit to pursuing everlasting treasures.

> *¹⁹Stop storing up treasures for yourselves on earth, where moths and rust destroy and thieves break in and steal. ²⁰Instead, store up treasures for yourselves in heaven, where moths and rust don't destroy and thieves don't break in and steal. ²¹Your heart will be where your treasure is.* (Matthew 6:19–21)

4. Remember that all we have, including our very lives, belongs to Almighty God, so recognize everything as a blessing from Him rather than as a product of our own doing.

A rich person's wealth is his strong city
and is like a high wall in his imagination. (Proverbs 18:11)

[17]It does no good to spread a net within the sight of any bird.
[18]But these people set an ambush for their own murder.
They go into hiding only to lose their lives.
[19]This is what happens to everyone
who is greedy for unjust gain.
Greed takes away his life. (Proverbs 1:17–19)

Daniel 11:17–24

11:17 *"Then the northern king will decide to invade with the power of his entire kingdom, and some decent men will invade with him. He will give the southern king his daughter as a wife in order to destroy the southern kingdom. But this will not succeed or help him.*

Antiochus III, who sought to enter his conquered territories with all the might of his entire kingdom, was also accompanied by upright people. These were likely the previously mentioned Jews who had forsaken their spiritual inheritance to pursue the carnal, material pleasures obtainable by swearing their allegiance to Antiochus.

Antiochus the Great, in a familiar scheme to gain the favor of the Egyptians without employing military force, offered his daughter Cleopatra to Ptolemy V, the king of the South, in order to promote an alliance with him and to secure some degree of influence in the affairs of Egypt. His daughter, however, would eventually grow sympathetic toward the Egyptian cause. Since Cleopatra did not remain loyal to her father, the whole scheme ultimately failed.[26]

11:18–19 *[18]Then he will turn his attention to the coastlands and capture many of them. But a commander will silence the insults that the northern king makes and even insult him. [19]He will turn back toward the fortresses in his own country, but he will stumble, fall, and disappear.*

Antiochus III steered his armies toward the islands of the Mediterranean Sea. Although he enjoyed some initial success in these endeavors, he was ultimately turned back and forced to retreat from Greece, where the Romans had joined forces with those who opposed the Seleucid campaign. The Roman army, led by a commander named Lucius Cornelius Scipio, pursued Antiochus' larger army back to Asia Minor and defeated him at the Battle of Magnesia.[27]

11:20 *"Another king will take his place. He will have a cruel official go out in royal splendor. But in a few days the king will be destroyed, although not in anger or war.*

Another ruler then arose within the kingdom of the North, Seleucus IV (Philopater), who was the son of Antiochus the Great. Seleucus IV extorted from the people and robbed them with heavy taxation.[28] He, like others before him, also stole from the temple in Jerusalem. Seleucus IV died having reigned over the kingdom of the North for only a short period of time.

11:21 *"A contemptible person will take his place. He will not be given royal splendor. He will invade when people are feeling secure, and he will seize the kingdom using false promises.*

When Seleucus IV died, the crown should have been passed to his son, the rightful successor, Demetrius I (Soter), who was held captive in Rome at that time. Seleucus IV had a younger brother, however, Antiochus IV (Epiphanes). This brother gained authority over the kingdom of the North through scheming and deceit.[29] Antiochus IV, wanting to appear as though he were acting out of duty and obligation, ascended the throne in Demetrius' absence, vowing to relinquish authority as soon as the rightful heir to the throne was freed from his captivity. Once his leadership was established, though, Antiochus secretly planned to gain the favor of the people through flattery and force. He had no intention of surrendering his power once he obtained it.[30]

11:22 *He will overwhelm large forces and defeat them, including the prince of the promise.*

After he had gained the kingdom, Antiochus Epiphanes earned a reputation for being very bloodthirsty, especially against any who opposed his authority or any whose destruction would benefit him. Armies that tried to invade his territories were completely overthrown.[31]

Interpretations vary regarding this reference to the "prince of the promise." Some identify this as the High Priest Onias III, who was also called Menelaus. Onias was sent to Syria for execution by Antiochus in order to stop him from organizing a revolt among the Jews.[32] More likely, though, this prince simply refers to Ptolemy VII (Philometer), the son of Cleopatra (Antiochus' sister), with whom Antiochus had formed a treaty.[33]

11:23–24 *[23]After an alliance has been made with him, he will act deceitfully and rise to power with only a few people. [24]When people feel secure, he will invade the richest parts of the provinces and do something that none of his predecessors ever did. He will distribute loot and wealth to his followers. He will invent new ways of attacking fortifications. But this will last only for a little while.*

Antiochus betrayed those with whom he had formed an alliance. He designed treaties and contracts to accomplish his own purposes, and when it suited him, he broke them. This verse likely refers specifically to the treaty he had formed with his nephew, Ptolemy VII, as described in the previous verse.

Once he had gained the trust of his nephew, Antiochus was able to invade the "richest parts of the provinces." Ptolemy, feeling secure and confident with his uncle's intentions because of the treaty, offered no resistance. Consequently, Antiochus was able to gain control over these territories despite his relatively small armies.[34] Such deceitful schemes were strategies possibly never considered and certainly never employed by his forefathers, who sought to conquer their adversaries through warfare. Furthermore, once he had obtained these regions, Antiochus distributed the wealth of his plunder among his lowly followers as a form of welfare to gain their favor.[35] Because of the early success he achieved from such ploys, he formulated plans to gain control over even larger strongholds of his opponent. Such conspiracies, however, were short-lived, and so were the successes he enjoyed from them.

Notes/Applications

Antiochus the Great was ultimately overcome in much the same way as he had conquered others. Similarly, every man's evil eventually revisits him. *"If you don't do all these things, you will be sinning against the Lord. You can be sure that you will be punished for your sin"* (Numbers 32:23). *"Make no mistake about this: You can never make a fool out of God. Whatever you plant is what you'll harvest"* (Galatians 6:7).

It is difficult to watch as the evil in our world continually escalates while evildoers prosper. We may wonder why a murderer is paroled before completing his sentence or why a doctor who performs abortions gains wealth. Where is the justice, especially for the victims of these crimes? Where is God in all of this?

Although life's scales often seem drastically unfair, God still reigns over it all. Evil runs its course only for the duration that Almighty God has preordained—no more and no less. What now appears to be prosperity for the evildoer is only temporal gain; in God's time, He will avenge all evilness. *"Don't take revenge, dear friends. Instead, let God's anger take care of it. After all, Scripture says, 'I alone have the right to take revenge. I will pay back, says the Lord'"* (Romans 12:19).

Instead of becoming disheartened by what appears to be injustice, we can rejoice in knowing that our God is perfect and that His ways and timing are also perfect. Though we cannot understand the ways of God, we can rest assured that God's perfect justice will ultimately prevail.

> [1]*Do not be preoccupied with evildoers.*
> *Do not envy those who do wicked things.*
> > [2]*They will quickly dry up like grass*
> > *and wither away like green plants.*
> [3]*Trust the Lord, and do good things.*
> *Live in the land, and practice being faithful. . . .*
> [9]*Evildoers will be cut off from their inheritance,*
> > *but those who wait with hope for the Lord will inherit the land.*
> > (Psalm 37:1–3, 9)

Daniel 11:25–31

11:25 *"With a large army he will summon his power and courage against the southern king, who will prepare for war with a large, strong army. But the southern king won't be able to withstand him because of the schemes devised against him.*

By the time Antiochus Epiphanes was prepared to abandon all treaties with Egypt and to confront the king of the South in unrestrained warfare, he had assembled a great army and increased his former strength tremendously. His nephew, Ptolemy VII (Philometer), was prepared for the battle with a great army of his own. Nevertheless, the king of the South was soundly defeated, although not by the hand of an overpowering opposition. Instead, he was defeated by having fallen too far into the traps of his uncle's deception before realizing that he was being played as a fool.[36]

11:26 *People who eat the king's rich food will ruin him. His army will be overwhelmed, and many will die in battle.*

The people, who Ptolemy VII once trusted, eventually betrayed him. Though Ptolemy had armies comparable in size and strength to those of Antiochus Epiphanes, his kingdom crumbled from within and many of his soldiers were slaughtered.

11:27 *The two kings will both plan to do evil. They will sit at the same table and tell lies. But they will not succeed, because the end must wait until the appointed time.*

These battles resulted in both parties gathering "at the same table," apparently a negotiation table, around which treaties were made and sure to be broken. Since both parties operated in the same ruthless and deceptive manner—the uncle being a treacherous conniver from the start and his nephew no longer willing to play the naive fool—neither one was able to gain clear advantage over the other.[37]

The angel that related all of these things to Daniel inserted a reminder of God's sovereignty over all matters so that Daniel would not forget in the midst of such suspenseful discourse that humanity's conniving and warring are relevant only in humanity's own eyes. Nothing in the world, regardless of how momentous it may seem, can or will ever come to pass until its "appointed time," which is solely determined by Almighty God and is not in the least influenced by the words, thoughts, intentions, or actions of mankind.

11:28 *The northern king will return to his country with a lot of wealth. He will be determined to fight against the holy promise. He will take action and return to his own country.*

The prophecies revealed by the angel up until this point, while dramatic and intriguing, seem to be merely background for the events that will follow. In a sense, the foundation was being laid for Daniel to understand the persecution of his people that would result from these events.

Antiochus IV returned to his own land with many riches but not as the triumphant victor he had anticipated. As a result, Antiochus Epiphanes took his fury out on Israel, perpetrating unspeakable atrocities "against the holy promise." Only after he had killed 80,000 Jews and had taken another 40,000 captive did he finally return to his northern homeland.[38]

11:29 *"At the appointed time he will again invade the south, but this time will be different from the first.*

When the time was right according to the Lord's providence, Antiochus IV again sought to march toward Egypt in battle. This campaign, however, differed from his others. This time, Antiochus advanced his armies toward the southern territories, but it would ultimately result in his doom.

11:30 *Ships will come from the west to attack him, and he will be discouraged and turn back. Angry at the holy promise, he will return, take action, and favor those who abandon the holy promise.*

Upon learning of Antiochus' plans to attack again, Ptolemy VII (Philometer) requested the assistance of Rome, who sent ambassadors such as Gaius Popilius Laenas in ships from Cyrus. These ambassadors met with Antiochus Epiphanes to threaten that he immediately retreat from Egypt or suffer the consequences.[39] Antiochus realized he had no realistic alternative, so he withdrew. With his pride crushed but his armies still intact, he once again decided to vent his frustration and rage by lashing out against Israel. He sent orders through one of his commanders, Apollonius, to randomly slay the Jews and to carry out the atrocities described in the verses that follow.

As indicated in the last part of this verse, the Jews who had renounced their Jewish heritage and readily complied with all that Antiochus demanded were likely the ones that enabled the king's successful execution of his campaigns against Israel. Therefore, their betrayal assisted Antiochus in his repeated attacks against Israel. These traitorous Jews, if not openly rewarded for such, at the very least escaped the slaughter and turmoil to which the faithful Jews were subjected.[40]

11:31 *His forces will dishonor the holy place (the fortress), take away the daily burnt offering, and set up the disgusting thing that causes destruction.*

We begin to see some of the horrible desecration for which Antiochus was responsible. According to the Law of Moses, the only people allowed in the temple were the priests of the tribe of Levi and the different families within that tribe that had been appointed to areas of service. More importantly, only the high priest was allowed to enter the Holy of Holies and only once a year. By order of Antiochus

Epiphanes, however, non-Jews entered the temple, even into the Holy of Holies, polluting it with their mere presence. Moreover, they disallowed proper ceremonial sacrifices to take place and made sacrilegious offerings that utterly desecrated the temple.[41]

Once again, God only allowed this defilement to take place for its appointed time and to fulfill His purposes. The enemies of God will always hate God and His people. However, this hatred is useless and cannot be acted out against the children of God unless God has preordained it.

Notes/Applications

Some people speak colorful lies and identify themselves as individuals of good, moral fiber when their hearts actually stir with mischievous intent. Although it is easy to be fooled by colorful rhetoric, we must cling to what is true. A change of heart always initiates a change of action. Therefore, time will ultimately reveal if a person's life points to the throne of God or to the throne of self.

Take a moment and remember what life was like before salvation. Each of us wandered hopelessly, bumping into worldly trend after worldly trend. In our quest for truth, we blindly and readily settled for worldly doctrines that pronounced our inherent goodness. Our total existence revolved around serving our selfish motives. Gripped by guilt and failure, we were physically alive but spiritually dead in our sins.

Our new life greatly contrasts that old life. We now confess our inability to obtain salvation apart from God's grace. Everything from our lifestyle to our temperament focuses on glorifying Christ, the abundant Life-giver. We now build our lives upon His solid-as-a-rock, eternal truth, and we live to love and serve the one who loved and served us even in His very death on the cross. The change that took place at our spiritual birth was more than a "changing of the guards" or "putting on a new face." It transformed us from within. God literally recreated us from a sinner to a saint. *"⁸Also get rid of your anger, hot tempers, hatred, cursing, obscene language, and all similar* sins. *⁹Don't lie to each other. You've gotten rid of the person you used to be and the life you used to live, ¹⁰and you've become a new person. This new person is continually renewed in knowledge to be like its Creator"* (Colossians 3:8–10).

As new creatures in Christ, no difference should exist between what we say and how we act. If there is not an obvious distinction between who we once were and who we now are, we need to examine ourselves to confirm whether or not we have truly died to the old self and live as a new creation in Christ. *"²²You were taught to change the way you were living. The person you used to be will ruin you through desires that deceive you. ²³However, you were taught to have a new attitude. ²⁴You were also taught to become a new person created to be like God, truly righteous and holy"* (Ephesians 4:22–24). What evidence in our lives shows that we are new creatures in Christ?

Daniel 11:32–38

11:32 *With flattery he will corrupt those who abandon the promise. But the people who know their God will be strong and take action.*

The Israelites who did not stand firmly upon God's truth were manipulated by the king's flatteries. Because of this, they allied themselves with the king in breaking the promise and in tyranny against their Jewish brethren. However, the Israelites who possessed a personal relationship with God were able to withstand the deceptions of the king. They remained faithful to the Lord despite their circumstances and would, therefore, accomplish great things in God's eyes.

11:33 *"People who are wise will help many to understand. But for some time they will be defeated by swords and flames. They will be captured and looted.*

Those Jews who recognized the spiritual trials that besieged them tried to encourage others to uphold their faith in God and not to be lured by the enemy's empty promises. They remained firm and strong, and they persuaded many others to remain likewise. As a result, many of these faithful ones suffered extreme persecution for their faith. They were subjected to the pillage of others, taken from their homes and families against their will, and in many cases, killed by sword and by fire.

> [36]*Some were made fun of and whipped, and some were chained and put in prison.* [37]*Some were stoned to death, sawed in half, and killed with swords. Some wore the skins of sheep and goats. Some were poor, abused, and mistreated.* [38]*The world didn't deserve these good people. Some wandered around in deserts and mountains and lived in caves and holes in the ground.* (Hebrews 11:36–38)

11:34 *As they are being defeated, they will get a little help, but many who are not sincere will join them.*

The faithful Jews received some degree of help in both their physical and spiritual battles against Antiochus IV. This is likely a reference to the early assistance the Jews received from Mattathias and his comparatively small number of Maccabean troops.[42] Despite this assistance, many additional Jews eventually abandoned the faith of their fathers when the struggle became too great. They joined forces with Antiochus' armies.

11:35 *Some of the wise people will be defeated in order to refine, purify, and make them white until the end times. But the appointed time is still to come.*

During this time of great suffering, some of those who were not deceived, "the wise people," also fell. However, this "falling" was not in the same sense as the apostate Jews who abandoned their faith and heritage. This use of "fall" is of a physical sense, indicating the suffering and persecution that befell these faithful Jews. Some of them were subjected to the full impact of Antiochus' schemes and were martyrs for their faith. Even so, this suffering occurred to glorify God and to "make them white," indicating the righteousness and holiness that they would gain by their deaths. Everyone who wins the victory this way will wear white clothes (*Revelation 3:5*).

Once again, the angel assured Daniel that all this persecution that would befall his people was appointed by the Lord within His sovereign plan and would only last for as long as God ordained it.

11:36 *"The king will do as he pleases. He will highly honor himself above every god. He will say amazing things against the God of gods. He will succeed until God's anger is over, because what has been decided must be done.*

A mask of ambiguity clouds the intention of the remaining verses of this chapter. As a result, this text has been the object of greatly varied interpretations throughout the ages. One thing is agreed upon almost unanimously: the remainder of this vision no longer refers to

Antiochus Epiphanes since he did not "succeed until God's anger is over," and the events mentioned hereafter do not consistently conform to historical events of his time. Since some, but not all, of the following descriptions can be fully reconciled in the person of Antiochus Epiphanes, other conclusions must be drawn. Some early commentators, such as Gill and Calvin, pose convincing arguments that the remaining verses do not depict a specific king so much as an entire kingdom prototype, namely the Roman Empire that would follow the fall of the Greco-Macedonian Empire.[43] Though such an argument serves as a definite possibility, the lack of precise matches between the textual prophecies and historical evidence leaves room for doubt and, consequently, room for speculation.[44] Most traditional interpretations contend the verses beginning here and concluding near the end of chapter twelve point not at any specific historical king but to the end-times global leader known as the antichrist.[45] Whether or not a particular historical figure is intended, the text describes characteristics and selfish actions that surely parallel with the ultimate embodiment of this antichrist figure. The commentary that follows, therefore, will approach these verses from this interpretation, although not with any intention of dismissing the validity of other reasonable interpretations.

Certainly, the character spoken of in this verse alludes to antichrist, also described as the "beast," which, as explained in the book of Revelation, will exalt himself above every god. *"³Don't let anyone deceive you about this in any way. That day cannot come unless a revolt takes place first, and the man of sin, the man of destruction, is revealed. ⁴He opposes every so-called god or anything that is worshiped and places himself above them, sitting in God's temple and claiming to be God"* (2 Thessalonians 2:3–4). He will speak horrible blasphemy against God, yet he will prosper only until God's appointed time for him is accomplished.

11:37 *He will have no interest in the gods of his ancestors or desire for women. He will have no interest in any god, because he will make himself greater than anyone else.*

More details of the true character of this figure are disclosed. He will not regard Almighty God as the Creator, Maker, or Sustainer of life. Because of the phrasing "gods of his ancestors" used in this verse, some commentators believe that the end-times antichrist will emerge from the Jewish race.[46] In a sense, this seems plausible since a false messiah of the Jews certainly could not be expected to arise from among Gentiles.

As with much of the remaining text, the phrase "desire for women" has been broadly interpreted. Possibly, it simply denotes this "king's" reluctance to share his glory, position, or power with anyone; perhaps he will not allow himself or his decisions to be influenced by anyone or anything else.

In addition, he will totally reject all other gods by ultimately forbidding the worship of anyone or anything other than himself; therefore, he will magnify himself above all men and all gods. *"Everyone living on earth will worship it, everyone whose name is not written in the Book of Life. That book belongs to the lamb who was slaughtered before the creation of the world"* (Revelation 13:8).

11:38 *Instead, he will honor the god of fortresses. With gold, silver, precious stones, and other expensive things he will honor a god his ancestors never heard of.*

The antichrist will believe himself to be a god more powerful than any other god. He will deceive many by his propaganda and, when necessary, by force. He will see himself and his influence as an impenetrable fortress. Once he is established in a position of global influence, he will demand mankind to worship him alone. His forefathers, meaning all those who will have existed before his emergence to power, will not recognize him as a god because they will have known nothing of his existence as such until his deity is self-proclaimed. As the ultimate act of self-glorification and blasphemy, he will worship and adorn himself with every symbol of wealth this world has to offer.

Notes/Applications

Verse thirty-five of this section states that God's people endured persecution for their faith "to refine, purify and make them white." Our finite minds can never fully comprehend all aspects of God's preordained plan for His creation, so we may struggle with understanding the purpose of persecution in our lives. Simply stated, God's purging prepares us for ministry by shifting our focus away from earthly preoccupations and onto the heavenly Father, so the purification of our faith equips us to accomplish all that God calls us to do.

No one enjoys the purification process. It is painfully costly because it usually requires that we lose something dear to us: our way, our dreams, or our loved ones. However, in losing, we gain. The waters of persecution erode our pride and remind us of God's wonderful, sustaining power to carry us through anything. Also, our obedience and faithfulness during a crisis will point others to Christ, so our trials will help us to better understand another's pain and to relate to him in his time of need. In His time, God will replenish what the waters of persecution sweep away from us. *"After Job prayed for his friends, the Lord restored Job's prosperity and gave him twice as much as he had before"* (Job 42:10). Despite the rising tides, He will preserve our souls and restore our joy.

God has not left us shipwrecked. As promised in His Word, the purification process is a part of His plan for us, and it only lasts "for the appointed time." Almighty God directs the flow of the purification waters, and He will not allow us to drown in them.

Daniel 11:39–45

11:39 *With the help of a foreign god, he will deal with strong fortresses. He will give high honors to those who acknowledge him, make them rulers over many people, and distribute land for a price.*

The antichrist will overcome the strongest governments of the world. This "foreign god" refers to his self-exalted status as god *(verse thirty-six)*; he is not foreign to himself, obviously, but to those who have never regarded him as a god.[47] The rulers that bow to him will be given some measure of authority and a portion of land to govern on the antichrist's behalf. These are likely the ten leaders depicted as the ten toes of the clay-and-iron image in Nebuchadnezzar's dream, and they serve as the antichrist's confederacy. Even though the antichrist will place himself in the temple as a god, he will never be God nor be omnipresent as only God is. Therefore, the antichrist will need these ten rulers to control their respective regions of the world for him so that he can ultimately obtain absolute control over the world's most powerful nations.

11:40 *"In the end times the southern king will attack him. The northern king will rush at him like a storm with chariots, horses, and many ships. He will invade countries, overwhelm them, and pass through their land.*

This verse further supports interpretations which conclude that this figure is not Antiochus but is the ultimate prophetic fulfillment of the antichrist in the last days, for once Antiochus retreated from Egypt after meeting with the ships from Cyprus, history reveals that he never again mounted a campaign against Egypt or any of its territories.[48]

In this verse, it is uncertain whether the king of the South will come against the king of the North in an attempt to overthrow him or if he will come against the "king" mentioned in verses thirty-six

through thirty-nine with the assistance of the king of the North. The
latter depiction seems more suitable in this context. The geographic
location of these kings and their kingdoms are likely given in relation
to their position to the antichrist, who at this point will be ruling
from his headquarters, which from all biblical indications will be in
Jerusalem, *"and they will trample the holy city for 42 months" (Revelation
11:2).* Though these kings come at him like a great wind with all
their available forces, they will be overthrown.

11:41 *He will invade the beautiful land, and tens of thousands will be defeated. But Edom, Moab, and the leaders of the
Ammonites will escape from his power.*

When the antichrist enters into Israel, there will be much worldwide
destruction. Many countries will be toppled in the process. A few,
however, will escape his hand. These countries are Edom, Moab,
and Ammon, which are all located in the area that is now known
as Jordan. The reason this territory escapes destruction is uncertain.
Perhaps, it will remain neutral in the conflict or will ally itself with
the antichrist, thereby avoiding the consequences of his wrath.[49]

11:42 *He will use his power against many countries. Even
Egypt will not escape.*

We are told that Egypt is one of the lands that will be overthrown.
The ruling hand of the antichrist will stretch around the world. His
influence and power will have a global impact.

11:43 *He will control gold and silver treasures and all Egypt's
treasuries. Libya and Sudan will surrender to him.*

This future "king" will ultimately control the economies of the
world, specifically the fiscal structures of Egypt, Libya, and Sudan.
These countries "will surrender" and be fully under his authority,
though it is uncertain whether this submission will be offered willingly or by coercion.

11:44 *But news from the east and the north will frighten him. He will leave very angry to destroy and exterminate many.*

Dissension will arise from the east and from the north. Therefore, the antichrist will go forth in a rage with great strength to destroy them. These kings will want to overthrow the antichrist because of his widespread oppression. These two leaders along with the leader from the South mentioned in verse forty possibly comprise the three leaders that will be subdued or overthrown by the antichrist, as previously described by Daniel. *"While I was thinking about the horns, another horn, a little horn, came up among them. It uprooted three of the other horns. This horn had eyes like human eyes and a mouth that spoke impressive things"* (Daniel 7:8).

11:45 *He will pitch his royal tents between the seas at a beautiful holy mountain. When he comes to his end, there will be no one to help him."*

We are told that the antichrist will build the tabernacles of his palace between "the seas," which most likely refers to the Mediterranean Sea and the Dead Sea, and the "beautiful holy mountain," which is Jerusalem.[50] This will function as his temporary royal quarters. The antichrist will place himself in the center of the world to rule over it all.

Notes/Applications

What a blessing it is that we are foretold how the end of the world will occur and what the result will be! Many terrible things will befall the earth during the last days. Therefore, regardless of the doctrinal view concerning Christ's Second Coming that one embraces, each of us must be prepared. *"Therefore, you, too, must be ready because the Son of Man will return when you least expect him"* (Matthew 24:44).

Part of being prepared includes understanding what the Word of God has to say about the end times. Scripture admonishes us to study and know the truth lest we be deceived or confused by any perversion of truth. *"False messiahs and false prophets will appear. They will work spectacular, miraculous signs and do wonderful things to deceive, if possible, even those whom God has chosen"* (Matthew 24:24). *"Beware of false prophets. They come to you disguised as sheep, but in their hearts they are vicious wolves"* (Matthew 7:15).

This will be a difficult time for all of creation, but praise the Lord for the assurance that He has already won the victory! *"⁷The mystery of this sin is already at work. But it cannot work effectively until the person now holding it back gets out of the way. ⁸Then the man of sin will be revealed and the Lord Jesus will destroy him by what he says. When the Lord Jesus comes, his appearance will put an end to this man"* (2 Thessalonians 2:7–8).

DANIEL 12

Daniel 12:1–7

12:1 *The person who looked like a human continued, "At that time Michael, the great commander, will stand up on behalf of the descendants of your people. It will be a time of trouble unlike any that has existed from the time there have been nations until that time. But at that time your people, everyone written in the book, will be rescued.*

This chapter continues the previous chapter's prophecy of the end times, wherein the angel had been explaining to Daniel the fate of his people, the Israelites. During the last days, the archangel Michael, protector of God's people, will stand guard over them especially during this time of tribulation worse than any nation has ever known.[1] *"There will be a lot of misery at that time, a kind of misery that has not happened from the beginning of the world until now and will certainly never happen again"* (Matthew 24:21).

Whereas the angel related the fate of the Jewish people in end times, he also conveyed the message of hope that exists for all mankind, both Jew and Gentile. Whether or not Daniel realized this unique intricacy is unclear. The angel appeared to refer to the "book," the collective, eternal record, called the Book of Life, in which the names of all people determined to be reconciled to God were revealed. The apostle John later recorded his vision:

> [10]He carried me by his power away to a large, high mountain. He showed me the holy city, Jerusalem, coming down from God out of heaven. [11]It had the glory of God. Its light was like a valuable gem, like gray quartz, as clear as crystal. . . .
>
> [27]Nothing unclean, no one who does anything detestable, and no liars will ever enter it. Only those whose names are written in the lamb's Book of Life will enter it. (Revelation 21:10–11, 27)

In describing the atrocious end-times affliction that will befall Daniel's people, and ultimately all who have their eternal inheritance guaranteed in heaven, the angel also delivered a message of hope: many, specifically those whose names are found "written in the book," will be "rescued." Details of this delivery, however, are unclear—whether by rapture, or by perseverance amidst turmoil or by ultimate delivery of physical death unto eternal life. However, to understand the reason for such ambiguity, one must remember to whom this message was originally intended—Daniel. The angel assured Daniel that, though his people would experience intense hardships in both the near and distant future, God would never abandon His faithful followers. We, as believers with the benefit of New Testament revelation, understand that this prophecy has far-reaching significance not limited to only Jewish believers.

12:2 *Many sleeping in the ground will wake up. Some will wake up to live forever, but others will wake up to be ashamed and disgraced forever.*

Daniel was not told that all of his people would inherit the kingdom of heaven, though he was assured that indeed many would. Rather, the angel then spoke about a resurrection whereby the dust of the ground would give up the dead, and all of Daniel's people would be judged either unto eternal life in heaven or unto eternal condemnation. Through the use of other scripture, Christians understand this judgment to be true for all mankind. Those who have died knowing Christ as their personal Lord and Redeemer, will finally meet Him face-to-face in all of His glory and will be united with Him for eternity.

> [13]Brothers and sisters, we don't want you to be ignorant about those who have died. We don't want you to grieve like other people who have no hope. [14]We believe that Jesus died and came back to life. We also believe that, through Jesus, God will bring back those who have died. They will come back with Jesus. [15]We are telling you what the Lord taught. We who are still alive when the Lord comes will not go into his kingdom ahead of those who have already died. [16]The Lord will come from heaven with a command, with the voice of the archangel, and with the trumpet call of God. First, the dead who believed in Christ will come back to life. (1 Thessalonians 4:13–16)

Those who did not receive Christ's gift of salvation—in other words, those whose names are not found written in the Book of Life—will be raised to "be ashamed and disgraced forever," and will be sentenced to the lake of fire, which is the second death spoken of in Revelation:

> [12]I saw the dead, both important and unimportant people, standing in front of the throne. Books were opened, including the Book of Life. The dead were judged on the basis of what they had done, as recorded in the books. [13]The sea gave up its dead. Death and hell gave up their dead. People were judged based on what they had done. [14]Death and hell were thrown into the fiery lake. (The fiery lake is the second death.) [15]Those whose names were not found in the Book of Life were thrown into the fiery lake. (Revelation 20:12–15)

Though this resurrection does not pertain exclusively to Jews, Daniel's people are surely included within it. Although the angel offered Daniel no further clarification regarding the ultimate fulfillment of this plan, the angel did explain that not all Jews would inherit righteousness simply because they were Jews but only those, as described in verse one, whose names are "written in the book."[2] There will be a distinct separation made at the time of the resurrection—some to everlasting life, the rest to everlasting contempt.

12:3 *Those who are wise will shine like the brightness on the horizon. Those who lead many people to righteousness will shine like the stars forever and ever.*

The wise, those who possess the truth of Christ Jesus, will shine forever in God's heaven "like the brightness on the horizon." God created the heavens, called the firmament, to embody light for the world. *"God put them in the sky to give light to the earth"* (Genesis 1:17). Therefore, these individuals who by their witness turn other men's hearts toward God will be a light to a lost world. They will be rewarded, and the legacy of their testimony will eternally glorify God. *"¹⁹My brothers and sisters, if one of you wanders from the truth, someone can bring that person back. ²⁰Realize that whoever brings a sinner back from the error of his ways will save him from death, and many sins will be forgiven"* (James 5:19–20).

12:4 *"But you, Daniel, keep these words secret, and seal the book until the end times. Many will travel everywhere, and knowledge will grow."*

God told Daniel to record all these things but, thereafter, to shut the words and seal them "until the end times," which refers to a period long after Daniel's lifetime: I have come to explain to you what will happen to your people in the last days, because the vision is about times still to come *(Daniel 10:14).*

Based upon this verse, many theologians contend that knowledge and world travel will increase during the end times.[3] However, that interpretation seems inept within this context and does not appear to be the true intention of the phrase "travel everywhere." Rather, the expression likely suggests the lengths that people will go in the end times to search for knowledge and understanding of the mayhem and turmoil occurring to them and around them.[4]

12:5 *When I, Daniel, looked up, I saw two men standing there. One man stood on one side of the river, and the other one stood on the other side.*

The two figures described in this verse appear to be angels. Daniel observed one of these angels standing on each side of the river, apparently the Tigris River, the same river Daniel was standing beside at the onset of the vision. *"On the twenty-fourth day of the first month, I was by the great Tigris River"* (Daniel 10:4). The appearance of these beings seems to launch us into the conclusion of this vision.[5]

12:6 *One of them asked the man dressed in linen clothes who was above the river, "How long will it be until these miracles are over?"*

One of these angels spoke to a person who stood upon the waters of the river between the two angels. Some interpreters are vague as to the identity of this "man dressed in linen clothes," leaving it open to speculation that this being was Gabriel, the angel that translated the prophecy to Daniel.[6] It seems more plausible to identify this person as the same preincarnate Christ Who appeared to Daniel before the beginning of this vision.[7] *"⁵When I looked up, I saw a man dressed in linen, and he had a belt made of gold from Uphaz around his waist. ⁶His body was like beryl. His face looked like lightning. His eyes were like flaming torches. His arms and legs looked like polished bronze. When he spoke, his voice sounded like the roar of a crowd"* (Daniel 10:5–6). An angel asked the one clothed in linen how long it would be until these prophecies were fulfilled.

12:7 *I heard the man dressed in linen clothes who was above the river. He raised his right hand and left hand to heaven and swore an oath by the one who lives forever. He said, "It will be for a time, times, and half of a time. When the power of the holy people has been completely shattered, then all these things will be finished."*

In the vision, the Lord stood upon the waters and lifted both of His hands to heaven, giving glory to God the Father by which there is no higher authority to swear the truth. *"⁵The angel whom I saw standing on the sea and on the land raised his right hand to heaven. ⁶He swore an oath by the one who lives forever and ever, who created heaven and everything in it, the earth and everything in it, and the sea and everything in it. He said, 'There will be no more delay'"* (Revelation 10:5–6). Christ then answered the angel for the purpose of ensuring Daniel's understanding of the vision, and He proclaimed that the period of tribulation would be "for a time, times, and half of a time." Many biblical scholars contend, based upon a common interpretation, that each appearance of the word *time* in this context signifies one year, and this interpretation corroborates all other scriptural accounts that the period of great tribulation will be three and a half years.[8] *"They will trample the holy city for 42 months"* (Revelation 11:2). *"Then the woman fled into the wilderness where God had prepared a place for her so that she might be taken care of for 1,260 days"* (Revelation 12:6). *"The beast was allowed to speak arrogant and insulting things. It was given authority to act for 42 months"* (Revelation 13:5).

When the "shattering" (destruction) of the "power" (unity) of the "holy people" (the Israelites) is completed, and they are finally forced to reconsider their rejection of the redemptive message of the Lord Jesus Christ, then the end will come.

Notes/Applications
Studying these Scriptures is like looking in a mirror and seeing reflections of our fast-paced world. As the Holy Spirit reveals the

meaning of these passages to us, we realize that we are living in the last days to which these verses refer, and we, therefore, desperately need to evaluate our spiritual condition.

By virtue of great technological achievements, we quickly approach an age where hearts are hardened against God's message. Mankind worships itself and believes that salvation lies in human accomplishment. Seemingly, the extent of what we can achieve is only limited by our imaginations. We have traveled to the moon and explored distant planets. Advances in medicine help us to live longer, healthier lives. Computers effortlessly spout reams of data, and intercontinental communication is instantaneous. However, with all of man's modern inventions, not one of them has been able to soothe a wounded heart. Not one has been able to prevent death altogether, and not one can deliver us from the inevitable judgment that awaits each of us at the end of time. *"People die once, and after that they are judged"* (Hebrews 9:27).

All of man's technological advances may enable him to attain virtually any level of temporary comfort at the touch of a button, but no amount of human knowledge will ever surpass that of the all-knowing Creator. No technological alternative will ever secure an eternal life in the presence of God. Nothing can ever secure an eternal hope except a vibrant relationship with a loving, personal, faithful Savior and Redeemer. *"Do not boast or let arrogance come out of your mouth because the Lord is a God of knowledge, and he weighs our actions"* (1 Samuel 2:3). *"Jesus answered him, 'I am the way, the truth, and the life. No one goes to the Father except through me'"* (John 14:6).

Daniel 12:8–13

12:8 *I heard him, but I did not understand. So I asked him, "Sir, how will these things end?"*

Daniel admitted that he did not understand the meaning of the things he had heard, so he addressed the Lord directly and asked for further explanation.

12:9 *He replied, "Go, Daniel. These words are to be kept secret and sealed until the end times.*

This prophecy conveyed events that would occur long after Daniel's lifetime. The meaning of the prophecy would become more apparent as its time of fulfillment drew near. Its relevance would become more evident for those to whom it would pertain. Until then, its meaning would be somewhat mysterious and vague, and therefore, Daniel was to go on his way and not to concern himself with the meaning of the vision.[9]

12:10 *Many will be purified, made white, and refined. But wicked people will do wicked things, and none of them will understand. Only wise people will understand.*

A warning is given in this verse that somewhat resembles the one given to the apostle John at the conclusion of the Revelation. *"Let those who don't have God's approval go without it, and let filthy people continue to be filthy. Let those who have God's approval continue to have it, and let holy people continue to be holy"* (Revelation 22:11). In both instances, "wicked people," the unrighteous condemned to separation from God, will not behave differently than what is generally expected of them—to "do wicked things."[10]

On the other hand, the numerous hardships of the last days will result in the purification of true believers. The more that something such as gold is purified, the more refined its strength and quality become. Those individuals who feign the role of a Christian will be purged out from true believers, and these true believers will mature spiritually as their faith is deepened through their suffering.

They will understand that the purpose of their suffering is ultimately for the glorification of God, whereas the wicked or unjust will have no biblical foundation to recognize these events as sovereign acts of Almighty God.

It would seem unwise to suggest that God will pour out increased discernment in the last days regarding the Word of God. Knowledge is not hidden within the Scriptures in the form of encrypted codes that only an enlightened few are able to decipher. One needs only to note the many varied interpretations that have been derived from this book because of such "decoding" as proof that confusion and doubt were not what God had intended. *"Scripture says, "I will destroy the wisdom of the wise. I will reject the intelligence of intelligent people""* (1 Corinthians 1:19).

In light of this, it seems most sensible to express simplicity in the interpretation of this passage. The wicked will continue as they always have—finding perplexity and ignorance in the Word of God and proclaiming lies and blasphemies against the things of God. But the "wise people," those whose faith is founded in the true God of Creation, will recognize the events that take place around them for what they truly are according to their understanding of God's Holy Word.

12:11 *From the time the daily burnt offering is taken away and the disgusting thing that causes destruction is set up, there will be 1,290 days.*

Though there are many theories regarding the content of these final three verses, clear explanation of their interpretations cannot be offered without employing a considerable measure of speculation. The first topic that is subject to debatable interpretation is the 1290 days mentioned in this verse. Of course, an explanation for this number of days is dependent upon the definition of the parameters that are given: "from the time that the daily burnt offering is taken away, and the disgusting thing that causes destruction is set up."

The traditional interpretation of this verse is that these days correlate with the end-times period of the great tribulation, which has already been determined to be three and a half years according to thirty-day months or 1260 days *(verse seven)*. The number we are given in this verse, though, consists of an additional thirty days that cannot be completely reconciled. Some expositors suggest that the three-and-a-half-year period given in other biblical references is a generalization and that the number given in this verse is the actual, specific number of days that the tribulation will entail.[11] However, this is contradicted by what we read in other Scripture verses. *"²But do not measure the temple courtyard. Leave that out, because it is given to the nations, and they will trample the holy city for 42 months. ³I will allow my two witnesses who wear sackcloth to speak what God has revealed. They will speak for 1,260 days" (Revelation 11:2–3)*. Others explain the extra thirty days as the span of God's judgment that will follow the tribulation.[12] Though interesting, this is unsubstantiated speculation. Still, other scholars contend that the events mentioned in this verse refer to the first advent of the Messiah *(see commentary on Daniel 9:24–27)*.[13] Whereas this point is compellingly defended, the duration of 1290 days that follow the resurrection of Christ do not appear to be substantiated by any specific historical event that would appear to fulfill this prophecy, and therefore, this seems an unlikely solution to this issue.

The resolution of these 1290 days is an uncertainty. Perhaps, as we are told in the previous verse, we will one day understand the significance of the number as the time draws near for this prophecy to be fulfilled. Until then, Christians can at least be comforted in knowing that all things that happen, no matter how horrible they may seem, will only last for an exact duration that God has predetermined.

12:12 *Blessed are those who wait until they reach 1,335 days.*

Once again, we are given a number that is not definable by anything we are told elsewhere in Scripture. Once again, we are offered a collage of explanations and calculations by a variety of scholars who favor theories that best suit their own interpretations. Yet once again, we are confronted with an ambiguous puzzle that cannot be resolved except for what is reachable through mere guesswork. Some speculate that these additional seventy-five days that exceed or extend beyond the 1260 days of tribulation will be used to set up the millennial government or to celebrate the reunion of Christ with His saints.[14] In reality, only God truly knows the perfect plan and reasoning of His divine timeline, and to present any theory as fact would be to read more into the verse than what is disclosed.

What we can presume with reasonable certainty is that this verse specifically and exclusively addresses Christians, those who will suffer the persecution already mentioned but also those who, in some unspecified manner, will be "blessed" by the Lord God Almighty, presumably for their perseverance during these trials.

12:13 *But go on until the end. You will rest, and you will rise for your inheritance at the end of time."*

Daniel was again admonished to cast any anxieties about these prophecies from his mind and to return to his normal life. Daniel was about ninety years old by this time, and God likely granted him peace and rest in his remaining years of life without giving him any additional revelations, which would seemingly have been included with the other accounts in this book. However, it can also be surmised with reasonable confidence that the "rest" God bestowed upon Daniel also described the peaceful tranquility that Daniel would experience after his physical life had ended and would experience until the end of this world's days, not just his days. This faithful servant will then "rise for your inheritance" with the other saints of God who possess the righteousness of Christ. "*7I have fought the good*

*fight. I have completed the race. I have kept the faith. ⁸The prize that shows
I have God's approval is now waiting for me. The Lord, who is a fair judge,
will give me that prize on that day. He will give it not only to me but also to
everyone who is eagerly waiting for him to come again"* (2 Timothy 4:7–8).

Notes/Applications

Over the course of his lifetime, Daniel observed the perils of his
people under the wiles of Babylonian captivity, and Daniel himself
endured severe discrimination for his Jewish ethnicity and for his
unwavering belief in the supremacy of Almighty God.

The Lord revealed to this faithful servant the progression of
the world's final days leading to the magnification of Jesus Christ as
King of kings and Lord of lords. However, these last days would be
overshadowed by peril unlike any the world had or has ever experienced. Daniel, no doubt, shuddered as he pondered the reality of
continued persecution of his people, but God's messenger assured
him that there would be an appointed end to these sufferings. Some
would be delivered from this time, some delivered out of it, and some
delivered through it, but ultimately, all whose names are written in
the Book of Life would receive their deliverance through the gift of
eternal life.

As we scan Christian history, our attention is captured by several
occurrences in which God's people have been miraculously delivered
from dire circumstances. However, countless believers have not been
delivered from similar circumstances and have died for their faith.
Why is there so much variation in the outcome? Does God favor
some over others? The only distinction between believers is God's
sovereignty. The Lord's purpose for some and plan for others varies
in course but not in result, which is the magnification of God. All
Christians are called to be martyrs, to die to self and ultimately to the
world and its system, yet the experiences of this call are as diverse as
the sands that line the seas.

A martyr is someone "who chooses to suffer death rather than
denounce religious principles." Although further definitions of this

term reduce its meaning to "one who endures great suffering," its purest definition couples the initial meaning of "being a witness" with "great sacrifice."[15] Contrary to rampant easy-believism philosophies that pervade much of modern Christian teaching, true Christianity demands martyrdom. We must die to our natural, selfish desires on a daily basis, never willing to renounce our faith in the Lord Jesus Christ our Savior even if at the cost of our own lives.

> [24]*Those who want to save their lives will lose them. But those who lose their lives for me will save them.* [25]*What good does it do for people to win the whole world but lose their lives by destroying them?* [26]*If people are ashamed of me and what I say, the Son of Man will be ashamed of those people when he comes in the glory that he shares with the Father and the holy angels* (Luke 9:24–26).

> *Those who love their lives will destroy them, and those who hate their lives in this world will guard them for everlasting life.* (John 12:25)

Daniel's faith was preserved and deepened through his sufferings as a servant of Almighty God. God charges us, as His saints, with the same challenge that He laid before this Old Testament saint, who was willing to die to self and to man and who by his unwavering commitment ultimately proclaimed, "In God I trust." Are we prepared to encounter persecution for our faith in Christ? Are we willing to be martyrs for Truth? Do we count our sufferings as opportunities to glorify God?

> [3]*Praise the God and Father of our Lord Jesus Christ! God has given us a new birth because of his great mercy. We have been born into a new life that has a confidence which is alive because Jesus Christ has come back to life.* [4]*We have been born into a new life which has an inheritance that can't be destroyed or corrupted and can't fade away. That inheritance is kept in heaven for you,* [5]*since you are guarded by God's power through faith for a salvation that is ready to be revealed at the end of time.*

⁶*You are extremely happy about these things, even though you have to suffer different kinds of trouble for a little while now.* ⁷*The purpose of these troubles is to test your faith as fire tests how genuine gold is. Your faith is more precious than gold, and by passing the test, it gives praise, glory, and honor to God. This will happen when Jesus Christ appears again.*

⁸*Although you have never seen Christ, you love him. You don't see him now, but you believe in him. You are extremely happy with joy and praise that can hardly be expressed in words* ⁹*as you obtain the salvation that is the goal of your faith.* (1 Peter 1:3–9)

TEXT NOTES

INTRODUCTION

1. *The New Encyclopaedia Britannica,* 15th ed., s.v. "Babylonia."

2. *The Complete Works of Flavius Josephus,* trans. William Whiston (Grand Rapids: Kregel Publications, 1960), 225.

3. J.B. Jackson, *A Dictionary of Scripture Proper Names* (Neptune, NJ: Loizeaux Brothers, 1909), 25.

CHAPTER ONE

1. J.B. Jackson, *A Dictionary of Scripture Proper Names* (Neptune, NJ: Loizeaux Brothers, 1909), 50.

2. Charles F. Pfeiffer and Everett F. Harrison, *The Wycliffe Bible Commentary* (Chicago: Moody Press, 1962), 773.

3. Jackson, *Proper Names,* 25, 38, 66, 13, 55.

4. Jackson, *Proper Names,* 16, 83, 65, 1.

5. James Strong, *Strong's Exhaustive Concordance of the Bible* (Iowa Falls: World Bible Publishers, 1986), 336.

CHAPTER TWO

1. Strong, *Exhaustive Concordance,* 866, 112

2. J.B. Jackson, *A Dictionary of Scripture Proper Names* (Neptune, NJ: Loizeaux Brothers, 1909), 10.

3. Alan Redpath, *Victorious Christian Living: Studies in the Book of Joshua* (Grand Rapids: Fleming H. Revel Co., 1993)

4. *American Heritage Dictionary,* 3rd ed., s.v. "knowledge" and "wisdom."

5. *American Heritage Dictionary,* 3rd ed., s.v. "specific gravity."

6. *VanNostrand's Scientific Encyclopedia,* ed. Douglas M. Considine (New York: VanNostrand Reinhold, 1989), 2653–2656, 1352, 2586, 764, 1599, 648.

7. Robert Jamieson, Andrew R. Fausset, and David Brown, *New Commentary on the Whole Bible: Old Testament Volume,* ed. J.D. Douglas (Wheaton, IL: Tyndale House Publishers, 1990), 1171.

8. Strong, *Exhaustive Concordance,* 919.

9. Charles F. Pfeiffer and Everett F. Harrison, *The Wycliffe Bible Commentary* (Chicago: Moody Press, 1962), 780.

10. John Gill, *Exposition of the Old and New Testaments,* vol. 6 (1810; reprint, Paris, AR: The Baptist Standard Bearer, 1989), 284.

CHAPTER THREE

1. John Gill, *Exposition of the Old and New Testaments,* vol. 6 (1810; reprint, Paris, AR: The Baptist Standard Bearer, 1989), 288.

2. J.D. Douglas, ed., *New Bible Dictionary,* 2nd ed. (Wheaton, IL: Tyndale House Publishers, 1962), 1075.

3. *New Geneva Study Bible,* ed. R.C. Sproul (Nashville: Thomas Nelson Publishers, 1995), 1335.

4. Gill, *Exposition of the Old and New Testaments,* 288.

5. Robert Jamieson, Andrew R. Fausset, and David Brown, *New Commentary on the Whole Bible: Old Testament Volume*, ed. J.D. Douglas (Wheaton, IL: Tyndale House Publishers, 1990), 1172.

6. James Strong, *Strong's Exhaustive Concordance of the Bible* (Iowa Falls: World Bible Publishers, 1986), 1101.

7. *New Geneva Study Bible*, 1335.

8. J. Vernon McGee, *Thru the Bible*, vol. 3 (Nashville: Thomas Nelson Publishers, 1982), 545.

9. Jamieson, Fausset and Brown, *New Commentary on the Whole Bible*, 1173.

10. Gill, *Exposition of the Old and New Testaments*, 291.

11. Strong, *Exhaustive Concordance*, 1095.

CHAPTER FOUR

1. John Calvin, "Commentaries on the Book of the Prophet Daniel," vol. 1, in vol. 12 of *Calvin's Commentaries*, trans. Thomas Myers (1843; reprint, Grand Rapids: Baker Books, 1999), 245.

2. Calvin, "Commentaries on the Book of the Prophet Daniel," vol. 1, *Calvin's Commentaries*, vol. 12, 244.

3. John Gill, *Exposition of the Old and New Testaments*, vol. 6 (1810; reprint, Paris, AR: The Baptist Standard Bearer, 1989), 297.

4. James Strong, *Strong's Exhaustive Concordance of the Bible* (Iowa Falls: World Bible Publishers, 1986), 1431.

5. Strong, *Exhaustive Concordance*, 1490, 656.

6. Matthew Henry, *Matthew Henry's Commentary on the Whole Bible* (Hendrickson Publishers, 1991), 1439.

7. J. Vernon McGee, *Thru the Bible*, vol. 3 (Nashville: Thomas Nelson Publishers, 1982), 556.

CHAPTER FIVE

1. John Calvin, "Commentaries on the Book of the Prophet Daniel,"
    vol. 1, in vol. 12 of *Calvin's Commentaries,* trans. Thomas Myers
    (1843; reprint, Grand Rapids: Baker Books, 1999), 305–306.

2. Charles F. Pfeiffer and Everett F. Harrison, *The Wycliffe Bible Com-
    mentary* (Chicago: Moody Press, 1962), 785.

3. Pfeiffer and Harrison, *Wycliffe Bible Commentary,* 785.

4. *The Complete Works of Flavius Josephus,* trans. William Whiston
    (Grand Rapids: Kregel Publications, 1960), 225.

5. Robert Jamieson, Andrew R. Fausset, and David Brown, *New
    Commentary on the Whole Bible: Old Testament Volume,* ed. J.D.
    Douglas (Wheaton, IL: Tyndale House Publishers, 1990), 1178.

6. Jamieson, Fausset and Brown, *New Commentary on the Whole Bible,*
    1179.

7. Calvin, "Commentaries on the Book of the Prophet Daniel," vol. 1,
    Calvin's Commentaries, vol. 12, 320.

8. Jamieson, Fausset and Brown, *New Commentary on the Whole Bible,*
    1178.

9. James Strong, *Strong's Exhaustive Concordance of the Bible* (Iowa Falls:
    World Bible Publishers, 1986), 296.

10. Jamieson, Fausset and Brown, *New Commentary on the Whole Bible,*
    1179.

11. Calvin, "Commentaries on the Book of the Prophet Daniel," vol. 1,
    Calvin's Commentaries, vol. 12, 328.

12. Pfeiffer and Harrison, *Wycliffe Bible Commentary,* 786.

13. John Gill, *Exposition of the Old and New Testaments,* vol. 6 (1810;
    reprint, Paris, AR: The Baptist Standard Bearer, 1989), 310.

14. *Josephus,* 225.

CHAPTER SIX

1. John Calvin, "Commentaries on the Book of the Prophet Daniel,"
    vol. 1, in vol. 12 of *Calvin's Commentaries*, trans. Thomas Myers
    (1843; reprint, Grand Rapids: Baker Books, 1999), 347–348.

2. J.D. Douglas, ed., *New Bible Dictionary*, 2nd ed. (Wheaton, IL:
    Tyndale House Publishers, 1962), 1075.

3. John Gill, *Exposition of the Old and New Testaments*, vol. 6 (1810;
    reprint, Paris, AR: The Baptist Standard Bearer, 1989), 312.

4. Warren W. Wiersbe, *Wiersbe's Expository Outline on the Old Testament*
    (Colorado Springs: Victor Books, 1993) 569–570.

5. Gill, *Exposition of the Old and New Testaments*, 313.

6. Corrie ten Boom, *Not I, But Christ* (Nashville: Thomas Nelson
    Publishers, 1984), 94.

7. James M. Freeman, *The New Manners and Customs of the Bible*, ed.
    Harold J. Chadwick (North Brunswick, NJ: Bridge-Logos Publishers,
    1998), 386.

8. Freeman, *The New Manners and Customs of the Bible*, 386.

9. Freeman, *The New Manners and Customs of the Bible*, 79.

CHAPTER SEVEN

1. John Gill, *Exposition of the Old and New Testaments*, vol. 6 (1810;
    reprint, Paris, AR: The Baptist Standard Bearer, 1989), 318.

2. Matthew Henry, *Matthew Henry's Commentary on the Whole Bible*
    (Hendrickson Publishers, 1991), 1446.

3. James Strong, *Strong's Exhaustive Concordance of the Bible* (Iowa Falls:
    World Bible Publishers, 1986), 1200.

4. Gill, *Exposition of the Old and New Testaments*, 319.

5. John Calvin, "Commentaries on the Book of the Prophet Daniel,"
    vol. 2, in vol. 13 of *Calvin's Commentaries*, trans. Thomas Myers
    (1843; reprint, Grand Rapids: Baker Books, 1999), 16.

6. Walter Chalmers Smith, "Immortal, Invisible" [ca. 1867] in *Baptist Hymnal* (Nashville: Convention Press, 1975), 32. Public Domain.

7. *New Geneva Study Bible,* ed. R.C. Sproul (Nashville: Thomas Nelson Publishers, 1995), 1343.

8. Robert Jamieson, Andrew R. Fausset, and David Brown, *New Commentary on the Whole Bible: Old Testament Volume,* ed. J.D. Douglas (Wheaton, IL: Tyndale House Publishers, 1990), 1184.

CHAPTER EIGHT

1. Charles F. Pfeiffer and Everett F. Harrison, *The Wycliffe Bible Commentary* (Chicago: Moody Press, 1962), 791.

2. John Gill, *Exposition of the Old and New Testaments,* vol. 6 (1810; reprint, Paris, AR: The Baptist Standard Bearer, 1989), 330.

3. James Strong, *Strong's Exhaustive Concordance of the Bible* (Iowa Falls: World Bible Publishers, 1986), 661.

4. John Calvin, "Commentaries on the Book of the Prophet Daniel," vol. 2, in vol. 13 of *Calvin's Commentaries,* trans. Thomas Myers (1843; reprint, Grand Rapids: Baker Books, 1999), 97–98.

5. Gill, *Exposition of the Old and New Testaments,* 334.

6. A.W. Tozer, *The Attributes of God* (Camp Hill, PA: Christian Publications, Inc., 1997), 43–45.

7. J.B. Jackson, *A Dictionary of Scripture Proper Names* (Neptune, NJ: Loizeaux Brothers, 1909), 32.

8. Gill, *Exposition of the Old and New Testaments,* 335.

9. William MacDonald, *Believer's Bible Commentary,* ed. Art Farstad (Nashville: Thomas Nelson Publishers, 1995), 1084.

10. Robert Jamieson, Andrew R. Fausset, and David Brown, *New Commentary on the Whole Bible: Old Testament Volume,* ed. J.D. Douglas (Wheaton, IL: Tyndale House Publishers, 1990), 1189.

11. Calvin, "Commentaries on the Book of the Prophet Daniel," vol. 1, *Calvin's Commentaries,* vol. 12, 122.

12. Calvin, "Commentaries on the Book of the Prophet Daniel," vol. 1, *Calvin's Commentaries*, vol. 12, 122.

13. Josephus, "Antiquities of the Jews," in *The Complete Works of Flavius Josephus*, trans. William Whiston (Grand Rapids: Kregel Publications, 1960), 245.

14. *Josephus*, 244.

15. Gill, *Exposition of the Old and New Testaments*, 336.

16. Jamieson, Fausset and Brown, *New Commentary on the Whole Bible*, 1189.

17. Josephus, 251-258; *New Geneva Study Bible*, ed. R.C. Sproul (Nashville: Thomas Nelson Publishers, 1995), 1153–1154.

18. Calvin, "Commentaries on the Book of the Prophet Daniel," vol. 1, *Calvin's Commentaries*, vol. 12, 128.

19. Gill, *Exposition of the Old and New Testaments*, 337.

20. *Josephus*, 262.

21. *Josephus*, 260.

CHAPTER NINE

1. Kenneth L. Barker and John R. Kohlenberger III, ed., *Zondervan NIV Bible Commentary*, Vol. 1: Old Testament (Grand Rapids: Zondervan Publishing House, 1994), 1386.

2. W. E. Vine, *Vine's Expository Dictionary of Old and Testament Words* (Nashville: Thomas Nelson Publishers, 1997), 120.

3. John Gill, *Exposition of the Old and New Testaments*, vol. 6 (1810; reprint, Paris, AR: The Baptist Standard Bearer, 1989), 342.

4. Gill, *Exposition of the Old and New Testaments*, 342.

5. "Antiquities of the Jews," in *The Complete Works of Flavius Josephus*, trans. William Whiston (Grand Rapids: Kregel Publications, 1960), 228.

6. Robert Jamieson, Andrew R. Fausset, and David Brown, *New Commentary on the Whole Bible: Old Testament Volume*, ed. J.D. Douglas (Wheaton, IL: Tyndale House Publishers, 1990), 1192.

7. Stephen R. Miller, *The New American Commentary*, ed. E. Ray Clendenen (Nashville: Broadman and Holman Publishers, 1994), 252.

8. Miller, *The New American Commentary*, 252–257.

9. James Strong, *Strong's Exhaustive Concordance of the Bible* (Iowa Falls: World Bible Publishers, 1986), 1499; Barker and Kohlenberger, *Zondervan NIV Bible Commentary*, 1388.

10. Miller, *The New American Commentary*, 259.

11. Jamieson, Fausset and Brown, *New Commentary on the Whole Bible*, 1193.

12. Pfeiffer and Harrison, *Wycliffe Bible Commentary*, 794; Barker and Kohlenberger, *Zondervan NIV Bible Commentary*, 1389; Gill, *Exposition of the Old and New Testaments*, 345.

13. Barker and Kohlenberger, *Zondervan NIV Bible Commentary*, 1389; *New Geneva Study Bible*, ed. R.C. Sproul (Nashville: Thomas Nelson Publishers, 1995), 1351.

14. Barker and Kohlenberger, *Zondervan NIV Bible Commentary*, 1389.

15. Gill, *Exposition of the Old and New Testaments*, 346.

16. Miller, *The New American Commentary*, 268.

17. R.C. Sproul, *The Last Days According to Jesus* (Grand Rapids: Baker Books, 1998), 38-41.

18. J. Vernon McGee, *Thru the Bible*, vol. 3 (Nashville: Thomas Nelson Publishers, 1982), 588–589; Barker and Kohlenberger, *Zondervan NIV Bible Commentary*, 1389–1390; Jamieson, Fausset and Brown, *New Commentary on the Whole Bible*, 1193.

19. *New Geneva Study Bible*, 1350.

20. John Calvin, "Commentaries on the Book of the Prophet Daniel," vol. 2, in vol. 13 of *Calvin's Commentaries*, trans. Thomas Myers (1843; reprint, Grand Rapids: Baker Books, 1999), 226–227.

21. John Newton, "Amazing Grace" [ca. 1779] in *Baptist Hymnal* (Nashville: Convention Press, 1975), 165. Public Domain.

CHAPTER TEN

1. Robert Jamieson, Andrew R. Fausset, and David Brown, *New Commentary on the Whole Bible: Old Testament Volume,* ed. J.D. Douglas (Wheaton, IL: Tyndale House Publishers, 1990), 1194.

2. Jamieson, Fausset and Brown, *New Commentary on the Whole Bible,* 1194–1195.

3. John Gill, *Exposition of the Old and New Testaments,* vol. 6 (1810; reprint, Paris, AR: *The Baptist Standard Bearer,* 1989), 348.

4. J. Vernon McGee, *Thru the Bible,* vol. 3 (Nashville: Thomas Nelson Publishers, 1982), 590.

5. J.D. Douglas, ed., *New Bible Dictionary,* 2nd ed. (Wheaton, IL: Tyndale House Publishers, 1962), 159.

6. Gill, *Exposition of the Old and New Testaments,* 349.

7. Charles F. Pfeiffer and Everett F. Harrison, *The Wycliffe Bible Commentary* (Chicago: Moody Press, 1962), 796.

8. Cleland B. McAfee, "Near to the Heart of God" [ca. 1901] in *Baptist Hymnal* (Nashville: Convention Press, 1975), 354. Public Domain.

9. John Calvin, "Commentaries on the Book of the Prophet Daniel," vol. 2, in vol. 13 of Calvin's Commentaries, trans. Thomas Myers (1843; reprint, Grand Rapids: Baker Books, 1999), 246.

10. Gill, *Exposition of the Old and New Testaments,* 351.

11. Matthew Henry, *Matthew Henry's Commentary on the Whole Bible* (Hendrickson Publishers, 1991), 1455.

12. *New Geneva Study Bible,* ed. R.C. Sproul (Nashville: Thomas Nelson Publishers, 1995), 1351.

13. Gill, *Exposition of the Old and New Testaments*, 353.

14. Jamieson, Fausset and Brown, *New Commentary on the Whole Bible,* 1196.

CHAPTER ELEVEN

1. Matthew Henry, *Matthew Henry's Commentary on the Whole Bible* (Hendrickson Publishers, 1991), 1457.

2. "Antiquities of the Jews," in *The Complete Works of Flavius Josephus,* trans. William Whiston (Grand Rapids: Kregel Publications, 1960), 229.

3. Kenneth L. Barker and John R. Kohlenberger III, ed., *Zondervan NIV Bible Commentary,* Vol. 1: Old Testament (Grand Rapids: Zondervan Publishing House, 1994), 1392–1393.

4. Barker and Kohlenberger, *Zondervan NIV Bible Commentary,* 1393.

5. Robert Jamieson, Andrew R. Fausset, and David Brown, *New Commentary on the Whole Bible: Old Testament Volume,* ed. J.D. Douglas (Wheaton, IL: Tyndale House Publishers, 1990), 1196.

6. John Gill, *Exposition of the Old and New Testaments,* vol. 6 (1810; reprint, Paris, AR: The Baptist Standard Bearer, 1989), 354.

7. Stephen R. Miller, *The New American Commentary,* ed. E. Ray Clendenen (Nashville: Broadman and Holman Publishers, 1994), 291.

8. Gill, *Exposition of the Old and New Testaments,* 355.

9. Miller, *The New American Commentary,* 293.

10. Jamieson, Fausset and Brown, *New Commentary on the Whole Bible,* 1196.

11. John Calvin, "Commentaries on the Book of the Prophet Daniel," vol. 2, in vol. 13 of *Calvin's Commentaries,* trans. Thomas Myers (1843; reprint, Grand Rapids: Baker Books, 1999), 246.

12. Gill, *Exposition of the Old and New Testaments,* 356.

13. Jamieson, Fausset and Brown, *New Commentary on the Whole Bible,* 1196–1197.

14. Calvin, "Commentaries on the Book of the Prophet Daniel," vol. 2, *Calvin's Commentaries*, vol. 13, 281–282.

15. Jamieson, Fausset and Brown, *New Commentary on the Whole Bible*, 1197.

16. Gill, *Exposition of the Old and New Testaments*, 357.

17. *New Geneva Study Bible*, ed. R.C. Sproul (Nashville: Thomas Nelson Publishers, 1995), 1352.

18. Jamieson, Fausset and Brown, *New Commentary on the Whole Bible*, 1197.

19. Calvin, "Commentaries on the Book of the Prophet Daniel," vol. 2, *Calvin's Commentaries*, vol. 13, 287–290.

20. Miller, *The New American Commentary*, 295; Gill, *Exposition of the Old and New Testaments*, 358.

21. Jamieson, Fausset and Brown, *New Commentary on the Whole Bible*, 1197.

22. Gill, *Exposition of the Old and New Testaments*, 358.

23. Jamieson, Fausset and Brown, *New Commentary on the Whole Bible*, 1197.

24. Henry, *Matthew Henry's Commentary*, 1457.

25. *Josephus*, 251–252.

26. Calvin, "Commentaries on the Book of the Prophet Daniel," vol. 2, *Calvin's Commentaries*, vol. 13, 296.

27. Miller, *The New American Commentary*, 296.

28. William MacDonald, *Believer's Bible Commentary*, ed. Art Farstad (Nashville: Thomas Nelson Publishers, 1995), 1089.

29. Miller, *The New American Commentary*, 298–299.

30. Henry, *Matthew Henry's Commentary*, 1458.

31. Henry, *Matthew Henry's Commentary*, 1458.

32. Gill, *Exposition of the Old and New Testaments*, 361.

33. Calvin, "Commentaries on the Book of the Prophet Daniel," vol. 2, *Calvin's Commentaries*, vol. 13, 306–307; Jamieson, Fausset and Brown, *New Commentary on the Whole Bible*, 1198.

34. Calvin, "Commentaries on the Book of the Prophet Daniel," vol. 2, *Calvin's Commentaries*, vol. 13, 308.

35. Gill, *Exposition of the Old and New Testaments*, 362.

36. Calvin, "Commentaries on the Book of the Prophet Daniel," vol. 2, *Calvin's Commentaries*, vol. 13, 311.

37. Jamieson, Fausset and Brown, *New Commentary on the Whole Bible*, 1199.

38. Jamieson, Fausset and Brown, *New Commentary on the Whole Bible*, 1199.

39. Gill, *Exposition of the Old and New Testaments*, 363–364.

40. Miller, *The New American Commentary*, 301.

41. Josephus, 257.

42. Barker and Kohlenberger, *Zondervan NIV Bible Commentary*, 1400.

43. Calvin, "Commentaries on the Book of the Prophet Daniel," vol. 2, *Calvin's Commentaries*, vol. 13, 338–393.

44. Charles F. Pfeiffer and Everett F. Harrison, *The Wycliffe Bible Commentary* (Chicago: Moody Press, 1962), 797.

45. Miller, *The New American Commentary*, 305.

46. Pfeiffer and Harrison, *Wycliffe Bible Commentary*, 797.

47. Miller, *The New American Commentary*, 308.

48. *Josephus*, 258–262.

49. Miller, *The New American Commentary*, 311.

50. Jamieson, Fausset and Brown, *New Commentary on the Whole Bible*, 1201.

CHAPTER TWELVE

1. Kenneth L. Barker and John R. Kohlenberger III, ed., *Zondervan NIV Bible Commentary*, Vol. 1: Old Testament (Grand Rapids: Zondervan Publishing House, 1994), 1403.

2. John Calvin, "Commentaries on the Book of the Prophet Daniel," vol. 2, in vol. 13 of *Calvin's Commentaries*, trans. Thomas Myers (1843; reprint, Grand Rapids: Baker Books, 1999), 375.

3. William MacDonald, *Believer's Bible Commentary*, ed. Art Farstad (Nashville: Thomas Nelson Publishers, 1995), 1091.

4. Stephen R. Miller, *The New American Commentary*, ed. E. Ray Clendenen (Nashville: Broadman and Holman Publishers, 1994), 321.

5. Robert Jamieson, Andrew R. Fausset, and David Brown, *New Commentary on the Whole Bible: Old Testament Volume*, ed. J.D. Douglas (Wheaton, IL: Tyndale House Publishers, 1990), 1202.

6. Barker and Kohlenberger, *Zondervan NIV Bible Commentary*, 1404.

7. John Gill, *Exposition of the Old and New Testaments*, vol. 6 (1810; reprint, Paris, AR: The Baptist Standard Bearer, 1989), 372.

8. Miller, *The New American Commentary*, 323.

9. Gill, *Exposition of the Old and New Testaments*, 373.

10. Henry, *Matthew Henry's Commentary*, 1462.

11. Miller, *The New American Commentary*, 325.

12. Miller, *The New American Commentary*, 325.

13. Calvin, "Commentaries on the Book of the Prophet Daniel," vol. 2, *Calvin's Commentaries*, vol. 13, 393.

14. Miller, *The New American Commentary*, 326.

15. Strong, *Exhaustive Concordance*, 889.

Commentaries available from
PRACTICAL CHRISTIANITY FOUNDATION

DANIEL
In God I Trust

MARK
Jesus Christ, Love in Action

JOHN
The Word Made Flesh

THE GENERAL EPISTLES
A Practical Faith

REVELATION
Tribulation and Triumph

For more information, please visit www.greenkeybooks.com